The Anglican Eucharist in Ecumenical Perspective

Doctrine and Rite
from Cranmer to Seabury

The Anglican Eucharist in Ecumenical Perspective

Doctrine and Rite from Cranmer to Seabury

Edward P. Echlin, S.J.

THE SEABURY PRESS
NEW YORK

Copyright © 1968 by The Seabury Press, Incorporated
Design by Carol Basen
602-338-C-2.5
Library of Congress Catalog Card Number: 68-11590
Printed in the United States of America

Ut mox unum sint

Preface

Theology proceeds from the perspective of a definite commitment. This book is no exception. My perspective is that of the Christian commitment. But there is something more. I write as a Catholic in union with Rome, a Jesuit, and a priest.

I doubt if any books of "purely objective" theology have been written. Nevertheless, this book is not about Roman Catholic doctrine. It is not a comparison with Roman dogma; nor is it a critical study. I have tried to show the development of Anglican Eucharistic thought from Cranmer to Seabury. In my research and writing, I have moved within the comprehensive mood known as the Anglican Way. And I have found myself very much at home.

I contend here, and have contended in this book, that there has been a definite development of Anglican Eucharistic thought from Cranmer to Seabury. I have contended that this development over four centuries has steadily drawn closer to Rome. I also contend that Roman Eucharistic thought has developed during this same period, and that Roman development has tended to converge with the insights of Anglicanism. Having said this, I will say little more about the development of Roman Eucharistic dogma. The subject would make an interesting book; but it would not be the book I have set out to write.

This book attempts to enlarge Christian understanding. Before we offer ourselves to each other, we must understand ourselves. Once we understand ourselves, we are in a position to understand each other. And once we understand each other, we are on the warm threshold of reunion. In writing this book, I have grown in understanding of the Anglican Communion. And I see no pre-emptive reason why the Rock of Peter and the flock of Canterbury should not again be one.

In this book, I have tried to show the historical development that culminated in the Episcopal Mass. I have concentrated on the doctrines of Sacrifice and Real Presence. In so doing, I had to omit many riches of Anglican Eucharistic thought. But these two doctrines were the points at issue in the sixteenth century; I consider them the paramount issues today.

Gratitude is due more people than I can mention here. I wish to thank Emilien Lamirande, of Saint Paul University, Ottawa, for suggesting this book in the first place, and the theology department of John Carroll University, Cleveland, for granting me leave of absence to finish it. Special mention is due the Jesuits of Campion Hall, Oxford, who offered me a home away from home while I did research in their towery city, and to A. M. Allchin, of Pusey House, for making available the incomparable collections in the Darwell Stone Room. I also wish to thank Dr. Niels Sonne, of General Theological Seminary, New York, for allowing me to use sources extant only in his library. Gratitude is due Mr. Arthur R. Buckley, of The Seabury Press, for invaluable suggestions, and to Union Theological Seminary for the grant of Visiting Scholar privileges at their fine institution. Finally, I wish to thank the Society of Jesus. The always mobile, ever adaptable Society teaches its members, even more than its legendary loyalty to the successors of Peter and the Apostles, a love of all Christian men—Protestant, Anglican, Orthodox, and Roman Catholic—and instills the ideal of going forward in unity to embrace the whole world and guard even heathen things.

EDWARD P. ECHLIN

John Carroll University
Feast of Edmund Campion, 1967

Contents

The Anglican Eucharist
in Ecumenical Perspective

Doctrine and Rite
from Cranmer to Seabury

Introduction

In 1548 Thomas Cranmer, Archbishop of Canterbury, startled England and Rome by his insertion of a vernacular rite for congregational Communion into the Latin Mass. Fittingly enough, this novel rite was called *The Order of the Communion*. It startled Christendom not only because it interrupted the Latin Mass with a vernacular insertion but also because it provided for the laity Communion in both species and implied that all present should communicate as at a meal.

Cranmer's innovation of 1548, however, was only the beginning. The following year, the Tudor cadences of the first complete Communion Service in English reverberated throughout the British Isles. This rite was also the work of the scholarly Cranmer. To this day scholars admire its prose and its adherence to ancient forms. But the rite also reflected Cranmer's theology, a theology which denied that the Eucharist offered Christ and considered Communion merely a spiritual reception of Divine benefits.

Naturally enough, the 1549 Service aroused considerable criticism and discussion throughout Europe. Roman Catholics found it objectionable, but, with the young Edward VI and his reforming advisers firmly entrenched in England, Roman Catholic objections were unheeded. Theologians of the reformed tradition found the service unsatisfactory because it did not proceed nearly far enough in satisfying the demands for reform prevalent at Geneva, Zurich, and Strasbourg. It was the moderates, however, those who accepted the Service with articulated reservations, who influenced—and, in the case of Stephen Gardiner, annoyed—Cranmer the most. In fact, two continental reformers of the moderate school, Martin Bucer and Peter Martyr, were invited by Cranmer to submit criticisms. But the moderate who seemed to exert the strongest influence was Stephen Gardiner, leading spokesman for the Henrician Catholic-without-Rome school and formerly Bishop of Winchester. In the clever polemical manner of that fissiparous century, he sarcastically complimented the 1549 Service for its teaching of Transubstantiation and propitiatory Sacrifice. Cranmer countered Gardiner's arguments with an equally polemical answer and, later, with a new Communion Service.

That new Service was the Communion rite of 1552 to replace that of 1549. In this Service Archbishop Cranmer went a long way to appease the reformers of the Swiss school, such as the fiery John Hooper of Gloucester. All overtones of propitiatory Sacrifice and corporal Real Presence were deleted. The altar was now a table; vestments were practically eliminated; a receptionist Communion formula replaced the more traditional 1549 formula. Significantly, every item that Gardiner had praised as teaching Transubstantiation and propitiatory Sacrifice was revised. Three-fifths of Bucer's written suggestions, to which Martyr had added his *fiat,* were incorporated in the new rite.

The 1552 Service was ill-starred from the outset. Because Cranmer had retained kneeling reception, reformers such as John Knox and Hooper were sharply displeased. Cranmer grudgingly countered their criticism with the insertion of the infamous "Black Rubric," which King and Council goaded him into appending just before the Service went to the printer. This rubric explained that kneeling reception signified no "reall and essencial" Presence of Christ's Body and Blood. But all this discontent mattered little in 1552. In a few months the formidable Mary Tudor, profoundly devoted to the Church of Rome, was to succeed to the throne.

During the Marian interlude, when the 1552 Service changed places in the English catacombs with the Roman rite, the real history of the Anglican Service was developing on the Continent. The exiles who fled to Frankfurt were soon enmeshed in dissension over Cranmer's Prayer Book. One faction advocated substantial conformity to the 1552 Office. Others, championed by John Knox, wanted a Lord's Supper along Genevan lines. Eventually, the conservatives prevailed. Knox and his followers adjourned to hospitable Geneva, where they composed the *Maner of the Lordes Supper,* a scriptural commemorative meal. The history of these exiles is important in Anglican Eucharistic development, not because they influenced Mary Tudor, but because future English monarchs would have to reckon with them.

Elizabeth, who succeeded Mary in 1558, was compelled to placate these Genevan exiles. In fact, Elizabeth fabricated a settlement which was an attempt to reconcile the many theological factions. Genevan exiles, now back in England, wanted the *Maner of the Lordes Supper* as the established Office. But Elizabeth's leanings were more Catholic than that. She also had to appease those who wanted to return to the rites of 1552 or of 1549.

The meager evidence available would seem to indicate that Elizabeth herself preferred the 1549 Service, but she had to assuage those partial to the Latin Mass, the 1552 Service, and the Genevan rite. Her compromise solution was the restoration of the 1552 Service—with three important changes, all in the direction of 1549. She abolished the "Black Rubric"; she restored vestments; and she juxtaposed Cranmer's 1549 Communion formula with his receptionist 1552 formula—a stroke of Anglican comprehensiveness. As a result of her settlement, there would be no further revisions of the English Service for a century.

Dissent, however, continued strong. The Puritans, as they were called, were demanding a scriptural meal according to "the word of God." When Elizabeth died in 1603, James Stuart became James I of England. The Puritans requested a conference on liturgical matters. James entertained their requests at Hampton Court but allowed no substantial concessions of any kind—and none in the Communion Service. His 1604 Service is described interchangeably with that of 1559 in these pages because it was apparently used interchangeably with the 1559 Service as long as printings of that Service lasted.

Another Stuart, the unfortunate Charles I, succeeded James in 1625, and his reign witnessed another mighty Archbishop of Canterbury, the towering William Laud. The Archbishop insisted on conformity to the English rite, and his Eucharistic theology exemplified in the Church of England what can be called Laudian theology.* He believed the Eucharist was a representative Sacrifice

---

* There is still pervasive confusion about terms to describe those whose theology was close to that of Rome and admitted little Protestantism. Laudian or Caroline seems to limit them to the seventeenth century; High Church is reminiscent of the age of Queen Anne; Anglo-

of consecrated elements. He denied Transubstantiation, but taught a "true and real" Presence. Laud fostered vestments, liturgical pageantry, and an altar position for the holy table. To the Puritans he was *bête noire* number one.

Meanwhile there were rumblings north of the Tweed. The Scottish Bishops demanded a native liturgy unique to the Highlands. Charles I and Laud preferred uniform use of the English Service. Eventually the Scottish Bishops prevailed. The King and Laud sanctioned a printing of a conservative revision of the 1604 Service. While this revision was still on the press, the scholarly Bishop of Dunblane, James Wedderburn, wrote Laud his famous letter advocating further and radical changes. His recommendations were, in brief, a return to 1549 and even to the ancient liturgies with which he was familiar. The Archbishop seized upon this opportunity for a Communion Service reflecting Laudian doctrine. The presses were halted. Laud and the King did not go the whole way with Wedderburn, but many of his recommendations were incorporated into a 1637 Service clearly teaching representative Sacrifice and perduring Real Presence.

Charles's promulgation of the new Service can only be described as tragically inept. He foisted the rite on the northern kingdom in such a high-handed manner that the Scottish people believed it emanated from him and Laud and not from their own Bishops. This Communion Service was greeted with a riot at its first reading, the spark that eventually consumed the whole kingdom in a bloody civil war, which saw Anglican Services outlawed and witnessed the horrendous executions of the Archbishop of Canterbury and the King of Great Britain.

In the two decades when Puritans and Independents held the upper hand, the Laudians industriously prepared for the eventual

---

Catholic is associated with the Oxford Movement; Catholic is too ambiguous and can be confused with the Church of Rome. All these terms are used in this study, but for lack of a universal epithet the most often used is Laudian. See Ernest C. Messenger, *The Reformation, the Mass, and the Priesthood. A Documented History with Special Reference to the Question of Anglican Orders,* 2 Vols., London, 1936–37, Vol. 1, p. 240.

restoration of the Stuart monarchy. John Cosin, a lifetime student
of Eucharistic theology and practice and future Bishop of Durham,
went into exile. Bishop Matthew Wren of Ely, in the Tower for
Laudian leanings, employed his forced leisure in composing Prayer
Book corrections. Wren had helped Laud review the 1637 Communion Service and was ready to advocate considerable revision.

When the inevitable Restoration occurred, Presbyterians has-
tened to cut their losings. Laudians emerged expectant of radical
revision. The Presbyterians requested a conference. Charles II
granted them one with his Bishops and divines at Savoy. Cosin, as
a delegate, was willing to allow some concession to Presbyterian
grievances. But the conservatives, in no mood to allow many concessions, prevailed. The once outlawed 1604 Communion Service,
which had been an occasion of martyrdom, now was held to be
sacrosanct. Moreover, the new Establishment intimately linked
the Prayer Book with the Church of England, with uniformity, and
peace. The Presbyterians were rebuffed, and the conservatives carried the day.

If too sacred for Presbyterian revision, the liturgy was also too
sacred for Laudian revision. Cosin and Wren revised their am-
bitious plans accordingly. Both were on the Convocation's revision
committee. But they were the only two in favor of revision. Other
Bishops, such as the influential Robert Sanderson of Lincoln, were
inimical to serious change. Considering the temper of the time,
it is amazing what Cosin and Wren did accomplish. Offertory
rubrics, similar to those of 1549 and 1637, emphasizing Sacrifice,
were restored. Several new concluding rubrics taught perduring
Real Presence. The resultant 1662 revision, approved by Convocation, King, and Parliament, has been the official Order for the Holy
Communion in the Church of England ever since.

When James II was deposed in 1688, William of Orange, a
staunch Protestant, ascended the throne; some Anglicans refused
the oath of allegiance to such a monarch. These recusants were
the Nonjurors, a group whose short history is important for Eucharistic theology out of all proportion to their numbers.

The Nonjurors soon realized that their unique freedom from
Erastianism offered them an opportunity for thorough Communion
Service revision. The man whose theology influenced them the
most was, paradoxically, a man who took the oath, John Johnson,

rector of Cranbrook in Kent. Johnson's influence on future High Church theology was immeasurable. In 1718 the Nonjurors framed their own Communion Service. Two important participants in this revision were Bishop Thomas Brett and Thomas Deacon.

For almost half a century, liturgical chaos continued to plague Scotland. Some used the established English Service; others used that of 1637; still others improvised their own. Finally, in 1764, the Scottish Bishops agreed to proposals for a new rite. The primary author of their 1764 Service was Bishop Robert Forbes, a follower of Johnson and the Nonjurors. The Service he produced resembled that of 1718 and reflected mature Nonjuror theology. It finally brought a measure of uniformity to the highlands.

This 1764 Service also influenced the New World. Without Bishops of its own, the Church of England in America paid only a shadowy allegiance to the Bishop of London. The desire of American Anglicans for their own Bishops was deepened by the War of Revolution. When peace was restored in 1783, Samuel Seabury of Connecticut journeyed to England for consecration. When the English Bishops temporized, Seabury travelled north for his consecration and signed a concordat with his Scottish consecrators in which he promised to advocate adherence to the 1764 Canon in the American Church. This agreement was easy for Seabury, for he was in the same tradition as Robert Forbes.

When the Protestant Episcopal Church of the United States —a title assumed in 1785—gathered in Convention in 1789, the only Bishops present were Seabury and William White. Together they formed the upper house committee for revision; indeed they *were* that house. White's theology was more evangelical than Seabury's, and he frequently criticized Laud, Johnson, and the Nonjurors. He was, nevertheless, somewhat influenced by their doctrine. He agreed to go along with Seabury's recommendation for the Scottish Canon. This was possible because the president of the lower house, William Smith, was also an advocate of Johnson's Eucharistic doctrine. When Convention adjourned, the American Church had a Communion Service, vividly sacrificial, and with emphasis on Real Presence in the elements. The long Eucharistic development that had begun at Thomas Cranmer's desk in Canterbury had reached a consummation in the New World.

The chapters that follow will trace in detail the historical evolution of Anglican Eucharistic doctrine from the time of Cranmer and the 1549 Service to the Communion Service of 1789 framed at Philadelphia. The emphasis will not be on history or liturgy as such, but on the developing doctrine embodied in that series of Eucharistic revisions. Church history and these Communion Service revisions will be considered only insofar as they influence or reflect this developing doctrine.

Although the Eucharist should be the sign and cause of Christian unity,[1] all too often it has been the sign and cause of strife and division. Hopefully, this study will be of some assistance to Roman Catholics, Anglicans, and other Christians in their audible yearnings for unity in the "breaking of the bread."

CHAPTER I

The Communion Service of 1549

And where heretofore there hath been great diversity in saying and singing in churches within this realm: some following Salisbury use, some others Hereford use, some the use of Bangor, some of York, and some of Lincoln: Now from henceforth the whole realm shall have but one use.[1]

So read the mellifluous words of Thomas Cranmer in the Preface to the first Book of Common Prayer. Henceforth there was to be uniformity of use in the realm. To achieve this uniformity, Cranmer chose to build on the Sarum, or Salisbury, rite, which was in most widespread use in sixteenth-century England.[2] It was this use of Sarum that Cranmer was to paraphrase, translate, adapt, and transform in his first reformed Communion Service "after the use of the Church of England." Sarum was his point of departure in 1549 for the first Anglican Lord's Supper,[3] a rite that was to reflect Cranmer's Eucharistic theology and influence all future Communion Services of Anglicanism. To facilitate our study of Cranmer's revision, let us first note the chief characteristics of the Sarum rite.

The Sarum Use

The Sarum Canon approximated, in word and rubric, the Roman rite today.[4] There was, however, more diversity in those parts of Sarum that preceded and followed the Canon. Cranmer transformed these parts too,[5] and his transformation of the whole reflected his theology.

In the Sarum use, the priest said several preparatory prayers while vesting, including a Collect for Purity and a *Pater Noster.* Among these prayers was a *Confiteor* in which mention was made of the saints. More private prayers followed as the priest ascended the altar and while, on festive occasions, he blessed the incense.

The Introit was followed by the *Kyrie, Gloria,* and several Collects including a Collect for the day. After the Epistle, the priest privately recited the prescribed Graduals, Alleluias, Tracts, and Sequences. On festive occasions the Gospel was followed by the Nicene Creed.

The Offertory was definitely and vividly sacrificial. After the prayer, the chalice, paten, and elements were presented to the celebrant. "Sacrifice" and "oblation" recurred frequently in the prayers and rubrics, and each time they referred to the elements. There was reference to offering the elements for living *and* deceased. Precise manual acts directed the celebrant to offer the "Sacrifice" to God. During the whole action, there were several more private priestly prayers.

Although the Sarum Canon differs little from its current Western descendant, the Communion tended to be a private devotion of the priest. Within the Sarum Mass there were no rubrics for Communion of the people. Practices differed not only within the various uses of the day, but even within different parts of a diocese that followed the same use. Sometimes the people did not communicate during Mass at all.[6] H. A. Wilson believes that in Sarum the people communicated during Mass and that they first recited a *Confiteor* and received absolution.[7]

Sarum, with its vivid emphasis on Sacrifice, reflected the belief of Catholics that the Mass was a propitiatory Sacrifice. It encouraged adoration of and belief in a corporal Real Presence in the elements. This was to be changed by Cranmer in 1549, and still more in 1552, to reflect his own doctrine of Sacrifice and Real Presence.

The Eucharistic Theology of Cranmer

Archbishop Cranmer was, in the words of the Reformation historian T. M. Parker, "by common consent the chief author of the new liturgy." [8] By 1548 his Eucharistic theology was definitive in its essentials.[9] It was in that year that he translated the Nuremberg Catechism. In his subtle translation of the "Sermon of the Communion of the Lord's Supper," he used translator's license to the extent of altering the text to mean a real presence to Faith *in usu Sacramenti.*[10]

In that same year he publicly stated that Christ's Body was not in the bread, and that what man received in Communion was the Sacrament.[11] Traheron described Cranmer's position to Bullinger: the "archbishop of Canterbury, contrary to general expectation, most openly, firmly, and learnedly maintained your opinion on this subject. His arguments were as follows: The body of Christ was taken up from us into heaven. Christ has left the world. . . ."[12] In his polemical *Answer to Gardiner,* Cranmer expostulated that the Communion Service of 1549 contained his doctrine.[13]

CRANMER AND SACRIFICE

Cranmer maintained two types of Sacrifice. This teaching appears vividly in his *Answer to Gardiner:*

> One kind of sacrifice there is, which is called propitiatory or merciful sacrifice, that is to say, such a sacrifice as pacifieth God's wrath and indignation, and obtaineth mercy and forgiveness for all our sins, and is the ransom for our redemption from everlasting damnation. . . .
>
> Another kind of sacrifice there is which doth not reconcile us to God, but is made of them that be reconciled by Christ, to testify our duties unto God, and to show our selves thankful unto him. And therefore they be called sacrifices of laud, praise, and thanksgiving.

Without hesitation Cranmer admitted that the Eucharist was a Sacrifice. But he denied that it was an oblation of Christ or propitiatory. He contended that God was already pacified by the Sacrifice of Christ, that sins were remitted thereby, and that we availed ourselves of this by faith. The Eucharist was an offering of laud, praise, commemoration, and thanksgiving for the reconciliation wrought by Christ. He scored private Masses whereby "they may remit sin, and redeem souls out of purgatory":

> The controversy is not whether in the Holy Communion be made a Sacrifice or not (for herein both Doctor Smith and I agree with the foresaid Council at Ephesus), but whether it be a propitiatory sacri-

fice or not, and whether only the priest make the said sacrifice—these be the points wherein we vary.[14]

The Mass was *not* an offering of Christ for sin. "We make not of Christ a new sacrifice propitiatory for remission of sin. . . . They therefore which gather of the doctors, that the mass is a sacrifice for remission of sin, and that it is applied by the priest to them for whom he saith or singeth," misrepresent the teaching of the Doctors.[15] The only propitiation for sins was the Sacrifice of Christ. The Masses were offerings by those already reconciled:

To defend the papistical error, that the daily offering of the priest in the Mass is propitiatory, you extend the word "propitiation" otherwise than the apostles do, speaking of that matter. I speak plainly, according to St Paul and St John, that only Christ is the propitiation for our sins by His death. You speak according to the papists, that the priests in their masses make a sacrifice propitiatory. I call a sacrifice propitiatory, according to the scripture, such a sacrifice as pacifieth God's indignation against us, obtaineth mercy and forgiveness of all our sins, and is our ransom and redemption from everlasting damnation. And, on the other side, I call a sacrifice gratificatory, or the sacrifice of the Church, such a sacrifice as doth not reconcile us to God, but is made of them that be reconciled to testify their duties and to show themselves thankful unto him. And these sacrifices in scripture be not called propitiatory, but sacrifices of justice, of laud, praise and thanksgiving.[16]

No priest could apply Christ's Sacrifice. Every man must receive the benefit at Christ's hands through faith:

The prophets, apostles, and evangelists do say that Christ himself in his own person made a sacrifice for our sins upon the cross, by whose wounds all our diseases were healed, and our sins pardoned; and so did never no priest, man, nor creature, but he, nor he did the same never more than once. And the benefit hereof is in no man's power to give any other, but every man must receive it at Christ's hands himself, by his own faith and belief, as the prophet saith.[17]

Even at the grim Oxford disputations, Cranmer clung to the position that Christ's Sacrifice "upon the altar of the cross is the only sacrifice and oblation for the sins of all mankind." [18]

Yet Christians had long believed the Mass was a Sacrifice.

Cranmer was eager to preserve this belief. Although the Sacrifice "upon the altar of the cross" was the sole propitiatory one, the Eucharist *was* a sacrifice.

This other Sacrifice was *not* an offering of Christ. It was a commemoration and a giving of ourselves:

Nor Christ never gave this honour to any creature, that he should make a sacrifice of him, nor did not ordain the sacrament of his holy supper, to the intent that either the priest or the people should sacrifice Christ again, or that the priests should make a sacrifice of him for the people: but his holy supper was ordained for this purpose, that every man, eating and drinking thereof, should remember that Christ died for him, and so should exercise his faith, and comfort himself by the remembrance of Christ's benefits, and so give unto Christ most hearty thanks, and give himself also clearly unto him.[19]

The people were involved in this offering as much as the priest. Their Sacrifice "of laud and praise" was no less acceptable than the Sacrifice of the priest: ". . . the humble confession of all penitent hearts, their acknowledging of Christ's benefits, their thanksgiving for the same, their faith and consolation in Christ, their humble submission and obedience to God's will and commandments, is a sacrifice of laud and praise. . . ."[20]

Although our offering of ourselves was not a propitiatory Sacrifice, there was a connection between our Sacrifice and the unique propitiatory Sacrifice of Christ. Our Sacrifice was acceptable "by that his sacrifice":

. . . all our obedience unto God's will and commandments is a sacrifice acceptable to God, but not a sacrifice propitiatory: for that sacrifice Christ only made, and by that his sacrifice all our sacrifices be acceptable to God, and without that none is acceptable to him. And by those sacrifices all christian people offer themselves to God, but they do not offer Christ again for sin; for that did never creature but Christ himself alone, nor he never but upon Good Friday.[21]

In what may have been an attempt to dissociate the Eucharist from death, Cranmer expostulated that we killed not our bodies but mortified "beastly and unreasonable affections":

And forasmuch as he hath given himself to death for us, to be an oblation and sacrifice to his Father for our sins, let us give ourselves again unto him, making unto him an oblation, not of goats, sheep, kine, and other beasts that have no reason, as was accustomed before Christ's coming, but of a creature that hath reason, that is to say, of ourselves. . . .[22]

Because our Sacrifices were not separated from the one propitiatory Sacrifice, they were acts of recompense and gratitude to God for Christ's Sacrifice:

Almighty God grant that we may truly lean to one sacrifice of Christ, and we to him again may repay our sacrifices of thanksgiving, of praise, of confessing his name, of true amendment, of repentance, of mercifulness towards our neighbours, and of all other good works of charity! [23]

Cranmer had to counter the objection that the Old Testament spoke of patriarchal sacrifices for sins. He declared these were "ceremonies" to foreshadow and prefigure the true and perfect Sacrifice to come:

. . . they were ceremonies ordained to this intent, that they should be, as it were, shadows and figures, to signify beforehand the excellent sacrifice of Christ that was to come, which should be the very true and perfect sacrifice for the sins of the whole world.[24]

Nor was the Last Supper a Sacrifice in addition to that of Calvary. It was the institution of a perpetual memory of Calvary: "at the time of his holy supper [Christ] did institute a perpetual memory of his death, to be celebrated among christians in bread and wine." [25] Although he instituted this memory that night in Jerusalem, "yet he made not at that time of the sacrifice of our redemption and satisfaction for our sins, but the next day following." [26]

Cranmer expressed willingness to retain the word "Mass" for the sacrifice of all Christian people. But he denied that the "Mass" was for the priest alone or that it was propitiatory:

I have denied that it is a sacrifice propitiatory for sin, or that the priest alone maketh any sacrifice there. For it is the sacrifice of all christian people to remember Christ's death, to laud and thank him for it, and to publish it and shew it abroad unto other, to his honour and glory.[27]

Cranmer was not disdainful of tradition and ceremonies,[28] but he feared a false understanding of the role of the priest had arisen in recent centuries. The priest had become an offerer of propitiatory Sacrifice. "For if only the death of Christ be the oblation, sacrifice, and price wherefore our sins be pardoned, then the act of the priest cannot have the same office." [29]

He contended these priestly Sacrifices meant that the priests destroyed Christ every day and were more guilty than the Jews who killed Christ but once:

For if they make every day the same oblation and sacrifice for sin that Christ himself made, and the oblation he made was his death, and the effusion of his most precious blood upon the cross, for our redemption and price of our sins; then followeth it of necessity, that they every day slay Christ, and shed his blood. . . .[30]

Every man should apply Christ's Sacrifice to himself. This application came only through the merits of Christ and the faith of the Christian. The oblations of priests did not merit redemption:

. . . he may trust to have remission of his sins, and be delivered from eternal death and hell, by the merit only of the death and blood of Christ; and that by his own faith every man may apply the same unto himself, and not take it at the appointment of popish priests, by the merit of sacrifice and oblations.[31]

By Divine ordinance every man should receive communion himself. It was detestable idolatry to trust in priestly oblations for remission of sins and release from purgatory:

And if we put the oblation of the priest in the stead of the oblation of Christ, refusing to receive the sacrament of his body and blood ourselves, as he ordained, and trusting to have remission of our sins by the sacrifice of the priest in the mass, and thereby also to obtain release of the pains in purgatory, we do not only injury to Christ, but also commit most detestable idolatry.[32]

The doctrine of "unbloody sacrifice" made no sense to Cranmer. Only when Gardiner set this doctrine forth in plain terms would Cranmer answer him fully:

. . . if you would not deceive simple people, but teach them such doctrine as they may understand, that you should in plain terms set forth and declare what the daily offering of the priest without blood-shedding is, in what words, deeds, crosses, signs, or gestures it standeth, and whether it be made before the consecration or after, and before the distribution of the sacrament or after, and wherein chiefly resteth the very pith and substance of it.[33]

The priest was Minister of the Sacrament. But the laity must communicate for themselves if they wished to enter the kingdom of heaven: ". . . he that thinketh to come to the kingdom of Christ himself, must also come to his sacraments himself, and keep his commandments himself, and do all things that pertain to a christian man himself. . . ."[34]

Every man "eating and drinking thereof, should remember that Christ died for him, and so should exercise his faith, and comfort himself by the remembrance of Christ's benefits, and so give unto Christ most hearty thanks."[35] This was the practice of the primitive Church when all gathered for the remembrance and thanksgiving. Private Masses were a recent accretion, an invention of clergy in search of lucre and a denial of the efficacy of Christ's Sacrifice.[36]

In one sentence Cranmer dismissed Roman Catholic appeals to the authority of ecclesiastical writers who taught the Mass was a propitiatory Sacrifice.

But all those authors be answered unto in this one sentence, that they call it not a sacrifice for sin, because that it taketh away our sin, which is taken away only by the death of Christ, but because the holy communion was ordained by Christ to put us in remembrance of the sacrifice made by him upon the cross.[37]

This "one sentence" is important for an understanding of Cranmer's acceptance of Peter Lombard's definition of Sacrifice:

. . . the Master of the sentence, of whom all the school-authors take their occasion to write, judged truly in this point, saying: "That which is offered and consecrated of the priest is called a sacrifice and oblation, because it is a memory and representation of the true sacrifice and holy oblation made in the altar of the cross."[38]

Cranmer interpreted Lombard's definition as teaching that we offer a *remembrance* of Christ's Sacrifice.* He interpreted Chrysostom's writings the same way:

---

* B. J. Kidd refers to this acceptance of Lombard by Cranmer, and concedes that "he takes this language to mean a commemoration

As though he should say: although in a certain kind of speech we may say that every day we make a sacrifice of Christ, yet in very deed, to speak properly, we make no sacrifice of him, but only a commemoration and remembrance of that sacrifice which he alone made, and never none but he.[39]

Therefore, Christ's ordinance should be followed: "the priest to minister the sacrament to the people, and they to use it to their consolation. And in this eating, drinking, and using of the Lord's supper, we make not of Christ a new sacrifice propitiatory for remission of sin." [40]

CRANMER AND REAL PRESENCE

The great Tractarian E. B. Pusey wrote: "The doctrine of the Eucharistic sacrifice depends upon the doctrine of the real objective presence." [41] Cranmer's doctrine on the Real Presence resembled that of such continental reformers as Zwingli, Bucer, and Oecolampadius. His doctrine departed sharply from that of the Church of Rome.

In Book I of the reply to Gardiner, Cranmer dismissed Transubstantiation as nonscriptural.

Now if you can prove that your transubstantiation, your fleshly presence of Christ's body and blood, your carnal eating and drinking of the same, your propitiatory sacrifice of the mass, are taught us as plainly in the scripture, as the said articles of our faith be, then I will believe, that it is so in deed.[42]

---

before men, and not before God," in *The Later Medieval Doctrine of the Eucharistic Sacrifice* (London, 1958), p. 21. But later in the same work, Kidd writes, "With Lombard's conception of the Sacrifice of the Eucharist, Cranmer as we have seen, professes himself ready to agree. The doctrine, then, that the Reformers repudiated was not that put forward by the earlier Scholastics." (*Ibid.*, p. 34.) If Cranmer understood Lombard as meaning "a commemoration before men, and not before God," it is hardly true to say he did not repudiate the doctrine of the earlier scholastics. However, Kidd is certainly correct in asserting that Cranmer held that the Eucharist was a Sacrifice.

Cranmer argued that a proliferation of articles of Faith would result if a tenet was proposed as dogma simply because God in His omnipotence could effect a change.

> . . . you might so, under pretence of God's omnipotencey, make as many articles of our faith as you list, if such arguments might take place, that God by his omnipotent power can convert this substance of bread and wine into the substance of his flesh and blood: ergo he doth so indeed.[43]

The result of this nonscriptural teaching was that people sought their dogma not in the clear light of Scripture "but at the Romish antichrist, believing whatsoever he prescribed unto them, yea, though it were against all reason, all senses, and God's most holy word also." [44]

The fact of the matter was that Christ spoke in figures when He called the bread and wine His Body and Blood. "Christ at that time spake in figures when he did institute that sacrament seeing that it is the nature of all sacraments to be figures." [45] Christ did not teach that the substance of bread was changed into His Body. He was speaking figuratively: "Christ spake these words of the bread, calling it his body, as all the old authors also do affirm." [46]

The Communion Service of 1549, according to Cranmer, did not teach Transubstantiation. "The book of common prayer neither useth any such speech nor giveth any such doctrine, nor I in no point improve that godly book. . . ." [47]

Cranmer denied that Christ was present in the bread either by conversion or inclusion. But Christ was present in the ministration. Cranmer agreed with Martin Bucer who "denieth utterly that Christ is really and substantially present in the bread, either by conversion or inclusion, but in the ministration he affirmeth Christ to be present, and so do I also." [48]

The Archbishop explained what he meant by a true presence in the ministration of the Sacrament. Christ and the Holy Spirit were present *in the recipients* by sanctifying power, virtue, and grace:

> Christ and the Holy Ghost be present in the sacraments; not meaning by that manner of speech, that Christ and the Holy Ghost be present in the water, bread, or wine (which be only the outward

visible sacraments,) but that in the due ministration of the sacraments according to Christ's ordinance and institution Christ and his holy Spirit be truly and indeed present by their mighty and sanctifying power, virtue, and grace, in all them that worthily receive the same.[49]

Christ therefore was present *in the recipients*. This was not a corporal presence. Cranmer held "that the force, the grace, the virtue and benefit of Christ's body that was crucified for us and of his blood that was shed for us, be really and effectually present with all them that duly receive the sacraments." [50] The feeding was a spiritual feeding that did not require corporal presence: "Outwardly we see and feel bread and wine with our outward senses, but inwardly by faith we see and feed upon Christ's true body and blood. But this is a spiritual feeding by faith that requireth no corporal presence." [51]

The substance of the Sacrament was bread and wine. The thing signified was Christ's Body and Blood. "I deny that Christ's body is the substance of the visible sacrament. For the substance of the sacrament is bread and wine, and the thing thereby signified is Christ's body and blood." [52]

Cranmer believed Christ's Risen Body was "the self-same visible and palpable body" that had walked in Galilee and died on the Cross with the same limitations of time and space. With these same limitations he ascended into heaven: "With this self-same body he forsook this world, and ascended into heaven . . . and now sitteth at the right hand of his father. . . ." [53]

Since Christ was limited to heaven until the Last Day, his presence in the Sacrament was similar to the sun's presence on earth. "We say that as the sun corporally is ever in heaven, and no where else, and yet by his operation and virtue the sun is here in earth . . . so likewise our Saviour Christ bodily and corporally is in heaven, sitting at the right hand of his Father." Although he is corporally in heaven, we eat His Flesh and drink His Blood spiritually. We grow to perfection "spiritually by faith eating his flesh, and drinking his blood, although the same corporally be in heaven, far distant from our sight." [54]

The Real Presence meant that the grace and efficacy of his passion was truly present to his true members: "If ye understand by this word 'really,' *re ipsa*, i.e., 'in very deed and effectually,' so Christ by the grace and efficacy of his passion, is in deed and truly present to all his true and holy members." He could not be present corporally because both Scripture and the early Church "professed from the beginning Christ to have left the world, and to sit at the right hand of the Father till he come unto judgment." [55]

The spiritual feeding was a true feeding on the Body and Blood of Christ that surpassed a corporal feeding:

> . . . this feeding is a spiritual feeding, and an heavenly feeding, far passing all corporal and carnal feeding and therefore there is a true presence and a true feeding upon the body and blood, and not "in figure only or not at all" as you most untruly report me as saying to be. This is the true understanding of the true presence, receiving and feeding upon the body and blood of our Saviour Christ, and not, as you deprave the meaning and true sense thereof, that the receiving of Christ is the receiving corporally with the mouth corporal, or that the spiritual receiving is to receive Christ, only by his divine nature. . . .[56]

Although Christ's Body and Blood were united to the "faithful receiver, and not to dumb creatures of bread and wine," [57] the elements were more than nude tokens. The broken loaf was a reminder that Christ was "to them spiritually and effectually given, and of them spiritually and fruitfully taken and eaten, to their spiritual and heavenly comfort, sustentation and nourishment of their souls, as is the bread of their bodies." When the priest distributes the bread, we "must think that inwardly by faith we see Christ feeding both body and soul to eternal life." [58]

Cranmer saw no value or comfort in a corporal presence. "What benefit, I beseech you, is it to us, if Christ be really and corporally in the forms of bread and wine a month or two, a year or two?" [59]

Cranmer interpreted the Roman Catholic position as teaching that Christ left the recipient when the elements were digested. He contrasted that interpretation to his position that Christ remained with the recipient as long as the latter was a member of Christ's Body:

> After the receiving thereof, he flieth up from the receiver into heaven, as soon as the bread is chewed in the mouth or digested in the stomach. But we say, that after what manner Christ is received of us, in the same wise he remaineth in us, so long as we remain the members of Christ.[60]

Since the elements were more than bare tokens, Cranmer did not "utterly deprive the outward sacraments of the name of holy things, because of the holy use whereunto they serve." In the due ministration of these elements Christ was present, "working with his word and sacraments." There was nothing to be worshipped in the bread and wine, "yet in them that duly receive the sacraments is Christ himself inhabiting, and is of all creatures to be worshipped." [61]

Christ was present in the Eucharist as He was present in His Word when He worked in the hearts of His hearers.

By which manner of speech it is not meant that Christ is corporally present in the voice or sound of the speaker (which sound perisheth as soon as the words be spoken), but this speech meaneth that he worketh with his word, using the voice of the speaker, as his instrument to work by; as he useth also his sacraments, whereby he worketh, and therefore is said to be present in them.[62]

Those who approached Communion with Charity and Faith "carnally eat with their mouths this sacramental bread, and drink this wine, so spiritually they may eat and drink the very flesh and blood of Christ which is in heaven, and sitteth at the right hand of his Father." [63]

As partakers of the same table, men were reminded of their unity in one Body of which Christ is the Head: "For when we be made partakers of this one table, what ought we to think, but that we be all members of one spiritual body, whereof Christ is the head." [64]

A key tenet in Cranmer's system was that Christ was "dwelling in us, and we in him." Just as the elements became one with our bodies, so we became one Body with Christ.

And the true eating and drinking of the said body and blood of Christ is, with a constant and lively faith to believe, that Christ gave his body, and shed his blood upon the cross for us, and that he doth so join and incorporate himself to us, that he is our head, and we his members, and flesh of his flesh, and bone of his bones, having him dwelling in us, and we in him.[65]

In Eucharistic doctrine, as in other matters, Cranmer was a man who looked at every side of a question. In the words of Stephen Neill, "his mind moved slowly and cautiously, but . . .

when he came to a decision, the decision was his own." [66] His Eucharistic teaching resembled that of the Swiss school of reformers, and he was demonstrably influenced by their insights.

Cyril Richardson, Gregory Dix, and others have contended that Cranmer moved "within the basic framework of Zwingli's opinions," [67] but the independent Archbishop departed from the Zurich humanist on certain points and it would be false to label him a Zwinglian. Cranmer's doctrine also approached that of Martin Bucer of Strasbourg, but C. H. Smyth certainly overstated his case when he labeled Cranmer a consistent "Suvermerianist." [68]

Cranmer was open to the insights of other thinkers; his mind was the mind of a scholar at work.[69] It seems safe to say that a precise "label" for Cranmer's doctrine is still *sub judice*. He was influenced by Zwingli and Bucer (and by Oecolampadius, Peter Martyr, John a Lasco, and his compatriot Bishop Ridley), but he was also a keen student of Scripture and the Fathers, a man with an independent bent of mind. Perhaps the proliferating plethora of labels for Cranmer's thought stems from a hesitancy to credit him with an individuality of his own. Perhaps he should be labelled a "Cranmerian," one influenced by many streams of thought, but one who sought Eucharistic doctrine which has "been declared to the Church from the beginning by such evident and manifest passages of Scripture, and the same has also been subsequently commended to the ears of the faithful . . . by the first ecclesiastical writers." [70]

Cranmer, a liturgical genius of the first rank, drew up rites with thundering repercussions, rites that reflected not only the doctrine of Zurich or Basle or Strasbourg, but varied streams of doctrine from several sources, not least of which was the beleaguered but still mighty Church of Rome.

The Order of the Communion, and the Lord's Supper "Commonly Called the Masse"

THE ORDER OF THE COMMUNION

In March, 1548, the *Order of the Communion* was issued by royal proclamation.[71] This vernacular rite for congregational Communion was to be inserted into the historic Mass. An opening exhortation was also provided to be delivered by the priest at least one day *prior* to the Communion Service. The rest of the *Order* was a uniform rite in Cranmerian prose for Communion of the people.

The *Order,* cautious in its wording, departed abruptly from past tradition in three particulars: first, it inserted a whole new rite within the Mass itself; second, the rite was in the vernacular; finally, Communion was to be distributed in both species.

Except for the preliminary exhortation, the *Order* consisted of rites to be inserted into the Mass immediately after the Celebrant's Communion.

Rubrics were provided instructing the priest to consecrate only as much bread as was required for the people, and to fill a large chalice or some "fair and convenient Cup or Cuppes" with wine.[72] The priest was instructed to partake sparingly of the consecrated wine, and to leave both consecrated species covered on the altar. Immediately after his own Communion, he was to turn and deliver still another exhortation "without the varying of any other Rite or Ceremony in the Masse (untill other order shalbe provided)." [73]

After this long exhortation, the communicants were invited to approach the altar. The priest or one of the assembly then recited a general confession. There followed a general absolution and the reading of consoling passages from Scripture called the "Comfortable Words." The priest next said the "Prayer of Humble Access," [74] distributed the Communion, and terminated the vernacular *Order* with a blessing.

When the *Order of the Communion* was forwarded to the hierarchy, the document stated that "sundry of his majesty's most grave and well learned prelates, and other learned men in Scripture," [75] agreed on the rite. Scholars, however, have been unable to unearth any evidence of such a meeting,[76] and it has been agreed generally that Cranmer was the author of the rite.[77]

There is abundant evidence, however, that the authors of the *Order of the Communion* had before them a document that had originated at Cologne.[78] After the Imperial Diet of Regensburg (1541), Archbishop Hermann von Wied of Cologne had summoned Martin Bucer, Philipp Melanchthon and others to prepare for him the necessary ordinances for a reformation of his diocese.[79]

These were published in 1543 under the title *Einfaltigs bedencken.*
A Latin edition, *Simplex ac pia deliberatio* appeared in 1545. Two
English editions followed, in 1547 and 1548, entitled *A Simple
and Religious Consultatio.*[80]

The Communion rite of the *Consultatio* should not be considered a Lutheran work; it was the work of Martin Bucer.
Melanchthon himself wrote: ". . . I read of the ceremonies of Baptism and the Lord's Supper which he [i.e., Bucer] composed." [81]

Nor should it be presumed that the *Consultatio* Communion
rite was followed slavishly by the authors of the *Order of the
Communion.*[82] Although these authors followed the general outline
of the *Consultatio,* the *Order of the Communion* was for the most
part an original composition.

The insertion of this vernacular rite into the Prayer Books
and Missals of the realm was a momentous beginning in the
revision of the central act of Christian worship. The theological
implications of the *Order of the Communion* are seen best only
in relation to the "Supper of the Lorde, and the Holy Communion,
Commonly Called the Masse," of which it was destined to be an
integral part.

The *Order of the Communion* and the new Communion
Service of which the *Order* would be a part reflected the Eucharistic theology of Thomas Cranmer.[83] Through his talented pen key
tenets of Zurich and Strasbourg also influenced the English rite.

"COMMONLY CALLED THE MASSE"

T. M. Parker wrote that "theology can never be a purely
theoretical science, and it is therefore vain to imagine that differences in religious outlook can fail to find expression in outward
observance. For religion centres in worship, and worship is the
expression of belief." [84] Christian worship itself centers in the
Lord's Supper. And the Lord's Supper of 1549 reflects the belief
of Thomas Cranmer.

In a notable example of conservatism, Cranmer retained
"Masse" in "The Supper of the Lorde, and the holy Communion,
commonly called the Masse." [85] According to Heiko Obermann,
"any reform in nonessentials would only confuse and thus mislead
the simple folk. The so-called 'liturgical conservatism' of the
magisterial reformers, where present, stems from this pastoral

concern." [86] The title was conservative. But the Service was different.

The Service opened with two rubrics reflecting Cranmer's belief that the Lord's Supper was not a work of the priest alone. All present were urged to communicate. Since the efficacy of the Service derived from personal dispositions, all were urged to repentance and Charity.

The "vestments rubric" that followed was a cautious attempt to diminish sacrificial overtones without disturbing the laity. The priest was to wear an alb with vestment *or* cope.[87] Deacons were to wear albs and tunicles. The latter were to help "in the ministration" and vest "for their ministry." There was no reference to Sacrifice:

Upon the daie, and at the tyme appoincted for the ministracion of the holy Communion, the Priest that shal execute the holy ministery, shall put upon hym the vesture appoincted for that ministracion, that is to saye: A white Albe plain, with a vestement or Cope. And where there be many Priestes, or Deacons, there so many shalbe ready to helpe the Priest, in the ministracion, as shalbee requisite: and shall haue upon theim lykewise, the vestures appoincted for their ministery, that is to saye, Albes, with tunacles. Then shall the Clerkes syng in Englishe for the office, or Introite, (as they call it) a Psalme appointed for that daie.

This cautious retention of vestments was probably another example of liturgical conservatism. Bucer considered it a concession to antiquity and the infirmity of the day. Shortly after landing on English soil, he and Fagius wrote Strasbourg about the retention of vestments:

We hear that some concessions have been made both to a respect for antiquity and to the infirmity of the present age; such, for instance, as the vestments commonly used in the sacrament of the eucharist . . . they are only to be retained for a time, lest the people, not having yet learned Christ, should be deterred by too extensive innovations from embracing his religion, and that rather they may be won over.[88]

The Communion Service began with the intonation of the Introit by the choir. Almost all the private priestly prayers prescribed in the Sarum Mass were omitted. There were no rubrics for the *Veni Creator, Introibo, Judica,* the private *Kyrie, Con-*

fitemini, Confiteor, Misereatur, Absolutio, Aduitorium, Aufer a nobis, the kissing of the altar, and sign of the cross.[89]

In the context of the penitential tone of Cranmer's Service, the omission of the *Confiteor* is most significant. This prayer had formerly been regarded as a sacerdotal preparation for the Sacrifice.[90] Also there had been within the prayer confession to the Saints.[91] In the Communion Service of 1549 all confession would be to God, begging pardon through the merits of the one Mediator, Jesus Christ. Of the Sarum preparatory prayers, only the Lord's Prayer and the Collect for Purity were retained.

Following the Introit the priest was to say or the choir sing the *Kyrie.* Then the priest was to intone the *Gloria* and the choir to sing beginning with "And in Yearth peace. . . ." It is noteworthy that in the rubric for the priestly intonation, the priest was described as standing at "Goddes borde," whereas before the Collect for Purity he was before the "Altar."

At the conclusion of the *Gloria,* the priest turned for the salutation. The Collect for the day followed, with one of the two proposed Collects for the king.[92]

After the Collects, there were rubrics for the Epistle, Gospel, and Creed. The Minister was next directed to deliver a homily. If his homily did not exhort the congregation to worthy Communion, he was to read the first exhortation in the Communion Service. This exhortation was the same one that had immediately preceded the people's Communion in the *Order of the Communion.* It stressed spiritual reception, repentance, faith, and charity. The laity were reminded that unworthy reception made them guilty of the Body of Christ, but worthy reception was to "dwell in Christ and Christ in us."

But not all were approaching the Sacrament in Reformation England. For these unfortunate congregations, still another long exhortation was provided, this time the one that had introduced the *Order of the Communion.* This exhortation continued the emphasis on spiritual reception. The effects of Communion were comfort, remembrance of the Passion, and assurance of redemption. The Mass was a banquet; the marriage garment for such a banquet involved faith, repentance, and purpose of amendment. Since the Communion was receptionist, only the virtuous encountered the Body of Christ. The exhortation concluded with a nascent Anglican comprehensiveness urging tolerance for those who confessed publicly as well as for those who sought out a "Minister" privately.

In brief Offertory rubrics that followed the exhortation, Cranmer diminished sacrificial overtones.[93] It was the people who offered. And they offered not Christ, but alms for the poor and money for support of the Minister. All twenty Offertory verses directly or indirectly referred to almsgiving or support of the clergy.

In this part of the Service, the words "offer" and "offeryng" always referred to money. When brief reference was made to the elements, the people were partakers of the same, and "persons appoynted to receiue the holy Communion." In further emphasis that the elements were received and not offered, those unable or unwilling to communicate were excluded from the "quire."

Sarum referred to the elements as a Sacrifice. All such references were eliminated in 1549. There were no "manual acts" rubrics directing the priest to offer the elements. Private priestly prayers were deleted. The celebrant was simply to prepare bread, wine, and water. After this succinct directive, he was urged to intone the Preface.

The first two of the twenty scriptural Offertory sentences and the rubrics are printed below as an example of the almsgiving emphasis in the 1549 Offertory:

> Then shall folowe for the Offertory, one or mo, of these Sentences of holy scripture, to bee song whiles the people doo offer, or els one of theim to bee saied by the minister, immediatly afore the offeryng.

> Let your light so shine before men, that they maye see your good woorkes, and glorify your father whiche is in heaven. (Math. v.)

> Laie not up for your selfes treasure upon the yearth, where the rust and mothe doth corrupt, and where theues breake through and steale: But laie up for your selfes tressures in heauen, where neyther rust nor mothe doth corrupt, and where theues do not breake through nor steale. (Math. vi[.])

. . . .

> Where there be Clerkes, thei shall syng one, or many of the sentences aboue written, accordyng to the length, and shortenesse of the tyme, that the people be offeryng. In the meane tyme, whyles the

Clerkes do syng the Offertory, so many as are disposed, shall offer unto the poore mennes boxe euery one accordynge to his habilitie and charitable mynde. And at the offeryng daies appoynted: euery manne and woman shall Paie to the Curate, the due and accustomed offerynges. Then so manye as shalbe partakers of the holy Communion, shall tary still in the quire, or in some conuenient place, nigh the quire, the men on the one side, and the women on the other syde. All other (that mynde not to receiue the said holy Communion) shall departe out of the quire, except the ministers and Clerkes.

Than shall the minister take so much Bread and Wine, as shall suffice for the persons appoynted to receiue the holy Communion, laying the breade upon the corporas, or els in the paten, or in some other comely thyng, prepared for that purpose. And puttyng ye wyne into the Chalice, or els in some faire or cōueniente cup, prepared for that use (if the Chalice will not serue) puttyng thereto a little pure and cleane water: And settyng both the breade and wyne upon the Alter: Then the Prieste shall saye.

The Lorde be with you.

The Sarum Prefaces were beautiful hymns of praise and thanksgiving. Cranmer left them almost intact in his new Service.[94] However, he reduced the Proper Prefaces to five: one each for Christmas, Easter, Ascension, Whitsunday, and Trinity Sunday. The *Sanctus* and *Benedictus,* scriptural hymns of praise, were also left intact in 1549.

But the Canon was not left intact. In this central part of the Service, Cranmer's revision was most radical and most apparent. It was in the Canon that his own Eucharistic theology appeared clearly. Proceeding with caution, he maintained the external appearance of the Sarum rite. Most of the significant expressions were meticulously preserved. But through rearrangement of the prayers themselves and through changes in wording, he was able to embody his position on Sacrifice and Real Presence. Although his Canon adheres to the form of Sarum and the Eastern liturgies,[95] he rearranged and rewrote those parts that he considered vehicles of medieval misunderstanding.

To appreciate Cranmer's composition and its relation to Sarum, the two rites are provided below in vertical columns. For, as the Standing Liturgical Commission of the Protestant Episcopal Church states, "the only way in which one can assess what Cranmer was attempting to do, and how successful or unsuccessful he was in his manner of doing it, is by a side by side and point by point comparison of the Sarum original, and the resultant text of the First Prayer Book." [96] The italicizing of words in the 1549 Service[97] is provided by this writer in an attempt to illustrate how Cranmer's theology is reflected in the very wording of his text.

SARUM	1549

1549

When the Clerkes have dooen syngyng, then shall the Priest, or Deacon, turne hym to the people and saye.

Let us praie for the whole state of Christes churche.

Then the Priest turnyng him to the Altar, shall saye or syng, playnly and distinctly, this prayer folowyng.

SARUM

Therefore, most merciful Father, we humbly pray and beseech thee through Jesus Christ thy Son our Lord, to receive and bless these ✠ gifts, these ✠ offerings, these ✠ holy undefiled sacrifices which we offer unto thee,

1549

Almightie and euerliuyng God, whiche by thy holy Apostle haste taught us *to make prayers and supplicacions, and to geue thankes* for al menne: We humbly beseche thee moste mercyfully to *receiue these our praiers:* which we offre unto thy diuine Maiestie,

SARUM

first of all for thy holy catholic Church, which do thou vouchsafe to keep in peace, to defend, unite, and govern throughout all the world: together with thy servant our Pope N., and our Bishop N., and our King N., and all orthodox believers, and maintainers of the Catholic and Apostolic faith.

1549

besechyng thee to inspire cōtinually the uniuersall churche, with the spirite of truethe, unitie and concorde: And graunt that al they that do cōfesse thy holy name, maye agree in the trueth of thy holye worde, and liue in unitie and godly loue. Speciallye we beseche thee to saue and defende thy seruant, Edwarde our Kyng, that under him we maye be Godly and quietly gouerned. And graunt unto his whole cōusaile, and to all that be put in aucthoritie under

SARUM   1549

hym, that they maye truely and
indifferently minister iustice, to
the punishement of wickednesse
and vice, and to the maintenaunce
of Goddes true religion and vertue. Geue grace (O heauenly father) to all Bishoppes, Pastors,
and Curates, that thei maie bothe
by their life and doctrine, *set
furthe thy true and liuely worde,
and* rightely and duely *administer
thy holy* Sacramentes.

Remember, O Lord, thy
servants and handmaids N. and
N., and all here present, whose
faith is perceived, whose devotion
is known unto thee: for whom we
offer, or who themselves offer
unto thee this sacrifice of praise
for themselves and all who belong
to them, for the hope of their salvation and safety, and who pay
their vows unto thee, the eternal,
true and living God.

And to al thy people geue thy
heauenly grace, that with meke
heart and due reuerence, they
maye heare and receiue thy holy
worde, truely seruynge thee in
holyness and righteousnes, all the
dayes of their lyfe: And wee
moste hūbly beseche thee of thy
goodnes (O Lorde) to coumforte
and succour all them, whyche in
this transytory lyfe be in trouble,
sorowe, nede, syckenes, or any
other aduersitie. And especially
we commend unto thy mercifull
goodnes, this congregacion which
is here assembled in thy name,
*to celebrate the commemoracion
of the most glorious death* of thy
sonne:

In communion with and ven-
erating the memory of, first of
all, the glorious ever-virgin Mary,
mother of our God and Lord Iesu
Christ, and also thy Apostles and
Martyrs, Peter and Paul, Andrew,
James, John, Thomas, James,
Philip, Bartholomew, Matthew,
Simon, and Thaddeus; Linus

And here *wee doe geue unto thee
moste high praise, & hartie
thankes* for the wonderfull grace
and vertue, declared in all thy
sainctes, from the begynning of
the worlde: And chiefly in the
glorious and most blessed virgin
Mary, mother of thy sonne Jesu
Christe our Lorde and God, and

Cletus, Clement, Xystus, Cornelius, Cyprian, Lawrence, Chrysogonus, John and Paul, Cosmas and Damian: and of all thy saints: by whose merits and prayers grant we may in all things be defended by help of thy protection. Through the same Christ our Lord. Amen.

(See after Consecration)

in the holy Patriarches, Prophetes, Apostles and Martyrs, *whose examples* (O Lorde) *and stedfastnes* in thy fayth and kepyng thy holye commaundementes: *graunt us to folowe.*

We commend unto thy mercye (O Lorde) all other thy seruantes, which are departed hence from us, with the signe of faith, and nowe do reste in the slepe of peace: Graūte unto them, we beseche thee, thy mercy, and euerlasting peace, and that at the day of the generall resurreccion, we and all they whiche bee of the misticall body of thy sonne, maye altogether be set on his right hand, and heare that his most ioyful voyce: Come unto me, O ye that be blessed of my father, and possesse the kingdom, whiche is prepared for you, from the begynning of the worlde: Graunt this, O father, for Jesus Christes sake, *our onely mediatour and aduocate.*

We beseech thee, therefore, O Lord, graciously to accept this oblation of our service and of thy whole family, and to order our days in thy peace, and command that we be delivered from eternal damnation, and be numbered in the flock of thine elect. Through Christ our Lord. Amen.

O God heauenly father, whiche of thy tender mercie, diddest geue thine only sonne Jesu Christ, to suffer deathe upon the crosse for our redempcion, who made there (*by his one oblacion once offered*) *a full, perfect, and sufficient sacrifyce, oblacion, and satysfacyon, for the sinnes of the whole worlde,* and did *institute, and in his holy Gospell commaund*

SARUM   1549

us to celebrate a perpetuall mem-
ory, of that his precious death,
untyll his comming again:

Which oblation do thou, O   Heare us (o merciful father) we
God, we beseech thee, vouchsafe   besech thee: and with thy holy
to make altogether bles✠sed, ap✠   spirite & worde vouchsafe to bl✠
proved, rati✠fied, reasonable, and esse and sanc✠tifie these thy
acceptable, that it may be made   *gyftes, and creatures of bread and*
unto us the Bo✠dy and Bl✠ood   *wyne, that they maie be unto us*
of thy most dearly beloved Son   the bodye and bloude of thy
our Lord Jesus Christ.   moste derely beloued sonne Jesus
                                   Christe.

Who, the day before he suf-   Who in the same nyghte that he
fered, took bread into his holy   was betrayed: tooke breade,* and
and venerable hands, and lifting   when he had blessed, and geuen
up his eyes toward heaven unto   thankes: he brake it, and gaue it
thee, O God his Father almighty,   to his disciples, saiyng: Take,
giving thanks unto thee, he bles✠   eate, this is my bodye which is
sed, brake, and gave it to his dis- geuen for you; do this in remem-
ciples, saying: Take and eat ye all braunce of me.
of this, For this is my Body.

Likewise after supper, tak-   Likewyse, after supper he toke
ing also this glorious Cup into his the cuppe,† and when he had
holy and venerable hands, again   geuen thankes, he gaue it to them,
giving thanks unto thee, bles✠sed, saiing: drynk ye all of this, for
and gave it to his disciples, say- this is my bloude of the newe
ing: Take and drink ye all of this. Testament, whyche is shed for
For this is the Cup of my Blood   you and for many, for remission
of the new and eternal Testament,   of synnes: do this as oft as ye
a Mystery of the faith, which shall shall drinke it, in remembraunce
be shed for you and for many for   of me.
remission of sins. As often as ye
shall do these things, ye shall do
them in remembrance of me.

---

* Marginal rubric: "Here the Prieste must take the breade into
his hādes."

† Marginal rubric: "Here the Prieste shall take the cuppe into his
hādes."

SARUM

Wherefore also, O Lord, we thy servants, together with thy holy people, having in remembrance both the blessed Passion of the same Christ thy Son our Lord God, and His Resurrection from the dead, and also his glorious Ascension into heaven, do offer to thine excellent Majesty of thine own gifts and bounties a pure ✠ oblation,[98] a holy ✠ oblation, a spotless ✠ oblation, the holy ✠ Bread of eternal life, and the Cup ✠ of everlasting salvation.

Upon which do thou vouchsafe to look with a favorable and gracious countenance, and to hold them accepted, as thou didst vouchsafe to hold accepted the offerings of thy righteous servant Abel, and the sacrifice of our forefather Abraham, and that which thy High Priest Melchizedech offered unto thee, a holy sacrifice, a spotless oblation.

We humbly beseech thee, Almighty God: command these things to be brought up by the hands of thy holy Angel to thine Altar on high before the sight of thy divine Majesty: that as many of us as shall by this altar-partaking, receive the sacred Bo✠dy and Bl✠ood of thy Son, may be filled with every heavenly bene✠diction and grace. Through the same Christ our Lord. Amen.

1549

These wordes before rehersed are to be saied, turning still to the Altar, *without any eleuacion, or shewing the Sacrament to the people.* WHerfore, O Lorde and heauenly father, *accordyng to the Instytucion of thy derely beloued sonne,* our sauior Jesu Christ, *we thy humble seruantes do celebrate, and make here before thy diuine Maiestie, with these thy holy giftes, the memoryall whyche thy sonne hath wylled us to make: hauing in remembraunce* his blessed passion, mightie resurreceyon, and gloryous ascencion, *renderyng unto thee most hartie thankes,* for the innumerable benefites procured unto us by thesame,

entierely desiryng thy fatherly goodnes, mercifully to *accepte this our Sacrifice of praise and thankes geuing:*

moste humblye beseching thee to graunt, that *by the merites* and deathe *of thy sōne Jesus* Christ, *and through faith* in his bloud, wee and al thy whole church, may obteigne remission of our sinnes, and all other benefites of hys passyon. And here *wee offre and present unto the (O Lord) oure selfe, oure soules, and bodies, to be a* reasonable, holy, and liuely sacrifice unto thee: humbly besechying thee, that *whosoeuer shalbee partakers of thys holy*

SARUM   1549

Communion maye worthely receiue the moste precious body and
bloude of thy sonne Jesus Christe;
and bee fulfilled with thy grace
and heauenly benediccion, *and
made one bodye with thy sonne
Jesu Christe, that he maye dwell
in them, and they in hym.*

Remember also, O Lord, thy
servants, and handmaids N. and
N., who have gone before us with
the sign of faith, and rest in the   (See before consecration)
sleep of peace. Grant unto them,
we beseech thee, O Lord, and to
all that have fallen asleep in
Christ, a place of refreshment,
light, and peace. Through the
same Christ our Lord. Amen.

And to us sinners also, thy   And although we be unworthy
servants who trust in the multi-   (through our manyfolde synnes)
tude of thy mercies, vouchsafe to *to offre unto thee any Sacryfice:*
grant some part and fellowship   *Yet we beseche thee to accepte*
with thy holy Apostles and Mar-   *this our bounden duetie and*
tyrs: with John, Stephen, Mat-   *seruice,* and *commaunde these our*
thias, Barnabas, Ignatius, Alexan- *prayers and supplicacions* by the
der, Marcellinus, Peter, Felicity, Ministery of thy holy Angels, to
Perpetua, Agatha, Lucy, Agnes,   be brought up into thy holy *Tab-*
Cecilia, Anastasia, and all thy   *ernacle* before the syght of thy
Saints: into whose company ad-   dyuine maiestie: not waiing our
mit us, we beseech thee, not as a merites, but pardonyng our of-
weigher of merits, but as a be-   fences, through Christe our Lorde,
stower of pardon. Through Christ
our Lord.

Through whom, O Lord,   by whome, and with whome, in
thou dost create, sanc✠tify, quic✠ the unitie of the holy Ghost, all
ken, bl✠ess, and bestow upon us   honour and glory, be unto thee,
all these good things.   O father almightie, world without
By ✠ him, and with ✠ him,   ende. Amen.
and in ✠ him, in the unity of the

Holy Ghost, all honour and glory
is unto thee, O God the Father
✠ Almighty, world without end.
Amen.

Cranmer rearranged the Sarum Canon into three long prayers, a prayer of general intercession, a prayer of Consecration, and a prayer of oblation. A few phrases of the historic Canon he eliminated completely; others he rewrote or transferred to novel contexts; and in some places he made additions of his own.

In the first prayer of general intercession, there was no mention of Sacrifice. This was probably occasioned by fear that mingling the intercession with mention of Sacrifice could lead to a propitiatory interpretation. There would have been added danger of the laity interpreting the new rite in a piacular sense, because Cranmer transferred the prayer for the dead to before the Consecration. Cranmer began the prayer "for the whole state of Christes churche" not with a petition to receive these "gifts, these offerings, these holy undefiled sacrifices which we offer," but with an offering of "prayers and supplicacions," a giving of thanks, a request "to receiue these our praiers: which we offre."

In a typical example of rearrangement and omission for doctrinal reasons, Cranmer departed from the Sarum Canon's supplication for those in authority. Sarum prayed first for the Pope, then the Bishop, and finally the King. Cranmer's prayer omitted the Pope, prayed first for the King and Council, and finally for Bishops, Pastors, and Curates.

The intercession for the clergy teaches their role in Cranmer's theology. They were not ordained to offer Sacrifice, but "to set furthe thy true and liuely worde" and "duely administer thy holy Sacramentes."

In the prayer for all present, they were not gathered to "offer unto thee this sacrifice of praise for themselves and all who belong to them, for the hope of salvation and safety." They were assembled "to celebrate the commemoracion of the most glorious death of thy sonne."

Cranmer skilfully combined both Sarum lists of saints into one brief litany. He mentioned by general classification only those who appear in Scripture, beginning with "the glorious and most blessed virgin Mary." There was no mention of veneration of the saints nor of their merits and prayers. By implication, this part of the new Canon cleverly taught the "one, only Mediator" doctrine.[99] Mention of the saints was part of giving praise and thanksgiving. We give "unto thee moste high praise, & hartie thankes" for the saints. The prayer requested assistance in following their steadfast example in keeping the commandments and in faith.

The intercession for the deceased, which appears after the thanksgiving for the saints, again teaches Cranmer's dogma that Christ is "our onely mediatour and aduocate." This clause was added to the prayer almost as an afterthought. It probably reflected apprehension on Cranmer's part that, despite his cautious wording, the very mention of the dead could imply the "superstition" of purgatory, suffrages, and a satisfactory Sacrifice. The prayer carefully avoided description of the state of those deceased. They were simply "departed hence from us, with the signe of faith, and nowe do reste in the slepe of peace." Yet there was still a prayer for "thy mercy." This prayer also reflected Cranmer's strong eschatology and Mystical Body tenets.

The Sarum rite made a double oblation immediately before the Consecratory prayer. The first prayer presented "this oblation of our service." The second asked that the "oblation" be made blessed, approved, ratified, reasonable, and acceptable.

Cranmer changed this *Hanc Igitur* and *Quam Oblationem* considerably. He had no mention of the people making an oblation. Rather, it was Christ who died on the Cross for our Redemption, and made there "(by his one oblacion once offered) a full, perfect, and sufficient sacrifyce, oblacion, and satysfaccyon, for the sinnes of the whole worlde." In his eagerness to emphasize the uniqueness of Christ's propitiation and mediation, Cranmer even used the nonscriptural word "satisfaccion." [100] Instead of wishing us to make an oblation, Christ instituted and commanded us to "celebrate a perpetuall memory, of that his precious death."

The preliminary invocation of the Trinity reveals Cranmer's teaching on the Real Presence. The Trinity was asked to sanctify the elements, "these thy gyftes and creatures of bread and wyne." [101] Where Sarum prayed *"ut nobis corpus et sanguis fiat,"* Cranmer's rite asked that "they maie be unto us the bodye and bloude." As he, Zwingli, and Bucer had contended in their writings, the elements would be the Body and Blood *to the faithful recipient.*

But they were still "creatures of bread and wyne." There was no substantial change.

In the narration of the Institution, the Consecratory prayer itself, Cranmer eliminated all nonscriptural embellishments of the Sarum rite. Gone were "into his holy and venerable hands," "lifting up his eyes toward heaven," "unto thee, O God his Father almighty, giving thanks unto thee," "brake," "glorious Cup," "eternal," "a Mystery of the Faith." What remained was a conflation of all four New Testament accounts, an account which formed almost the fullest possible combination of Our Lord's acts and words.

The "manual Acts" for the Consecration were stark and simple. The priest's hands would accomplish approximately what Christ would have done at the Last Supper. Only two manual blessings were retained, both in the preliminary invocation. There was no action or gesture indicating Sacrifice or adoration. In fact the prescription was definite that the priest was to say the words "without any eleuacion, or shewing the Sacrament to the people." What was being symbolized was a memorial meal, a Sacrifice of ourselves, our praise and thanksgiving.

In the final third of his Canon, the prayer of oblation, Cranmer offered a Sacrifice of ourselves, praise, and thanksgiving —a different Sacrifice than that of Sarum. The Sarum prayer offered "a pure oblation, a holy oblation, a spotless oblation." Cranmer's rite "accordyng to the Instytucyon" made "with these thy holy giftes, the memoryall whyche thy sonne hath wylled us to make." It rendered "unto thee moste hartie thankes."

In a striking omission, Cranmer dropped the comparison with the offerings of Abel, Abraham, and Melchizedech, despite the Scriptural basis for these oblations. His prayer simply requested God "mercifully to accepte this our Sacrifice of praise and thankes geuing." Another change to be noted was that the "Altar" on high of the Sarum Canon became "thy holy Tabernacle."

Cranmer did not offer "these . . . things" to God. His Sacrifice was an offering of "oure selfe, oure soules, and bodies, to be a reasonable, holy, and liuely sacrifice unto thee." Such a total commitment led to a reception of "the most precious body and bloude." The communicants were "made one bodye with thy sonne Jesu Christe, that he maye dwell in them, and they in hym."

The intercession for the dead was transferred to before the

Consecration, where there was no mention of Sacrifice. This re-arrangement reduced the dangers of propitiatory interpretations. The concluding section of Cranmer's oblation offered "our bounden duetie and seruice" and "our prayers and supplicacions." Our offenses would be pardoned not by God's "waiyng our merites," but through "Christe our Lorde." On a final note of rendering all glory to Christ for the Redemption, Cranmer's Canon closed with a single doxology and the all-important "Amen."

After the *Pater Noster* and *Pax,* the rubrics prescribed the *Pascall Lambe* prayer. In this prayer we see once again Cranmer's conviction that Christ was offered "once for al" on the Cross, that He took away the world's sins, that the Communion Service was a feast:

> The Priest.
> CHrist our Pascall lambe is offred up for us, once for al, when he bare our sinnes on hys body upon the crosse, for he is the very lambe of God, that taketh away the sinnes of the worlde: wherfore let us kepe a joyfull and holy feast with the Lorde.

In the priest's invitation that followed, those who repented and had charity and purpose of amendment were invited to take the Sacrament for their comfort. The Confession to follow immediately was made to "God, and to his holy church." In the light of subsequent developments, it should be noted that the communicants approached kneeling.

Following the absolution the priest pronounced the "coumfortable woordes." The three passages selected by Cranmer served to emphasize the doctrine of justification by faith in the merits of Christ and the unique mediation of the Lord.

> Then shall the Priest also say.
> Heare what coumfortable woordes our sauior Christ sayeth, to all that truely turne to him.
> Come unto me all that trauell and bee heauy laden, and I shall refreshe you. So God loued the worlde that he gaue his onely begotten sonne, to the ende that al that beleue in hym, shoulde not perishe, but haue lyfe euerlasting.
> Heare also what saint Paul sayeth.
> This is a true saying, and woorthie of all men to bee receiued, that Jesus Christe came into thys worlde to saue sinners.

Heare also what saint John sayeth.

If any man sinne, we haue an aduocate with the father, Jesus Christ the righteous, and he is the propiciacion for our sinnes.

The Prayer of Humble Access followed. The priest was located at "gods boord." The altar was a table; the context was one of an approaching meal. Once again the eating of Christ's Flesh and Blood was approximated to dwelling in Him and He in us.

Then shall the Priest turnyng him to gods boord knele down, and say in the name of all of them, that shall receyue the Communion, this prayer folowing.

WE do not presume to come to this thy table (o mercifull lord) trusting in our owne righteousnes, but in thy manifold & great mercies: we be not woorthie so much as to gather up the cromes under thy table, but thou art the same lorde whose propertie is alwayes to haue mercie: Graunt us therefore (gracious lorde) so to eate the fleshe of thy dere sonne Jesus Christ, and to drynke his bloud in these holy Misteries, that we may continuallye dwell in hym, and he in us, that oure synfull bodyes may bee made cleane by his body, and our soules washed through hys most precious bloud. Amen.

In the Communion, the priest was one of the "Ministers"; the elements were "the Communion" and "the Sacramente." Significantly, the administrative prayer was that the Body "whiche was geuen" and the Blood "which was shed" preserve body and soul.

Then shall the Prieste firste reciue the Communion in both kindes himselfe, and next deliuer it to other Ministers, if any be there presente (that they may bee ready to helpe the chiefe Minister) and after to the people.

And when he deliuereth the Sacramente of the body of Christe, he shall say to euery one these woordes.

The body of our Lorde Jesus Christe whiche was geuen for thee, preserue thy bodye and soule unto euerlasting lyfe.

And the Minister deliuering the Sacramēt of the bloud, and geuing euery one to drinke once and no more, shall say.

The bloud of our Lorde Jesus Christe which was shed for thee, preserue thy bodye and soule unto euerlasting lyfe.

If there be a Deacon or other Priest, then shal he folow with the Chalice: and as the priest ministreth the Sacramēt of the body, so shal he (for more expediciō) minister the Sacrament of the bloude, in fourme before written.

In the Communion tyme the Clarkes shall syng.

ii. O lambe of god that takeste away the sinnes of the worlde: haue mercie upon us.
i. O lambe of god that takeste away the synnes of the worlde: graunt us thy peace.

Beginning so soone as the Prieste doeth receyue the holy Communion:

Immediately following the Communion the choir was to sing a "post Communion" verse. The twenty-two Scriptural selections had a marked tone of future amendment. The first two are listed here to give an indication of that tone.

Sentences of holy scripture, to be sayd or song euery day one, after the holy Communion, called the post Communion.

If any man will folowe me, let him forsake hymselfe, and take up his crosse and folowe me. (Math. xvi.)
Whosoeuer shall indure unto thende, he shalbe saued. (Mar. xiii.)

The 1549 Communion Service concluded with a fixed Collect following the "post Communion" verse, and a final blessing. The final Collect was one of thanksgiving for the "spirituall foode of the most precious body and bloud of thy sonne," and assurance of salvation and mystical oneness that results from partaking of the Body and Blood of Christ.

The seven rubrics following the Communion Service leave no doubt that to the framer of the new Service the Lord's Supper was just that, a *Supper*, a Communion. The rubrics revealed a concerted effort to avoid all hints of propitiatory Sacrifice or real corporal Presence.

If there were no communicants, there was to be no Communion Service. Instead Cranmer proposed a truncated Service concluding at the Offertory. He provided eight intercessory prayers to conclude this abbreviated Service. To make sure there was no misunderstanding, the priest was to wear slightly different vestments for this Service and give the final blessing immediately after one of the Collects provided. Since the Collects are of a general nature, only the first one is given below.

Collectes to bee sayed after the Offertory, when there is no Communion, euery such day one.

ASsist us mercifully, O Lord, in these our supplicacions & praiers, and dispose the way of thy seruantes, toward the attainement of euerlasting saluacyon, that emong all the chaunges and chaunces of thys mortall lyfe, they maye euer bee defended by thy moste gracious and readye helpe: through Christe our Lorde. Amen.

. . . .

Upon wednesdaies & frydaies, the English Letany shalbe said or song in all places, after suche forme as is appoynted by the kynges maiesties Iniunccions: Or as is or shal bee other wyse appoynted by his highnes. And thoughe there be none to cōmunicate with the Prieste, yet these dayes (after the Letany ended) the Priest shall put upon him a playn Albe or surplesse, with a cope, and say al thinges at the Altar (appoynted to bee sayde at the celebracyon of the lordes Supper) untill after the offertory. And then shall adde one or two of the Collectes afore written, as occasion shall serue by his discrecion. And then turning him to the people shall let them depart, with the accustomed blessing. And the same order shall be used all other dayes, whensoeuer the people be customably assembled to pray in the churche, and none disposed to communicate with the Priest.

Lykewyse in Chappelles annexed, and all other places, there shalbe no celebracion of the Lordes supper, except there be some to communicate with the Priest. And in suche Chapelles annexed where ye people hath not bene accustomed to pay any holy bread, there they must either make some charitable prouision for the bering of the charges of the Communion, or elles (for receyuyng of the same) resort to theyr Parish Churche.

There was also provision for the type of bread to be used. It was still unleavened and round, although now "somethyng more larger and thicker then it was." There was to be no print, probably to avoid the "superstition" of a true Presence subsequent to the time of lawful use. The bread was to be broken, as it was at the Last Supper and as is fitting for a meal. There was also the fateful concluding remark that men must not think less to be received in part of the bread than in the whole, but in each part the whole Body of Christ.

For aduoyding of all matters and occasyon of dyscencyon, it is mete that the breade prepared for the Communion, bee made through all thys realme, after one sort and fashion: that is to say, unleauened, and rounde, as it was afore, but without all maner of printe, and somethyng more larger and thicker then it was, so that it may be aptly deuided in diuers peices; and euery one shall be deuided in two pieces, at the leaste, or more, by the discrecion of the minister, and so distributed. And menne muste not thynke lesse to be receyued in parte, then in the whole, but in eache of them the whole body of our sauiour Jesu Christ.

A rubric provided that the people "offer" at the "Offertory" the price of the elements. This rubric is interesting because, although the people offer money to their Ministers instead of elements to God, there *is* still a connection between their "offering" and the elements. This connection did not go unnoticed by future advocates of a return to 1549 "usages."

And forsomuche as the Pastours and Curates within thys realme, shal continually fynd at theyr costes and charges in theyr cures, sufficient Breade and Wyne for the holy Communion (as oft as theyr Parishoners shalbe disposed, for theyr spiritual comfort to receyue the same) it is therefore ordered, that in recompense of suche costes and charges, the Parishoners of euerye Parishes, shall offer euery Sonday, at the tyme of the Offertory, the iuste valour and price of the holy lofe (with all suche money, and other things as were wont to be offered with the same) to the use of theyr Pastours and Curates, and that in suche ordre and course, as they were woont to fynde and pay the sayd holy lofe.

There were two final prescriptions that "there shal alwaies some Communicate with the Prieste." There was a strange provision for appointed communicants, so eager was Cranmer that the "reciuing" of the Sacrament be "most agreable to the institucion thereof." If there was no way to have communicants present, the priest himself on weekdays was *not* to communicate.

There was a penalty of excommunication attached for those who without good reason "doeth absent themselues" for longer than a year:

Also, that the reciuing of the Sacrament of the blessed body and bloud of Christ, may be most agreable to the institucion thereof, and to the usage of the primatiue Churche: In all Cathedrall and Collegiate Churches, there shal alwaies some Communicate with the Prieste that ministreth. And that the same may bee also obserued every where abrode in the countrey: Some one at the least of that house in euery

Parishe, to whome by course after the ordinaunce herein made, it apperteyneth to offer for the charges of the Communiō, or some other whom they shall prouide to offer for them, shall reciue the holye Communion with the Prieste: the whiche may be the better doen, for that they knowe before, when their course commeth, and maie therefore dispose thēselues to the worthie receiuyng of the Sacramente. And with hym or them who doeth so offre the charges of the Communion: all other, who be then Godly disposed thereunto, shall lykewyse receiue the Communion. And by this meanes the Minister hauyng alwaies some to communicate with him, maie accordyngly solemenise so high and holy misteries, with all the suffrages and due ordre appoynted for the same. And the Priest on the weke daie, shall forbeare to celebrate the Communion excepte he haue some that will communicate with hym.

Furthermore, euery man and womā to be bound to heare and be at the diuine seruice, in the Parishe churche where they be resident, and there with deuout prayer, or Godlye silence and meditacion, to occupie themselues. There to paie their dueties, to communicate once in the yeare at the least, and there to receyue, and take all other Sacramentes and rites, in this booke appoynted. And whosoeuer willyngly upon no iust cause, doeth absent themselues or doeth ungodly in the Parishe church occupie thēselues: upon proffe thereof, by the Ecclesiasticall lawes of the Realme to bee excomunicate, or suffre other punishement, as shall to the Ecclesiastical iudge (accordyng to his discrecion) seme conuenient.

The 1549 Service "after the use of the Churche of England" closed appropriately with a rubric explaining why reception was in the mouth. Cranmer had no theological objections to reception in the hands. Christ had not commanded the contrary; and ancient writers testified to the practice. Yet the pensive Archbishop feared the "superstition" of corporal presence, adoration, and illicit reservation of the elements. Where Communion was distributed in the hands, "they many times conueyghed the same secretelye awaye, kept it with them, and diuersly abused it to supersticion and wickedness." Therefore, he prescribed reception in the mouth.

The 1549 Communion Service was a skillful blend of the *Order of the Communion* and Cranmer's subtle adaptation of the Sarum Mass. Scholars still admire its unwonted adherence to ancient forms and its sonorous prose. Cranmer intended it to reflect his doctrines of Sacrifice "of ourselves, our souls and bodies, our praise and thanksgiving," and a "true" Presence of the efficacy of

Christ's heavenly Body in the *recipient*. But in the last analysis the revision was basically conservative. Cranmer did not want to offend the Catholic party. To this day Catholic Anglicans prefer it to Cranmer's final revision in 1552. Evangelical Anglicans seemingly prefer his 1552 Service. And it is to the genesis of 1552 that we now turn.*

---

* In 1550 Cranmer's most fateful work, the Anglican Ordinal, was officially issued. We limit our remarks on this delicate subject to a footnote because this book deals principally with the Anglican Eucharist and because the subject of Anglican Orders has been treated adequately (and inadequately) elsewhere. Nevertheless, the first two chapters of this book should throw some light on a confused issue. For the point at issue in Roman teaching on Anglican Orders is Cranmer's concept of priesthood and Sacrifice and its reflection in the Ordinal. His Ordinal was used for the remaining three years of Edward's reign, discarded under Mary Tudor, revived under Elizabeth, and (with slight revisions added in 1552) used at the ordination of Matthew Parker at Lambeth Chapel in 1559. The Roman Church has consistently taught that Parker's ordination was void from defect of form (sacrificial signification) in the Ordinal and from the defect of intention in Parker's consecrators. The Roman Church has not denied that a correct intention has prevailed in many or most Anglican ordinations of more recent times. But the Anglican Ordinal was always used, and the Ordinal, so Rome has ruled, is still incapable of signifying sacrificial priesthood, despite a few alterations made in 1662. There is also much confusion about ceremonies in which Old Catholics, Orthodox, or others participated as consecrators. It should be stated forcefully that even in these cases, the Anglican Ordinal was used, and therefore Rome still considers the form defective.

We would like to make three points here and then refer the reader to detailed writings on this subject. First, it seems to us that the question will never be settled with absolute certainty. The ways of God and the intentions of men are too inscrutable for such certitude. Second, there is a respectable opinion in Catholic theology that Anglican Orders are indeed valid. One cogent argument often used is the working of the Spirit in the Church. Who is to say the Spirit will be frustrated by the lack of signification of a book? Third, we ourselves propose a conditional reordination of Episcopalians to settle this issue forever. Anglicans who themselves have scruples toward the historic episcopate in other churches have often expressed willingness to undergo such a ceremony for a "wider ministry." A widely read Anglican work on this subject is Gregory Dix, *The Question of Anglican Orders* (London, 1944); but the reader should also refer to E. L. Mascall, "Intention and Form in Anglican Orders," *Church Quarterly Review,* No. 158, 1957, pp. 4–20. The most influential Roman Catholic book is Francis Clark, *Anglican Orders and Defect of Intention* (London, 1956). This latter work also contains an 8-page bibliography. Another Roman Catholic scholar, John Jay Hughes, challenges Clark's conclusions for the invalidity of Anglican Orders on both historical and sacramental grounds in "Ministerial Intention in the Administration of the Sacraments," *Clergy Review,* No. 51, 1966, pp. 763–776; "Two English Cardinals on Anglican Orders," *Journal of Ecumenical Studies,* Winter, 1967, pp. 1–26; "The Papal Condemnation of Anglican Orders: 1896," *Ibid.,* Spring, 1967, pp. 235–267; and "Stewards of the Lord: A Reappraisal of Anglican Orders," Unpublished Doctoral Dissertation, Faculty of Theology of the University of Munster, 1967.

CHAPTER II

Reactions to the 1549 Service

Cranmer's crowning Eucharistic work was the 1552 Communion Service. Unambiguously reflecting reformed doctrine, it sharply departed from the cautious comprehension of the 1549 rite. Elizabeth was to restore some comprehensiveness with three significant adjustments in 1559, but the English rite remained basically that of 1552. Her successor, James I, made no further changes in the Communion Service in the 1604 Prayer Book settlement.

The Communion Service of 1552

To understand the genesis of the 1552 Communion Service, it is necessary to know something of the varied reactions to Cranmer's earlier production in 1549. His first Service was met with three general responses: favorable; favorable with reservations; and aggressively unfavorable. Those who had reservations towards 1549 and those who received it with militant distaste influenced Cranmer in his final revision.

FAVORABLE REACTION

Protector Somerset proclaimed the 1549 Service with enthusiastic eulogy. In June, 1549, he wrote Reginald Pole that a Lord's Supper had been "allowed, set forth and established by act and statute, and so published and divulged to so great a quiet as ever was in England and as gladly received of all parts." [1]

In the same month Dryander wrote Bullinger from Cambridge that "a new book has now been published a month or two back which the English churches received with the greatest satisfaction." [2]

Cranmer himself believed the 1549 rite adequately reflected true Eucharistic doctrine. He was grateful "to the eternal God [that] the manner of the holy Communion, which is now set forth within this realm, is agreeable with the institution of Christ." [3] In the *Answer to Gardiner* he frequently defended that "godly book." [4]

There was no stimulus to change from these enthusiasts. If the reaction that Somerset and Dryander had described were as widespread as they implied, there probably would have been no immediate revision at all.

JOHN HOOPER

But the favorable reaction was not as widespread as they implied. No later than Pentecost Monday, the tottering government of Somerset faced a conservative revolt. Half of the agrarian sector of Cornwall and Devon rose in arms and demanded a return to the religion of Henry VIII. The new Prayer Book they denounced as a mere "Christmas game." They demanded a return to the Latin Mass, Communion in one species, the reservation of the Sacrament, and the restoration of ceremonies. The rebellion was crushed in August, but it represented the extreme conservative reaction against the new services. [5]

There was another extreme reaction, equally vehement, but neither physically violent nor conservative. This was the reaction of those for whom Cranmer had not gone nearly far enough. These extremists wanted the last traces of the Mass eliminated and a new Communion Service instituted along the lines of the Zurich communal Supper. Among these zealots, the eloquent John Hooper was most prominent. [6]

Although it is probably true that the primary impetus for revision emanated from the moderate criticism of Bucer and the clever interpretations of Gardiner, [7] Hooper's influence was considerable. [8] This was notably true of his eloquent London sermons.

His primary objection to the new Service was that it departed from the dictates of the Bible. He urged that the nonscriptural overtones of Sacrifice and Real Presence be eliminated utterly, and the teaching of a commemorative meal be stressed. Although not always consistent on the point, he taught that additions not found in Scripture were not indifferent, but plain erroneous. [9]

Hooper's life indicated an obduracy that would make him a formidable opponent to whatever he attacked. After the promulgation of the six "Catholic Articles" of Henry VIII, he withdrew to

Zurich. There he imbibed theology from Bullinger until the English climate improved under Edward VI. Soon after his return to London, he became a forceful preacher with large and prominent audiences.[10]

His obduracy *vis-à-vis* nonscriptural accretions manifested itself in the case of his tempestuous Episcopal consecration. Against his will, Council appointed him Bishop of Gloucester. Not only was he commanded to accept the bishopric, but also the vestments and ceremonies. Hooper refused. He remained adamant for a year, and indeed won the concession that he would not have to swear by the Saints.[11] But his opponents insisted on vestments. In 1550 Micronius wrote Bullinger that "they are all of them intent upon subjecting Hooper to their ceremonies, so he opposes them with all his might, and refers every thing to the apostolic ceremonies."[12]

After long and heated wrangling,[13] Hooper was committed to the Fleet by Privy Council in 1551. Under such duress he submitted to reduced ceremony. Even then, although he preached in rochet and chimere before the King, he won the concession that he would not have to wear this dress on all occasions in his diocese.[14]

As early as December, 1549, Hooper wrote Bullinger that "the public celebration of the Lord's Supper is very far from the Order and institution of our Lord"; he objected to vestments and candles, and complained that mass priests "carefully observe the same manner and tone of chanting to which they were heretofore accustomed in the papacy."[15]

He attacked vestments as against the sufficiency of the Word of God. "He that will be admitted to the ministry of God's word or his sacraments, must come in white vestments, which seemeth to repugn plainly with the former doctrine that confessed the only word of God to be sufficient."[16] Micronius described Hooper's attitude towards vestments: "Hooper denies . . . that they are matters of indifference, inasmuch as they obscure the dignity of the priesthood of Christ, and nurture hypocrisy, superstition &c."[17]

Hooper urged the removal of altars. He considered them foreign to the institution of Christ, and an enticement to the superstition of propitiatory Sacrifice:

It were well then, that it might please the magistrates to turn the altars into tables, according to the first institution of Christ, to take away the false persuasion of the people they have of sacrifices to be done upon the altars; for as long as the altars remain, both the ignorant people, and the ignorant and evil-persuaded priest, will dream always of sacrifice.[18]

He thought altars interfered with the people's participation in the Service. If tables replaced altars, then "such as would receive the holy communion of the precious body and blood of Christ might both hear and see plainly what is done, as it was used in the primitive church. . . ."[19]

The more simple the Service was, the closer it accorded with the institution of Christ:

The outward preparation, the more simple it is, the better it is, and the nearer unto the institution of Christ and his apostles. If he have bread, wine, a table, and a fair table cloth, let him not be solicitous nor careful for the rest, seeing they be not things brought in by Christ, but by popes. . . .[20]

In 1549 he referred to Bishops who restored the Lord's Supper to Scriptural simplicity: "There are here six or seven bishops who comprehend the doctrine of Christ as far as relates to the Lord's Supper. . . . The altars are here in many churches changed into tables."[21]

In *A Declaration of the Ten Holy Commandments,* Hooper described what he considered Scriptural simplicity. The Sabbath involved not an altar and Sacrifice, but prayer, preaching, almsgiving, and the "blessed supper of the Lord":

For as he hath appointed six days for us to exercise ourselves in the business and travails of the world; so hath he appointed the seventh to exercise the ceremonies of the church, which are instituted for the preservation of the ministry of the church: as to use common prayer, hear the sermon, use the blessed supper of the Lord, and to give alms.[22]

The obdurate reformer never mollified in his opposition to altars, even when awaiting execution under Queen Mary. In a mood of discouragement, he wrote Bullinger from prison: "The altars are again set up throughout the kingdom: private masses are frequently celebrated in many quarters; the true worship of God, true invocation, the right use of the sacraments are all done away with."[23]

Consistently with his campaign for simplicity in the use of plain tables, Hooper urged that bread be distributed according to Christ's institution, that is, leavened, broken, and in the hand:

When the minister is thus well prepared with sound and godly doctrine, let him prepare himself to the distribution of the bread and wine; and as he giveth the bread, let him break it, after the example of Christ. He should give the bread and not thrust it into the receivers mouth. . . .[24]

Hooper urged a sitting reception of Communion, both as a precaution against idolatry and as a sacramental imitation of the Last Supper:

I wish it were commanded by the magistrates, that the communicators and receivers should do it standing or sitting. But sitting, in mine opinion, were best, for many considerations. . . . Christ with his apostles used this sacrament, at the first sitting; declaring that he was come that should quiet and put at rest both body and soul.[25]

He thought kneeling gave the false impression that Transubstantiation had occurred, that the elements were changed in their substance and should now be adored. It was Scriptural teaching that bread and wine remained "in their substantial essence and nature without changing." [26]

In answer to Gardiner's book, Hooper scored Transubstantiation as against Scriptural teaching on Christ's Ascension. His position on the local confinement of Christ's Body to heaven was similar to that of Cranmer. He claimed it was against the nature of Christ's ascended Body that at every Lord's Supper He "can be or may be, against the nature of a true body, present bodily at the commandment of every priest, when he speaketh these words, *Hoc est corpus meum.* . . ." [27]

Close adherence to Scripture and apostolic usage would liberate the Sacrament from pomp and ceremony. The Minister "doeth best his office and is best instructed to minister the sacrament, if he in the ministration thereof go as near as is possible to the first institution of Christ and the apostles." [28]

But Ministers were not so disposed in England. Ceremony-prone prelates outdid the Aaronical rites of Judaism. Even Seneca would be appalled at the proliferating accretions. "What would he say, if he saw our churches, that have not the ceremonies commanded by God, but by man to the dishonouring of God?" [29]

The new Communion Service was so manifestly impious that Hooper threatened a boycott. "I am so much offended with that book, and that not without abundant reason, that if it be not corrected, I neither can nor will communicate with the church in the administration of the supper." [30]

The duties of a Minister were circumscribed. He was to be prepared inwardly and outwardly. For inward preparation it was necessary that a Minister's "mind and soul be instructed and furnished with godly doctrine, and a fervent spirit and zeal to teach his audience, to establish them in the truth, and to exhort them." Outwardly, "the more simple it is, the better it is and the nearer unto the institution of Christ and his apostles." [31]

The duties of the recipient were likewise circumscribed. Hooper divided them into before receiving, while receiving, and after receiving.[32]

Before receiving he was to examine himself according to the Pauline mandate. Then he was to confess his sins, but Hooper made "no mention here of auricular confession, as though that were a thing necessary to be done before, or after the receiving of the sacrament." Only after such penitential preparation—and reconciliation with his neighbor—did a man "eat worthily the body of Christ; and he that doth not thus prepare himself, eateth nothing but the sacrament to his everlasting damnation."

While receiving "the mind is elevated and lift up into heaven." The recipient was persuaded "by faith that as truly appertaineth unto him the promises and grace of God, through the merits and death of Christ, as he sensibly and outwardly receiveth the sacrament and witness of God's promise." Only "after the manner and phrase of scripture" was the bread called Body, the wine Blood. Therefore Communion should be received sitting.

After receiving, "there should be thanksgiving of all the church for the benefits of Christ's death; there should be prayer made unto God, that they might persevere and continue in the grace of God received: they should help the poor with their alms."

All sacrificial overtones should be deleted. "Thus should the perfection of Christ's institution be had in honour, and the memory of the dead left out, and nothing done in the sacrament that had not God's word to bear it." [33] As for Saints' days, the honor "should be given only unto God. In the old testament was no feast ever dedicated unto any saints, neither in the new." [34] In the primitive Church, the Ministers were "preachers of God's word, and ministers of Christ's sacraments." In that pristine age it was not their function "to sacrifice for dead nor live, not to sing a mass, or any such like." [35]

Hooper was disgruntled with the 1549 Mass because it was not in accord with Christ's institution. There remained vestiges of Sacrifice and Transubstantiation which were unfitting for a Scriptural commemorative meal. How effective a crusader Hooper was is still a matter of conjecture. There is no known document delineating the extent of his influence on the Archbishop of Canterbury. But it is a fact that the Communion Service of 1552 moved in the direction to which Hooper's crusade had pointed.

STEPHEN GARDINER

In Stephen Gardiner, sometime Bishop of Winchester, Cranmer encountered a tongue-in-cheek defender of the new Communion Service. That is, Gardiner claimed the Book of Common Prayer could be interpreted in the traditional Catholic sense. At the time of the book's publication, Gardiner languished in prison for his recalcitrance towards the English Reformation. He was at that time in no position to exert official or public influence. But he believed he could, if necessary, maintain and enforce the new Service.[36] What angered Cranmer were the reasons Gardiner tendered for his approval. It was a classic case of the moderate "friend" being more an irritant than the extremist enemy.

The Gardiner-Cranmer "Supper strife" already had a history. Their verbal arrows first began to fly in 1546, when Gardiner published a book entitled *Detection of the Devil's Sophistry,* and in 1548 when he preached a sermon before the King that displeased the Archbishop of Canterbury.[37] In apparent answer to Gardiner's rhetoric, Cranmer's *Defense* appeared. Gardiner countered instantly with his *Explication and Assertion of the True Catholic Faith touching the most blessed Sacrament of the Altar with Confutation of a book Written against the Same.*[38] It was in this book that Gardiner alleged the new Communion Service taught "true Catholic Faith" in the sense of Transubstantiation and propitiatory Sacrifice. Cranmer heatedly replied with his definitive Eucharistic writing, the *Answer to Gardiner.*

In this book, Cranmer replied to Gardiner topic by topic—reprinting the bulk of his opponent's book in the process. The Archbishop presented his own doctrine, defended the new Communion Service as reflecting that doctrine, and flayed Gardiner's arguments in the discourteous language of that turbulent era.

Gardiner argued first for Transubstantiation, and secondly for propitiatory Sacrifice. This was a direct confrontation with Cranmer who derided these two doctrines as the roots of evil:

> . . . the very body of the tree, or rather the roots of the weeds, is the popish doctrine of transubstantiation, of the real presence of Christ's flesh and blood in the sacrament of the altar (as they call it), and of the sacrifice and oblation of Christ made by the priest, for the salvation of the quick and the dead.[39]

What apparently angered Cranmer the most and goaded him to abusive language were Gardiner's contentions that the 1549 Service taught these two doctrines. Cranmer lashed back by faulting Gardiner's book as a product of ignorance. In the *Preface,* Cranmer asserted that Gardiner "thinketh that he hath sufficiently proved transubstantiation . . . yet how far he is deceived, and doth vary from the doctrine of other papists, and also from the the principles of philosophy . . . the reader hereby may easily perceive." [40] Gardiner was not above the use of subtle sophistry. Cranmer derided him for this in a broadside against Winchester's book: "For your book is so far from an explication and assertion of the true catholic faith in the matter of the sacrament, that it is but a crafty cavillation and subtle sophistication. . . ." [41]

Without doubt Gardiner was a clever, if not always scholarly, polemicist. He argued that sometimes writers contradict themselves. Those who propound false doctrines sometimes teach the truth despite themselves. Then, apparently with tongue in cheek, he prayed that Transubstantiation be taught uniformly as well as it was propounded in the Book of Common Prayer.

> . . . God of his infinite mercy have pity on us, and grant the true faith of this holy mystery uniformly to be conceived in our understandings, and in one form of words to be uttered and preached, which in the book of common prayer is well termed, not distant from the catholic faith in my judgment.[42]

With more sophistry than scholarship, Gardiner even alleged that Zwingli taught Transubstantiation. "Zuinglius taketh it truly for a necessary consequence of the truth, if there be in the sacrament the real presence of Christ's body, as there is in deed." [43]

Gardiner discussed the problem of profligate communicants. He denied they received Christ spiritually, but they did receive Him sacramentally.[44] Since a substantial change had taken place in the elements, Christ was bodily present not only in use, but before reception.[45]

Gardiner believed the conversion of substance was true Catholic teaching of which Cranmer was well aware: ". . . the substance of which natures of bread and wine is converted into his most precious body and blood, as it is truly believed and taught in the Catholic Church, of which teaching this author cannot be ignorant." [46] In his ponderous style, Gardiner alleged that Cranmer had taught a corporal reception in his Catechism and in the Prayer Book:[47]

. . . we receive in the sacrament the body of Christ with our mouth; and such speech other use, as a book set forth in the archbishop of Canterbury's name, called a Catechism, willeth children to be taught that they receive with their bodily mouth the body and blood of Christ; which I allege, because it shall appear it is a teaching set forth among us of late, as hath been also, and is by the book of common prayer. . . .[48]

Gardiner may have been referring to the 1549 distribution formula and the rubrics for a kneeling reception.

The Body of Christ was the substance of the sacrament. This, claimed Gardiner, was the teaching of Martin Bucer who "saith, we must believe Christ's body to be there, the same that did hang upon the cross, our Lord himself." Bucer taught that Christ "said not, this is my spirit, this is my virtue, but 'this is my body.' " [49]

Cranmer's rubric that the whole Christ was present in each part of the broken host delighted Gardiner. Again and again he beleaguered the Archbishop with this rubric: "In the book of common prayer, now at this time set forth in this realm, 'It is ordered to teach the people, that in each part of the bread consecrate, broken, is the whole body of our Saviour Christ,' which is agreeable to the Catholic doctrine." [50] "In the book of common prayer it is truly said, in each part of the bread consecrate broken to be Christ's whole body. . . ." [51] Gardiner used this rubric still a third time when discussing substance and accident. It was the glorious Christ that was present in the Sacrament. Therefore Christ's Body was not broken when the priest divided the hosts: ". . . it is in the book of common prayer set forth, how in each part of that is broken of the consecrate bread is the whole body of our Saviour Christ." [52]

There were three types of reception. The first was spiritual. The second "both sacramentally and spiritually, which is when men worthily communicate. . . ." The third "sacramentally only which is by men unworthy, who eat and drink in the holy supper to their condemnation. . . ." [53]

Gardiner brushed aside Cranmer's translation of *fiat nobis*. The Invocation "made" the creatures of bread and wine the Body and Blood of Christ. In his argument Gardiner was undeterred by the "unto us" of the Communion Service:

> The body of Christ is by God's omnipotency, who so worketh in his word, made present unto us at such time, as the church pray it may please him to do so, which prayer is ordered to be made in the book of common prayer now set forth.[54]

Once again Gardiner referred to the epiclesis. He implied that it reflected his doctrine of Real Presence:

> And therefore when the church by the minister, and with the minister, prayeth that the creatures of bread and wine set on the altar (as the book of common prayer in this realm hath ordered), may be unto us the body and blood of our Saviour Christ; we require then the celebration of the same supper, which Christ made to his apostles. . . .[55]

These elements were consecrated by God's omnipotence even *before* reception: "how they be so changed into the body and blood of Christ, which is a work wrought by God before we receive the sacrament." [56]

Gardiner drew two rapid conclusions. If the Sacrament was Christ's Body even before reception, the Sacrament should be adored. And the 1549 Communion Service taught just that:

. . . in the book of common prayer . . . the priest is ordered to kneel and make a prayer of his own, in the name of all that shall communicate, confessing therein that is prepared there; at which time nevertheless that is not adored that the bodily eye seeth, but that which faith knoweth to be there invisibly present . . .[57]

In the latter section of his book Gardiner discussed Sacrifice. Scripture taught "that the oblation and sacrifice of our Saviour Christ was and is a perfect work, once consummate in perfection without necessity of reiteration. . . ."[58]

Though this consummated Sacrifice was not reiterated, the Lord's Supper was a frequent commemoration and "shewing" of the perfect Sacrifice. The "sacrifice once consummate was ordained by Christ's institution in his most holy supper to be in the church often remembered and shewed forth in such sort of shewing as to the faithful is seen present the most precious body and blood of our Saviour Christ under the forms of bread and wine. . . ."[59]

Gardiner did not hesitate to state explicitly that Christ's Body was offered in the Mass. It was the same Body that was offered on Calvary. But the manner of offering was different; the Eucharist was without bloodshed: ". . . the same body is offered daily on the altar, that was once offered on the altar of the cross; but the same manner of offering is not daily that was on the altar of the cross, for the daily offering is without bloodshed. . . ."[60]

Gardiner's reference to the placing of the elements on the table may have been a subtle thrust that the Communion Service taught propitiatory Sacrifice. For the Church "prayeth that the creatures of bread and wine set on the altar (as the book of common prayer in this realm hath ordered) may be unto us the body and blood of our Saviour Christ. . . ."

The proximity of the prayer for the Church to the Consecration indicated that the Eucharist was a propitiatory Sacrifice. Gardiner did not state this in so many words, but the meaning of his ponderous polemics did not escape Cranmer:

Whereupon this persuasion hath been duly conceived, which is also in the book of common prayer in the celebration of the holy supper retained, that it is very profitable at that time, when the memory of Christ's death is solemnized, to remember with prayer all the estates of the church, and to recommend them to God.[61]

Gardiner annoyed Cranmer and even provoked him to antagonistic language by claiming that the new Communion Service taught Transubstantiation and propitiatory Sacrifice. Once again, there is no extant document in which Cranmer admits he made changes in 1552 to obviate Gardiner's polemics. But it is a fact that in the 1552 revision there were changes in every part of the rite that Gardiner had alleged taught Transubstantiation or propitiatory Sacrifice.

MARTIN BUCER

In 1550 the Archbishop of Canterbury invited Martin Bucer to submit his verdict on the 1549 Prayer Book.[62] Bucer presented his response to Thomas Goodrich, Bishop of Ely, on January 5, 1551, under the title: *Censura Martini Buceri super libro sacrorum seu ordinationis Ecclesiae atque ministerii ecclesiastici in regno Angliae.*

The *Censura* approved of the new Communion Service.[63] Nevertheless, Bucer suggested several corrections and explanations.

For better lay participation, Bucer urged that the altar be closer to the people. He preferred a Service enacted in a central place; "from that place the sacred and Divine things might be presented to the people present that all might easily hear and understand the words." [64] He believed the simple expedient of moving the Service to a more central location would increase attendance: ". . . the whole Church will communicate, as often as the Service is openly performed, and not just a few people." [65]

Bucer desired stringent rubrics for the exclusion of sinners. He allowed no exceptions: ". . . let those who with graver sins offended the Church or detracted from the Faith be excluded to do their penance, as well as those who do not wish to make restitution to their offended brethren or forgive those who have offended them." [66]

He saw nothing "objectively wrong" with vestments; but he wanted the vestments rubric eliminated "not because I believe there is anything objectively wrong in them so that instructed men are unable to use them ordinately, but I see they are a cause of superstition to many." [67]

His moderate attitude is exemplified in a letter to the uncompromising Hooper: "It is clear that Our Lord Jesus Christ prescribed only the substance of the ministry of Word and Sacraments in His own words. All other things pertaining to the decent and useful administration of the ministries he permitted the Church to ordain." [68]

Peter Martyr compared Bucer's position to his own in a letter to Bullinger: ". . . since that diversity of apparel possesses little or no edification and very many persons superstitiously abuse it, I therefore considered that it ought to be removed. Bucer made very nearly the same answer. . . ." [69]

Burcher pointed out the divergence of Bucer's view from that of Hooper. "Hooper has Jean a Lasco and a few others on his side; but against him many adversaries, among whom is Bucer. . . ." [70]

Despite this moderate attitude towards vestments, Bucer feared appearances of the Mass remained.[71] He urged further elimination of private Masses and offerings for the departed. He cautioned against the preservation of private altars. This was especially repugnant when the altars were in the same building where corporate worship took place. The priests still offered Mass on these altars even during the Communion Service. He also opposed private chapels in great houses; these too encouraged the superstition of propitiatory Sacrifice.

Bucer ineffectually dissented from some reformers in his opposition to the Ante-Communion Service. He called this practice a carryover from the perversity of the Roman anti-Christians. He feared that the truncated Service appeared to the unlettered a private Mass. It was only to say "a truncated Mass, but with all the trappings of a Mass."

He urged uniformity in vestments and location for all services. If Morning and Evening Prayer took place in different vestments and at a different spot in Church than the Communion Service, it might give the impression that the Communion Service was a lofty Sacrifice. The solution was to enact all Services at the same place, and in "common vestments."

Nor was Bucer pleased with the Offertory procession. He urged, in its place, a collection for the poor. This collection would be the "sacrifice and oblation" of the congregation. Everyone present should offer, not only for Divine blessing, but "because of his Charity toward Christ's members. . . . His least ones, the hungry, the thirsty, the homeless, the naked, the sick, the incarcerated." [72]

Bucer suggested that "Deacons and Subdeacons collect these offerings of the faithful, and let them distribute them depending on the necessity of the poor and the discretion of the priest and Bishop."

Apparently a sturdy conservatism still flourished. The rubrics of Cranmer's Service did not explicitly forbid certain historical gestures; and conservative priests took advantage of this loophole. They clung to such Roman remnants as "to genuflect, to make a sign of the cross in the air, to lift up the hands, to strike the breast, and other such gestures of the Mass never adequately forbidden, which they do in administration of the holy supper." [73]

As for bread, "there is nothing narrated by the evangelists" that prescribed round wafers.[74] And the reception of the elements in the mouth was an invitation to superstition.[75]

Bucer proposed consecrating plentiful bread and wine. Limiting these elements to an adequate supply for the congregation gave a false impression of Transubstantiation. Actually the elements had "no more holiness in themselves than other bread and wine has." Christ was not enclosed in consecrated bread, but "offered to disposed minds through the words of the Lord and these symbols." [76]

Bucer recommended using the superfluous elements for ordinary sustenance. "Some have the superstition of thinking it's evil, if something is left over from the bread and wine of the Service, to allow it to return to profane use: as if there were anything holy in the bread and wine outside of the use of Communion." [77]

As a true Strasbourg reformer, he approved of protracted teaching and exhorting. Therefore, he desired an increase of homilies and exhortations in the English Service. He urged Ministers to "teach, admonish, and exhort" the people on the prime importance of the Lord's Supper.[78] Because of his suspicion of many ordained Ministers in the realm, he discouraged the selective reading of certain *parts* of provided homilies and exhortations.[79] Apparently, he suspected some Ministers of reading certain paragraphs out of context so as to teach propitiatory Sacrifice and Real Presence.

For the same reason, he was not content with prescribed reading of Scriptures. He thought prewritten homilies and exhortations paramount. "For here and there either Epicureans or Papists preside at the Services who do not wish, even if they were capable, to faithfully expound the mysteries of Christ to the populace." [80]

He appealed to Cyprian and Justinian in objecting to Cranmer's commemoration of the departed in his prayer of intercession. "There is no mention of it in the description of the Lord's Supper," in Cyprian or Justinian.[81]

Bucer recommended deletion of Cranmer's words in the epiclesis to bless and sanctify "these thy gyftes and creatures of bread and wine." [82] He feared invoking God's blessings on the elements would lead many to the superstition of Transubstantiation. He proposed a prayer of his own composition, invoking Divine blessing on the *recipients*. He urged Cranmer to substitute it for the epiclesis in the new Service:

> Hear us, o merciful God the Father, and bless and sanctify us with your word and Holy Spirit, that we might truly perceive by faith the Body and Blood of your Son from His hand in these mysteries for the food and drink of eternal life.[83]

He thought even the sparse rubrics Cranmer had retained at the Consecration were too many. Despite the express prohibition of elevation, he feared manual acts rubrics could induce that superstitious practice. If elevations continued, so would the superstition of Transubstantiation.[84] As a substitute for the two signs of the cross Cranmer had retained, he suggested a very Scriptural rubric for "breaking of the bread." [85]

Bucer considered the mention of angelic ministry inimical to the doctrine of Christ's unique mediation.[86] Again he urged his own composition as a substitute: "benevolently accept because of your Son, our Mediator, these our prayers and supplications, not weighing our merits." [87]

Cranmer was urged to incorporate more Scriptural *logia* into the Service as an excellent safeguard for the doctrine of spiritual Presence. "So let us not fear to use words of the Divine Presence, by which the Lord testified Himself, to be, remain, and dwell among us and within us. . . ." [88]

Bucer feared the extreme symbolism of the left wing of the reformed tradition. He expressed the sincere hope to Peter Martyr that "the Anglican Church never come into suspicion as if you recognize nothing in the Lord's Supper except mere signs of Christ, through which a recording of the absent Christ should be somehow aroused. . . ." [89]

Hooper and Gardiner were not invited to launch criticisms of the new Communion Service. Bucer was. It is one of the ironies of Anglican Eucharistic history that all parts of the Service that Gardiner praised were changed; whereas the invited criticisms of Bucer were accepted only in part, albeit the greater part. Bucer did not survive for the promulgation of the 1552 Prayer Book. Had he lived, he would have been gratified to see the majority of his suggestions incorporated in a radically new Communion Service.

PETER MARTYR

Peter Martyr was an Italian canon who had been expelled from his homeland by the Inquisition. For some time thereafter, he resided in Zurich and Strasbourg. At the accession of King Edward, he joined other Protestant refugees in the salubrious climate of Cranmer's England. In May, 1549, he accepted the appointment of Regius Professor of Divinity at Oxford.[90]

Cranmer solicited criticism from Martyr as well as Bucer. Martyr is known to have submitted his written animadversions, although there is no extant copy of the document.[91]

Since the Italian reformer never mastered English, he was unable to read the original. However, John Cheke presented him with a copy, probably translated into Latin. Martyr wrote his criticisms on this copy and presented it to Cranmer.

Only after Martyr had studied Cheke's rendition of the Service and submitted his corrections to Cranmer, did he read Bucer's *Censura*. He was delighted with Bucer's laborious treatise and felt he now fully comprehended the contents of the 1549 Book. He added his approval to Bucer's work.[92]

However, Martyr noticed something Bucer had apparently overlooked. In studying the Communion Service, Martyr had also perused the rite for Communion of the Sick. Apparently Bucer had not noticed the rubrics there for reservation of the Sacrament:

> But if the sick person be not able to come to the church, and yet is desirous to receive the Communion in his house, then he must give knowledge over night, or else early in the morning to the curate, signifying also how many be appointed to communicate with him. And if

the same day there be a celebration of the holy Communion in the church, then shall the Priest reserve (at the open Communion) so much of the sacrament of the body and blood as shall serve the sick person, and so many as shall communicate with him. . . .[93]

Martyr objected to reservation. He feared this practice would imply a sacredness in the elements. In a statement similar to Bucer's remarks about Cranmer's epiclesis, Martyr wrote: "the words of the supper pertain more to men than to bread and wine."

I am surprised that you omitted a criticism of the Communion of the Sick, where it is prescribed if it is had on a Sunday when the Lord's Supper is celebrated, the Minister should take part of the bread with him, and so administer communion in the house of the sick person. It bothers me that in that part they do not repeat what pertains essentially to the Lord's Supper. The reason is that, as you also believe, or at least I think you do, the words of the supper pertain more to men than to bread and wine.[94]

Martyr assured Bucer that he had admonished Cranmer to repeat those things "which are necessarily required at the Lord's Supper." [95] He had nothing more to add to Bucer's criticisms. "These are the things I thought of some moment. Why you omitted them, I do not know. But in all other things, I wrote my agreement with your opinion. . . ." [96]

He expressed gratitude for Cranmer's invitation to himself and Bucer. Cranmer had assured him extensive changes were in the making, but what they were specifically he had not "revealed to me, nor did I dare ask him." [97]

In another remark reminiscent of Bucer's *Censura,* Martyr witnessed to a still rugged conservatism in the realm. John Cheke had boasted that if certain bishops "do not wish . . . to arrange that the things that should be changed will be changed, the King on his own will do it; and when it comes to parliament he will interpose his kingly authority." [98]

This revealing letter of Martyr's reveals two things. First, the Italian reformer was in agreement with Bucer's *Censura,* save only that book's lack of criticism of reservation. Second, Cranmer, Cheke, and the King himself were prepared for an extensive revision.

CHAPTER III

The Communion Services of 1552, 1559, and 1604

"The Lordes Supper or Holye Communion"

On April 6, 1552, a new Prayer Book broke upon the land. Appended was the stipulation that the Book was to come into use on the feast of All Saints following.

The Second Act of Uniformity testified to its approval by King and Parliament.[1] Whether or not Convocation approved is still a mystery. But there was at least *post factum* approval in the enthusiastic Thirty-Fifth Article of 1553:

> The Book which of very late time was given to the Church of England by the King's authority and the Parliament, concerning the manner and form of praying and ministering the Sacrament in the Church of England, likewise also the book of Ordering Ministers of the Church set forth by the foresaid authority, are godly and in no point repugnant to the wholesome doctrine of the Gospel, but agreeable thereunto, furthering and beautifying the same not a little. . . .[2]

A letter of Cranmer to Council concerning the final rubric in the Communion Service indicated royal and parliamentary approval. The letter also gives good indication of authorship; Cranmer informed Council that ". . . not only we, but a great many Bishops and others of the best learned within this realm . . ." considered the problem of kneeling for Communion. From this testimony, the authorship consisted of Cranmer, other Bishops, and learned Divines. As for the Book's approval, he wrote: ". . . the book being read and approved by the whole state of the Realm, in the High Court of Parliament, with the King's majesty his royal assent. . . ."[3]

The Uniformity Act tried to connect the new Book with the 1549 rite. The latter was "a very godly order, agreeable to the Word of God and the primitive Church, very comfortable to all Christian people desiring to live in Christian conversation, and most profitable to the state of this realm." [4]

THE NATURE OF THE 1552 REVISION

With such commendation of 1549, it was necessary to explain why any revision was needed at all. Certainly it was not the fault of that "godly order," but "rather by the curiosity of the ministers and mistakers, than of any other worthy cause." The same 1549 Book had been by order of King and Parliament "faithfully and godly perused, explained and made fully perfect." The Curate was to read these words of praise four times a year.

Cranmer's *Preface* expressed similar reasons for revision. It was certainly not because of serious defects in previous Services. But "there was never any thing by the wit of man so well devised, or so sure established, which (in continuance of time) hath not been corrupted; as (among other things) it may plainly appear by the common prayers in the Church. . . ." [5] Therefore, if doubts arise and the local Bishop cannot solve them, the hesitant one should seek a resolution from the Archbishop.[6]

When the 1552 Prayer Book appeared, it was obvious that the Communion Service had been more than "faithfully and godly perused." It was changed considerably. As in 1549, Cranmer retained essential rites and prayers. But the striking rearrangement, rewording, and new rubrics reflected a desire to meet Gardiner's contentions, and to placate reformers such as Hooper, Bucer, and Martyr.

The very title of the new book pointedly indicated that changes had been made. In 1549 the title read *The booke of the common praier and administracion of the Sacramentes, and other rites and ceremonies of the Churche: after the use of the Churche of Englande.*[7] The new title, ignoring other uses, was simply: *The Boke of common praier, and administracion of the Sacramentes, and other rites and ceremonies in the Churche of Englande.*[8]

Another significant change was the transferral of Cranmer's treatise on ceremonies from the closing pages of the 1549 book to a prominent place right after the Preface in the new edition.[9] This prominent location indicated that attention had focused on ceremonies in the new edition, that some had been eliminated, and others preserved. Cranmer explained why some ceremonies were maintained, others abolished:

> . . . some at the first were of Godly intent and purpose devised, and yet at length turned to vanity and superstition: some entered into the church by undiscreet devotion, and such a zeal as was without knowledge, and for because they were winked at in the beginning, they grew daily to more and more abuses; which not only for their unprofitableness, but also because they have much blinded the people, and obscured the glory of God, are worthy to be cut away, and clean rejected. Other there be, which although they have been devised by man, yet it is thought good to reserve them still. . . .[10]

Although he indicated that considerable changes in ceremonies had been made, Cranmer stoutly defended the preservation of others. It was an effort on his part to assuage radicals of the left as well as Henrician conservatives:

> But now as concerning those persons, which preadventure will be offended, for that some of the old ceremonies are retained still: if they consider that without some ceremonies it is not possible to keep any order or quiet discipline in the church, they shall easily perceive just cause to reform their judgments.[11]

SOME FEATURES OF THE NEW SERVICE

The Archbishop feared agitation for a total abandonment of all ritual. He asked the extreme group to respect ceremonies at least for their antiquity and to avoid "innovations and newfangleness, which (as much as may be with true setting forth of Christ's religion) is always to be eschewed." Nonetheless, if these ceremonies were abused, they should be eliminated. In embryonic Anglican comprehensiveness, Cranmer indicated the direction of ceremonies in the new liturgy:

> For we think it convenient that every country should use such ceremonies, as they shall think best to the setting forth of God's honour or glory, and to the reducing of the people to a most perfect and godly living, without error or superstition: and that they should put away other things, which from time to time they perceive to be most abused, as in men's ordinances it often chanceth diversely in diverse countries.[12]

The title of the new Communion Service was an omen of what was to follow. As Cranmer had indicated in the treatise on ceremonies, something was retained. But something was also changed.

In 1549 the title read: *The Supper of the Lorde, and the holy Communion, commonly called the Masse.*[13] In the new title, Cranmer minimized the danger of distinguishing the Lord's Supper from the Holy Communion. They were clearly stated to be the same thing. And the Service was no longer "the Masse." The new title was: *The order for the administracion of the Lordes Supper or holye Communion.*[14]

Cranmer retained the original penitential rubrics. Prospective communicants were still required to give their names to the Minister. The Curate was again directed to exclude notorious and unrepentant sinners. Those at enmity with their neighbors were not to communicate.

A striking new rubric followed. It prescribed a Service conducted at a *table*. The priest was to stand at the north side of the table.

> The Table hauyng at the Communion tyme a fayre white lynnen clothe upon it, shall stande in the body of the Churche, or in the chauncell, where Morninge prayer, and Eueninge prayer be appoynted to bee sayde. And the Priest standing at the northsyde of the Table, shal saye the Lordes prayer with thys Collecte folowinge.
>
> ALmightie God, unto whom al heartes be open . . .[15]

Within the Service itself, there was no vestments rubric. However, the Communion Service usually followed Morning Prayer. In that section of the new liturgy, there was an extremely interesting rubric prescribing the apparel supposed to be worn at the Lord's Supper.

> And here is to be noted, that the Minister at the time of the communion, and at all other times in his ministration, shall use neither Alb, Vestment, nor Cope: but being Archbishop, or Bishop, he shall have and wear a rochet: and being a priest or Deacon, he shall have and wear a surplice only.[16]

No one could attend the new Service without noticing these striking changes. The altar had become a table in the midst of the people. The priest stood not at the far end of the church, but at the north side of the new table. Gone were chasuble, alb, and even cope. The average parish priest wore only a simple surplice.

The lack of music also distinguished this Service from the Mass. There was no Introit. Practically every trace of singing was removed. But there was an interesting preservation of the old order in the rubrics for Morning Prayer.

And (to the end the people may the better hear) in such places where they do sing, there shall the Lessons be sung in a plain tune, after the manner of distinct reading; and likewise the Epistle and Gospel.[17]

After the Collect for Purity there was another marked change, this time in the *Kyrie*. Instead of the accustomed ninefold *Kyrie,* the Minister was instructed to rehearse the Decalogue and the people to respond by asking God's mercy.[18]

The result was an examination of conscience combined with the traditional *Kyrie* in such a way as to form a penitential Litany. This new practice provided an examination in preparation for the general confession. The communal air emphasized the waning of private Penance in England.

The public examination-litany inaugurated the new Service on a strong note of penitential preparation. The rubric and the first two petitions are given below:

Then shal the Priest rehearse distinctly all the .x. Commaundementes: and the people knelyng, shall after euerye Commaundement aske Gods mercy for theyr transgresssion of thesame, after thys sorte.

Ministre
God spake these wordes, and sayd: I am the Lorde thy God. Thou shalt haue none other Goddes but me.

People
Lorde haue mercye upon us, and encline oure heartes to kepe thys lawe.

Ministre
Thou shalte not make to thy selfe any grauen ymage, nor the lykenes of any thing that is heauen aboue, or in the earth beneath, nor in the water under the earth. Thou shalte not bowe downe to them, nor worshyppe them: for I the Lorde thy God am a gelous God, and visite the sinne of the fathers upon the children, unto the thyrde and fourth generacion of them that hate me, and shewe mercy unto thousandes in them that loue me and kepe my commaundementes.

People
Lorde haue mercy upon us, and encline our heartes to kepe thys lawe.

Within such a penitential atmosphere, there was no room for the traditional *Gloria* which was transferred to the end of the Service.

There was no salutation before the Collects. The priest simply began "Let us praye" immediately after the penitential Litany. As in 1549, the Collect for the day preceded two alternate Collects for the King.[19]

In 1552 a low Mass format provided the basic structure. The priest alone read Epistle and Gospel. This less solemn format facilitated Cranmer's efforts to eliminate music and ceremonies reminiscent of the Mass with its theology of propitiatory Sacrifice.

The Creed was said, not sung. There was an interesting addition of the words "whose kingdom shall have no end."

The Sermon or prewritten homily followed the Creed. There was no permission to select a portion of one of the homilies. The rubrics for Epistle, Gospel, Creed, and homily were as follows:

Immediately after the Collectes, the priest shal reade the Epistle, begynnyng thus.

The Epistle written in the.   Chapter of.

And the Epistle ended, he shal saye the Gospel, beginninge thus.

The Gospell, wrytten in the.   Chapter of.

And the Epistle and Gospel beyng ended, shalbe sayed the Crede.

I Beleue in one god, the father almightie . . . .

. . . .

After the Crede, yf there be no sermon, shall folowe one of the homilies already set forth, or hereafter to be set forth by commune auctoritie.

THE OFFERTORY REVISION

In an almost desperate attempt to appease critics and obviate propitiatory overtones, Cranmer radically revised the Offertory. Gone were such words as "Offer," "Offertory," and "Offering" except in the context of support of the clergy.[20] Only a minimum of the former framework remained. There was no music, no procession, no depositing of alms in the poor box. In lieu of a procession, churchwardens collected alms for the poor and only these officials deposited them in the poor box. Instead of Offertory hymns, formerly chanted during the procession, the Minister was directed to recite one of the 1549 Offertory verses. The people were exhorted to "remember" the poor; it was their "devotion" that was placed in the poor box.

Within the Service itself, there were no rubrics providing for elements. The rubrics for consecrating only what was necessary for the communicants was eliminated.[21]

Another rubric to which Bucer had objected was the provision that only communicants remain in the "quire." This had given the impression that non-communicants were tolerated at the Service. In the new Service this rubric was dropped; the impression now given was that all present would communicate.

The 1549 and 1552 Offertory rubrics are provided below. Only the first Offertory verse is printed. Key words and phrases illustrating the changed emphasis have been italicized by this writer.

1549	1552
Then shall folowe for the Offertory, one or mo, of these Sentences of holy scripture, to bee song whiles the people doo offer, or els one of theim to bee saied by the minister, immediatly afore the offeryng.	After suche sermon, homelie, or exhortacion, the Curate shall declare unto the people whether there be any holye dayes or fasting daies the weke folowing: and earnestly exhorte them *to remembre the poore,* saying one or moē of these sentēces folowing, as he thinketh most cōuenient by his discrecion.
Let your light so shine before men, that they maye see your good woorkes, and glorify your father whiche is in heauen. (Math. v.)	Let your lyght so shine before men, that they maye see your good woorkes, and glorify your father whiche is in heauen. (Math. v.)
Where there be Clerkes, thei shall syng one, or many of the sentences aboue written, accordyng to the length and shortenesse of the tyme, that the people be offeryng. In the meane tyme, whyles the Clerkes do syng the Offertory,	Then shal the *Churche wardens, or some other* by them appointed, *gather the deuocion* of the people, and *put* the same into the pore

1549	1552
so many as are disposed, shall offer unto the poore mennes boxe euery one accordynge to his habilitie and charitable mynde. And at the offeryng daies appoynted: euery manne and woman shall Paie to the Curate the due and accustomed offerynges. Then so manye as shalbe partakers of the holy Communion, shall tary still in the quire, or in some conuenient place, nigh the quire, the men on the one side, and the women on the other syde. All other (that mynde not to receiue the said holy Communion) shall departe out of the quire, except the ministers and Clerkes.	mens boxe: and upon the *offering* daies appointed euery man and woman shall *paye to the curate* the due and accustomed *offeringes:*
Than shall the minister take so much Bread and Wine as shall suffice for the persons appoynted to receiue the holy Communion, laying the breade upon the corporas, or els in the paten, or in some other comely thyng, prepared for that purpose. And puttyng ye wyne into the Chalice, or els in some faire or cōueniente cup, prepared for that use (if the Chalice will not serue) puttyng thereto a little pure and cleane water: And settyng both the breade and wyne upon the Alter:	

Immediately subsequent to his stark Offertory, Cranmer interposed a diminished version of the prayer of general intercession. Gardiner had implied that this prayer proved the Supper was a propitiatory Sacrifice. Therefore Cranmer shortened the petitions, and removed the prayer from its former proximity to the Consecration.

He also made other significant changes. In the new version it was the priest who introduced the prayer. And it was no longer "for the whole state of Christes churche." The new introduction read: "Let us pray for the whole state of Christes Churche militant here in earth."

Consistent with the new introduction, there was no mention of the faithful departed now in the sleep of peace. The dead had been excluded. Cardwell believes this omission was meant to show that "the church not only did not practice intercession for the dead, but even carefully excluded it." [22]

The new version of the prayer was no longer intimately connected with the consecration. It was now inserted into a long penitential preparation. Accordingly, Cranmer dropped the words "to celebrate the commemoracion of the most glorious death of thy sonne." The words, "to accepte our almose" were added with the provisional rubric that they should not be read when no alms were given *to the poor.*

The commemoration of the Saints, including the Blessed Virgin, was gone from the new version of the prayer.

Rather than depart from his theme of penance and almsgiving, Cranmer also eliminated at this point reference to the general Resurrection and the Mystical Body.

The priest was no longer at "the Altar" nor was he allowed the option of singing. Both versions are listed below to indicate the extensive deletions. Significant additions have been italicized.

1549	1552
Let us praie for the whole state of Christes churche.	Let us pray for the whole state of Christes Churche *militant here in earth.**
Then the Priest turnyng him to the Altar, shall saye or syng, playnly and distinctly, this prayer followyng.	ALmightie and euerliuing God, which by thy holy Apostle haste taughte us to make prayers and supplicacions, and to geue thankes for all menne: we hum-
ALmightye and euerliuyng	

---

* Marginal rubric: "Yf there be none *almose geuen unto the poore* than shall ye wordes of *acceptyng our almes* be lefte out unsayed."

1549	1552
God, whiche by thy holy Apostle hast taught us to make prayers and supplicacions, and to geue thankes for all menne: We humbly beseche thee most mercyfully to receiue these our prayers: which we offre unto thy diuine Maiestie, besechyng thee to inspire cōtinually the uniuersal churche, with the spirit of trueth, unitie and concorde: And graunt that all they that doe cōfesse thy holye name, maye agree in the trueth of thy holye worde, and liue in unitie and godly loue. Speciallye wee beseche thee to saue and defende thy seruant, Edwarde our Kynge, that under him we maye be Godly and quietly gouerned. And graunte unto his whole coūsaile, and to all that bee put in authoritie under hym, that they maye truely and indifferently minister iustice, to the punishmente of vice, & to the maintenaunce of Goddes true religion & vertue. Geue grace (O heauenly father) to all Bishoppes, Pastors, and Curates, that they maie both by their life and doctrine, set furthe thy true and liuely worde, and rightely and duely administer thy holye Sacramentes.	bly beseche thee moste mercifully *to accepte our almose,* and to receiue these our prayers whiche we offre unto thy diuine Maiestie: beseching thee to inspire continuallye, the uniuersal churche with the spirite of trueth, unitie and concorde: and graunte that al they that doe confesse thy holy name, maye agree in the trueth of thy holy word, and lyue in unitie and Godly loue. We beeseche thee also to saue and defende all Christian kynges, Princes, and gouernours, and speciallye thy seruaunte, Edwarde our Kyng, that under hym we maye be Godlye and quietly gouerned: and graunte unto hys whole counsayle, and to al that be put in auctoritie under hym, that they may truely and indifferentlye minister iustice, to the punishmente of wickednesse and vice, and to the mayntenaunce of Gods true religion and vertue. Geue grace (O heauenly father) to all Bisshops, pastoures and Curates, that they may both by theyr lyfe and doctryne set forth thy true and lyuely worde, and rightly and duely administer thy holy Sacramentes: and to al thy people geue thy
And to all thy people geue thy heauenly grace, that with meke hearte and due reuerence, they maye heare and receiue thy holy worde, truely seruyng thee in holyness and righteousnes, all the dayes of their life. And wee moste hūbly beseche thee of thy	heauenly grace, and especially to thys congregaciō here present, that with meke hearte & due reuerence, they maye heare and receiue thy holy worde, truely seruynge thee in holynes and righteousnesse al the dayes of their lyfe. And we most humbly

1549	1552
goodnes (O Lorde) to coumfort and succour all them, whyche in this transytory lyfe be in trouble, sorowe, nede, sycknes, or any other aduersitie. And especially we commend unto thy merciful godnes, thys congregacion whiche is here assembled in thy name, to celebrate the commemoracion of the most glorious deathe of thy sonne:	beseche thee of thy goodnesse (O Lord) to coumforte and succoure al them whiche in thys transitorye life be in trouble, sorowe, nede, sickenes, or any other aduersitie: Graunt this O father, for Jesus Christes sake our onely mediatour and aduocate. Amē.

THE PENITENTIAL PREPARATION AND THE EXHORTATIONS

The penitential preparation became didactic as well when three exhortations followed the prayer for the Church. Cranmer responded to Bucer's suggestion for more penitential exhortations with an extensive, newly-composed exhortation for cases when people were negligent about communicating.

This new composition taught with a repetitiousness aimed at the uninstructed that the Lord's Supper was a communal meal, a Communion commemorative of Christ's death.

In this exhortation it became clear why the 1549 rubric about non-communicants departing from the "quire" was dropped. The new Service took a far stricter view of these "gasers and lokers on." They were not to remain while others communicated (as if a Sacrifice propitiatory were being offered) but were to depart altogether and "geue place to them that be Godly disposed."

In its emphasis on Communion, this exhortation sedulously avoided any inference of carnal real Presence. Even the brief narration of the Institution omits the all-important words "This is my Body" and "This is my Blood." The words employed throughout indicate the goal of Cranmer's teaching. He freely used "supper," "provuision," "communicate," "feaste," "holy Communion," "banquet," "eate," "Lordes table," "heauenly foode," and other expressions indicative of a meal.

Another exhortation followed, this time the second exhortation of 1549. Only two noteworthy changes were made.

The first was an added precaution against the danger of carnal

Real Presence interpretations. The cognate sections of the two exhortations are compared below:

1549	1552
. . . our dutie is to come to these holy misteries, with moste heartie thankes to bee geuen to almightie GOD, for his infinite mercie and benefittes geuen and bestowed upon us his unworthye seruantes, for whom he hath not onely geuen his body to death, and shed his bloude, but also doothe vouchsaue in a Sacrament and Mistery, to geue us his sayed bodye and bloud to feed upon spiritually.	. . . oure duetye is to rendre to Almightie God our heauēly father moste hartye thankes, for that he hath geuen his sonne our sauioure Jesus Christe, not onely to die for us, but also to be our spiritual fode & sustenaūce, *as it is declared unto us,* as wel by Gods worde, as *by the holy Sacramentes of* his blessed body, and bloud.

The second change involved Confession. In language still typically ambiguous, but less so than in 1549, Cranmer changed the priest from minister "of GOD and of the churche" to minister "of Gods worde." As another subtle deemphasis of private penance, the admonition not to judge those who confess privately was omitted. The apparent goal of the new wording was to obviate the danger of anyone considering Penance a means of salvation over and above Christ's Redemptive Act:

1549	1552
. . . yf there bee any of you whose conscience is troubled & greued in any thing, lackyng comforte or counsaill, let him come to me, or to some other dyscrete and learned priest, taught in the law of God, and confesse and open his synne & griefe secretly, that he maye receiue suche ghostly counsaill, aduyse and comfort, that his conscience maye be releued, and that of us (as of the Ministers of GOD and of the churche) he maye receiue comfort and abso-	. . . if there be any of you which by the meanes afore said, cannot quiet his own conscience, but requireth further confort or counsel: then let him come to me or some other discrete and learned *ministre of Gods worde,* and open his griefe, that he may receiue such gostly counsail, aduise, and coumfort, as his conscience may be relieued: & that by *ministery of Gods worde,* he maye receyue comforte & *the benefite of* absolucion, to the quietinge of his cō-

1549	1552
lucion, to the satisfaccion of his mynde, and auoyding of all scruple and doubtfulnes: requiryng such as shalbe satisfied with a generall confession, not to be offended with them that doe use, to their further satisfyng, the auriculer and secret confession to the Priest. . . .	science, & aduoiding of al Scruple & doubtfulnes.

Still a third exhortation followed, this time the introductory one of 1549. Once again only two notable changes were made.

The first was an elimination. In 1549 those guilty of "greuous cryme" were told to stay away from the Communion table. But there was one exception: "excepte he bee truly sory therefore, and earnestly mynded to leaue the same vices, and do trust him selfe to bee reconciled to almightie God, and in Charitie with all the worlde." In 1552 Cranmer eliminated this exceptive clause. The requirements were stiffened. It was an added indication that the reception was a spiritual one; there was no change in the elements.

The second change was another elimination in a further attempt to interpret the Divine Presence in a receptionist sense. In 1549 Cranmer had exhorted the people that the feeding was spiritual, involving comfort and consolation. But he had used the phrase "blessed body, & precious bloud, for us to fede upon spiritually." Even this statement was apparently too strong for his critics. He revised it in a more receptionist sense as follows:

1549	1552
. . . he hath lefte in those holy Misteries, as a pledge of his loue, & a continuall remēbraunce of the same his owne blessed body, & precious bloud, for us to fede upon spiritually, to our endles comfort & consolacion.	. . . *he hath instituted and ordayned holy misteries,* as pledges of his loue, and continual remembraunce of his death, to our great and endless comforte.

THE REVISED CONSECRATION AND COMMUNION

One of the paramount aims of the new revision was to transpose or eliminate every prayer that had intervened between Consecration and Communion. In 1549 the long prayers of oblation and preparation apparently had been interpreted as teaching Transubstantiation and adoration of the elements.

' Therefore Cranmer transferred most of these prayers. Those of preparation for Communion he placed immediately after the exhortations. Now they were preparation for Consecration as well as Communion. No one could mistake them as signifying Transubstantiation because no Consecration had taken place.

He placed the Invitation, Confession, Absolution, Comfortable Words, and Prayer of Humble Access immediately after the final exhortation. The priest was still "kneling," but Gardiner could hardly accuse him of worshipping this time. For everything that had taken place previously had been penitential preparation and alms-giving.

Only after the Prayer of Humble Access, when most of the Service was completed, did Cranmer make provision for the Consecratory prayer. Marked adaptations in the new prayer reflected the renewed emphasis on a receptionist Communion. Cranmer went to considerable effort to remove the few remaining vestiges that had been interpreted as teaching Transubstantiation and Sacrifice.

In the famous "one oblation, once offered" phrase, Cranmer added the words "of hymselfe" in further pointed emphasis of the unicity of Calvary. The most startling change of all was his elimination of the 1549 epiclesis invoking Trinitarian sanctification of the creatures of bread and wine. In a new receptionist epiclesis, reminiscent of Martyr's letter to Bucer, and Bucer's suggestion to Cranmer, he invoked God's blessings on the *recipients*. He also changed "to celebrate" as reminiscent of the Mass. The new phrase was "to continue" a perpetual memory.

The last of the traditional manual acts rubrics were removed, along with the only two blessings Cranmer retained from Sarum. Consistent with his emphasis on blessing the recipients, he even deleted mention of Christ's blessing of the food at the Last Supper.

In his determination to eliminate all prayers between Consecration and Communion, Cranmer transferred the commemoration of the Redemption to the Consecration prayer itself. The new and very diminished form was only "in remembraunce of his death and passion."

The two versions of the Consecratory prayer are printed below. Once again cognate mutations are italicized.

1549

O God heauenly father, which of thy tender mercie, diddest geue thine only sonne Jesu Christ, to suffre death upon the crosse for our redempcion, who made there (by his one oblacion once offered) a full, perfect, and sufficient sacrifyce, oblacion, and satysfacyon, for the sinnes of the whole worlde, and did institute, and in his holy Gospell commaund us, to celebrate a perpetuall memory, of that his precious death, untyll his comming again: Heare us (o merciful father) we besech thee: and with thy holy spirite & worde, vouchsafe to bl✠esse and sanc✠tifie these thy gyftes, and creatures of bread and wyne, that they maie be unto us the bodye and bloude of thy moste derely beloued sonne Jesus Christe. Who in the same nyght that he was betrayed:* tooke breade, and when he had blessed, and geuen thankes: he brake it, and gaue it to his disciples, saiyng: Take, eate, this is my bodye which is geuen for you, do this in remembraunce of me.

Likewyse after supper he toke the cuppe,† and when he had

1552

Then the priest standing up, shal saye as foloweth.

ALmighty God oure heauenly father, whiche of thy tender mercye dyddest geue thine onely sonne Jesus Christ, to suffre death upon the crosse for our redempcion, who made there (by hys one oblacion *of hymselfe* once offered, a full, perfecte and sufficiente sacrifice, oblacion, and satisfaccion for the synnes of the whole worlde: and dyd institute, and in hys holye Gospell commaunde us, to *continue* a perpetuall memorye of that his precious death, untyll hys comynge agayn. Heare us O mercyfull father wee beeseche thee: *and graunte that wee receyuing these thy creatures of bread and wyne, accordynge to thy sonne our Sauioure Jesu Christes holy institucion, in remembraunce of his death and passion, may be partakers of his most blessed body & bloud:* who in the same night that he was betrayed, toke bread, and when he had geuen thankes, he brake it, and gaue it to his Disciples, saying: Take, eate, this is my body which is geuen for you.

---

* Marginal rubric: "Here the [Pri]este must [ta]ke the [bre]ad into [his] hādes.'

† Marginal rubric: "Here the [Pr]iest shall [ta]ke the [cu]ppe into [hi]s hādes."

1549	1552
geuen thankes, he gaue it to them, saiyng: drynk ye all of this, for this is my bloude of the newe Testament, whyche is shed for you and for many, for remission of synnes: do this as oft as you shall drinke it in remembraunce of me.	Doe this in remembraunce of me. Likewise after supper he tooke the cup, and when he had geuen thankes, he gaue it to them, saying: drinke ye all of this, for this is my bloud of the new Testament, whiche is shed for you and for many, for remission of synnes: doe this as ofte as ye shal drinke it in remembraunce of me.
These wordes before rehersed are to be saied, turning still to the Altar, without any eleuacion, or shewing the Sacrament to the people.	

Since all intervening prayers between Consecration and Communion had been transferred or omitted, Communion immediately followed the Consecratory prayer. The rubrics and formulas for distribution were changed to a more receptionist sense, and Communion was now received in the hands.

In a preliminary rubric for distribution of the bread, Cranmer referred not to the "Sacramente of the body" but to the "Communion" and "the bread." The distribution formula no longer read the "body of our Lorde Jesus Christe," but "Take and eate this, in remembraüce that Christ dyed for thee, and feede on him in thy hearte by faythe, with thankes geuinge." In the preliminary rubric for the second species, it was no longer "the Sacramēt of the bloud," but "the cup" that was given. The formula no longer read "the bloud of our Lorde Jesus Christe" but "Drinke this in remembraunce that Christes bloud was shed for thee, and be thankefull." In a final stroke of receptionism, Cranmer even eliminated the traditional *Agnus Dei*.

The abrupt change in emphasis may be seen clearly when the two Services are compared in columns:

1549	1552
Then shall the Prieste firste receiue the Communion in both kindes himselfe, and next deliuer it to other Ministers, if any be there presente (that they may bee	Then shal the *minister* first receyue the Communion in bothe kyndes him selfe, and next deliuer it to other ministers, yf any be there present (that they may

1549	1552

ready to helpe the chiefe Minister) and after to the people.	help the chief minister) and after to the people *in their handes* kneling. And when he delyuereth *the bread,* he shall saye.
And when he deliuereth the Sacramente of the body of Christe, he shall say to euery one these woordes.	
The body of our Lorde Jesus Christe whiche was geuen for thee, preserue thy bodye and soule unto euerlasting lyfe.	Take and eate *this, in remembraūce* that Christ dyed for thee, and *feede on him in thy hearte by faythe, with thankes geuinge.*
And the Minister deliuering the Sacramēt of the bloud, and geuing euery one to drinke once and no more, shall say.	And the minister that delyuereth the *cup,* shall saye.
The bloud of our Lorde Jesus Christ which was shed for thee, preserue thy bodye and soule unto euerlasting lyfe.	Drinke *this in remembraunce* that Christes bloude was shed for thee, and *be thankefull.*
If there be a Deacon or other Priest, then shal he folow with the Chalice: and as the priest ministreth the Sacramēt of the body, so shal he (for more expediciō) minister the Sacrament of bloude, in fourme before written.	

THE PRAYER OF OBLATION

Cranmer still had to find a place for the last remnants of the prayers that had followed the Consecration in 1549. Therefore, the Our Father, with introduction deleted, immediately followed the Communion. The long prayer of oblation was substituted for the fixed Post-Communion of 1549, which was likewise deleted. The Paschal Lambe prayer was also eliminated.

In the new prayer of oblation, Cranmer no longer referred to "these thy holy giftes." The omission was easy in 1552 because the elements were gone. The commemoration of the Redemption was included in the Consecration itself. The petition for a worthy reception of the "moste precious body and bloude" was now directed merely to "thy grace & heauenly benediccion." The reference to angelic ministry, opposed by Bucer, was eliminated.

Cranmer's doctrine of the Mystical Body and holy fellowship of Christians did not cohere well with the new prayer of oblation. Therefore, he composed an alternative prayer to the oblation that could be recited at the discretion of the Minister.

1549	1552
WHerfore, O Lorde and heauenly father, accordyng to the Instytucyon of thy derely beloued sonne, our sauiour Jesu Christ, we thy humble seruauntes do celebrate, and make here before they diuine Maiestie, with these thy holy giftes, the memoryall whyche thy sonne hath wylled us to make, hauing in remembraunce his blessed passion, mightie resureceyon, and gloryous ascencion, renderyng unto thee most hartie thankes, for the innumerable benefites procured unto us by thesame, entierely desiryng thy fatherly goodnes, mercifully to accepte this our Sacrifice of praise and thankes geuing: most humbly beseching thee to graunt, that by the merites and death of thy sōne Jesus Christ, and through faith in his bloud, we and al thy whole church, may obteigne remission of our sinnes, and all other benefites of hys passyon. And here wee offre and present unto the (O Lorde) oure selfe, oure soules, and bodies, to be a reasonable, holy, and liuely sacrifice unto thee: humbly besechyng thee, that whosoeuer shalbee partakers of thys holy Communion, maye	Then shall the priest saye the Lordes prayer, the people repeating after him euery peticion. After shalbe sayde as foloweth. O Lorde and heauenly father, we thy humble seruauntes, entierly desyre thy fatherly goodnes, mercifully to accepte this our Sacrifice of prayse and thankes geuing: most humbly besechyng thee to graunt that by the merites & death of thy sonne Jesus Christ, and through faith in his bloud, we and al thy whole church, may obtaine remission of our synnes, & al other benefites of his Passion. And here we offre and present unto thee, O lord, our selfes, our soules & bodies, to be a reasonable, holy, & liuely Sacrifice unto thee: hymbly beseching thee, that all we which be partakers of this holy Communion, *may be fulfilled with thy grace & heauenly benediccion.* And althoughe we bee unworthy, throughe our manifolde sinnes, to offre unto thee any sacrifice: yet we beseche thee to accept this our bounden duetie and seruice, not

1549

worthely receiue the moste precious body and bloude of thy sonne Jesus Christe: and bee fulfilled with thy grace and heauenly benediccion, and made one bodye with thy sonne Jesu Christe, that he maye dwell in them, and they in hym. And although we be unworthy (through our manyfolde synnes) to offre unto thee any Sacryfice: Yet we beseche thee to accepte thys our bounden duetie and seruice, and commaunde these our prayers and supplicacions, by the Ministery of thy holy Angels, to be brought up into thy holy Tabernacle before the syght of thy dyuine maiestie: not waiyng our merites, but pardonyng our offences, through Christe our Lorde, by whome, and with whome, in the unitie of the holy Ghost: all honour and glory, be unto thee, O father almightie, world without ende. Amen.

1552

weighing oure merites, but pardoninge oure offences, through Jesus Christe oure Lord: by whom and with whom, in the unitie of the holy gost, al honour and glory be unto thee O father almightie, worlde withoute ende. Amen.

Or thys.

ALmightie and euerliuinge God, we most hartely thāke thee, for that thou dooeste vouchsafe to fede us, whiche haue duely receiued these holy misteries, with the spirituall foode of the most precious body and bloud of thy sonne our sauiour Jesus Chryst: and doest assure us thereby of thy fauoure and doodnesse towarde us, and that we bee very membres incorporate in thy mistical body, whiche is the blessed companie of al faithful people, and be also heyres throughe hope, of thy euerlasting kingdome, by the merites of the moste precious death and Passion of thy deare sonne: we now most humbly beseche thee, O heauenly father, so to assist us with thy grace, that we maye continue in that holy felowship, and doe all suche good workes as thou hast prepared for us to walke in, throughe Jesus Christ our Lorde: to whom with thee and the holy goste be al honour and glory, world without ende. Amen.

In the concluding *Gloria,* Cranmer added a second recitation of the significant words: "Thou that takest away the sinnes of the worlde, haue mercy upon us." In 1928 the Protestant Episcopal

Church argued that this phrase was a dittography when they removed it from their Prayer Book.[23] It seems more likely, however, that Cranmer added it deliberately. It emphasized the unicity of Christ's Sacrifice. And its repetition compensated for the deleted *Agnus Dei.*

The Service proper terminated with the final blessing and a list of the 1549 alternate Collects for a truncated Service "when there is no Communyon." Bucer's objection to this Ante-Communion was ignored.

Missing were terminal rubrics for singing and for celebrating the Communion "on the workeday or in priuate howses." [24]

THE NEW RUBRICS

In the rubrics for the abbreviated Ante-Communion the direction was now for "holy dayes" instead of "wednesdaies & frydaies, and all other daies." This Service was to conclude not at the "offertory" but at the prayer for the Church "militant here in earth." Significantly, there was no mention of vestments.

In 1549, a rubric prescribed that there should be no Supper unless "some" communicate with the priest. In 1552, this "some" was clarified. It was a "good noumbre"; this meant "aboue twentie persons" of discretion, of whom "foure, or three at the least" must communicate. In another blow at private Masses, the new rubric ordered all priests and deacons in Cathedral and College Churches to communicate with the Minister unless they had "reasonable cause to the contrary." The weird 1549 provision for communicants by proxy was eliminated.

Only in this section of his new Service did Cranmer see fit to mention the elements. He specified that Curate and Churchwardens provide them. Not only were the people excluded from providing the elements at the Service itself, but this time the laity were included only by the phrase "at the charges of the Parishe." This charge as well as others was to be paid by order of houses every Sunday.

The rubric that Gardiner had exploited so well about the whole Christ being present in each particle of broken bread was quietly dropped.

There was a final provision that each parishioner was to communicate not once, but three times a year, one of these occasions being Easter. But there was no longer any provision for ecclesiastical penalty.

Since Communion was now to be received in the hands, there was a conspicuous absence of the rubric explaining why Communion was *not* received in the hands.

THE BLACK RUBRIC

The Communion Service of 1552 was born under a cloud. While the Prayer Book was still at the printers, a storm broke.

It seems that, even at this late date, the extreme party was still attacking the practice of kneeling for Communion. Hooper's adamant position was well known from his London sermons.[25] The immediate catalyst for the new crisis, however, seems to have come from the turbulent north. There John Knox had set aside kneeling at the Communion Service. And he was distributing household bread to sitting communicants.[26]

Knox journeyed to London for a violent sermon before King and Council. He threw his weight behind Hooper in a sweeping attack against kneeling. Utenhovius described the situation to the well-informed Bullinger:

> Some disputes have arisen within these few days among the bishops, in consequence of a sermon of a pious preacher, chaplain to the duke of Northumberland, preached by him before the king and council, in which he inveighed with great freedom against kneeling at the Lord's supper, which is still retained by the English. This good man, however, a Scotsman by nation, has so wrought upon the minds of many persons that we may hope some good to the church will at length arise from it. . . .[27]

King and Council now realized that kneeling was *explicitly* prescribed in the new Service. Council thereupon suspended issuance of the Book, already partially in print. To temporize, they alleged certain printer's errors required emendation.[28]

In the meantime, Council wrote posthaste to Cranmer ordering him to reconsider his rubrics for kneeling. At this the Archbishop balked. He had gone as far as he was going to go in trying to please others. He would go no further. His works had been misinterpreted by Gardiner, ridiculed by Hooper, criticized by Bucer and Martyr, and now attacked by a non-conforming reformer from the northern mountains. Cranmer replied to Council respectfully but trenchantly:

> Where I understand by your Lordships' letters that the King's majesty his pleasure is that the Book of Common Service should be diligently perused, and therein the printers' errors to be amended. I shall travaile therein to the uttermost of my power. . . . And where I understand further by your Lordships' letters that some be offended with kneeling at the time of receiving of the sacrament, and would that I (calling to me the Bishop of London, and some other learned men as Mr Peter Martyr or such like) should with them expend and weigh the said prescription of kneeling, whether it be fit to remain as a commandment, or to be left out of the book. I shall accomplish the King's Majesty his commandment herein: albeit I trust that we with just balance weighed this at the making of the book, and not only we, but a great many Bishops and others of the best learned within this realm. . . .[29]

Cranmer's pique mounted at those extreme critics who had goaded him on Scriptural grounds:

> "But," say they, "it is not commanded in the Scripture to kneel, and whatsoever is not commanded in the Scripture is against the Scripture, and utterly unlawful and ungodly." But this saying is the chief foundation of the Anabaptists and divers other sects. This saying is a subversion of all order as well in religion as in common policy. If this saying be true, take away the whole Book of Service; for what should men travell to set in order in the form of service, if no order can be got but that is already prescribed by Scripture? And because I will not trouble your Lordships with reciting of many Scriptures or proof in this matter, whosoever teacheth anysuch doctrine. . . . I will set my foot by his, to be tried by fire, that his doctrine is untrue; and not only untrue, but also seditious and perilous. . . .

> "But it is not expressly contained in the Scripture," (say they) "that Christ ministered the sacrament to his apostles kneeling." Nor they find it expressly in Scripture that he ministered it standing or sitting. But if we follow the plain words of the Scripture we should rather receive it lying down on the ground—as the custom of the world at that time almost everywhere, and as the Tartars and Turks use yet at this day, to eat their meat lying upon the ground.[30]

While Cranmer groped for a compromise to please Council without actually changing his Service, Knox again took the offensive. On October 21, as a censor of the proposed Articles of Religion, he issued another criticism of ceremonies.[31]

Cranmer's exact measures are unknown. But almost certainly it was he who composed the "Black Rubric." There is a letter in the Council Register dated October 27, 1552, ordering "a letter to the Lord Chancellor to cause to be signed unto the Book of Common Prayer, lately set forth, a certain Declaration signed by the King's Majesty, and sent unto his Lordship, touching the kneeling at the receiving of the Communion." [32]

The style, the doctrine, the attitude toward critics expressed in the new rubric are those of Thomas Cranmer. This eleventh-hour addition provided a new and controversial conclusion to the 1552 Communion Service. Known to history as the infamous "Black Rubric," it succinctly expressed Cranmer's mature doctrine of the Real Presence.

Cranmer explicated why he prescribed kneeling. He did so as an acknowledgment of Christ's *benefits* which were received in a worthy reception. Apparently he was referring to the force, the grace, the efficacy of Christ that benefits the worthy communicant.

Cranmer made it absolutely clear that a kneeling acknowledgment of Christ's benefits implied no adoration of Christ in the elements, no ontological presence. The bread and wine were not to be adored; they remained in their natural substance. Adoration would be idolatry. As for the "naturall bodye and bloud" of Christ, they were in "heauen and not here." Cranmer still considered Christ's ascended Body bound by the same limitations of space as during His public life. It was "agaynst the trueth of Christes true naturall bodye, to be in moe places then in one at one time."

This rubric has provoked a plethora of criticism from Anglicans, Roman Catholics, and Protestants, but it is invaluable to the student of Cranmer's doctrine. A clearer statement of his teaching on the true Presence would be hard to imagine.

Key passages have been italicized:

ALthough no ordre can be so perfectlye deuysed, but it may be of some, eyther for theyr ignoraunce and infirmitie, or els of malice and obstinacie, mysconstrued, depraued, and interpreted in a wrong parte. And yet because brotherly charitie willeth, that so muche as conueniently may be, offences should be taken away: therfore we willing to dooe the same. Wheras it is ordeyned in the booke of common prayer, in the administracion of the Lordes Supper, that the Communicantes kneelynge shoulde receiue the holye Communion: whiche thyng well mente, for *a sygnificacyon of the humble and gratefull acknowledgeynge of the benefites of Christe, geuen unto the woorthye receyuer,* and to auoyde the prophanacion and dysordre which about the holye communion myghte elles ensue. Lest yet the same kneelynge myght be thought or taken otherwyse, we dooe declare that *it is not mente thereby, that any adoracion is doone, or oughte to bee doone, eyther unto the Sacramentall bread or wyne* there bodelye receyued, *or unto anye reall and essenciall presence there beeyng of Chrystes naturall fleshe and bloude.* For as concernynge the Sacramentall bread and wyne, they *remayne styll in theyr verye naturall substaunces,* and therfore may not bee adored, for that were Idolatrye to be abhorred of all faythfull christians. And *as concernynge the natural bodye and bloud of our sauior Christ, they are in heauen and not here: for it is agaynst the trueth of Christes true naturall bodye, to be in moe places then in one at one tyme.*

In retrospect the turbulent birth of the 1552 Service, with the furor over kneeling, reads like an omen of its short life. Council's last-minute letter to the Chancellor meant that the printers had but a few days to revise and distribute the Service. It is not surprising that some copies were issued without the new rubric, and some with the "Black Rubric" hastily pasted on a flyleaf.[33]

The Book made its deadline in London, but it is uncertain how far it supplanted 1549 in the countryside.[34] When Bishop Ridley officiated at the first Service in St. Paul's, his young King and the Communion Service itself had about eight months to live.

But the 1552 Communion Service was the basis of all future revisions within the Anglican Communion. It would be considerably adapted in England and Scotland. Through these diverse paths it would provide the framework for the American Service some two centuries later.

The Communion Service of 1559

THE MARIAN INTERLUDE

Shortly after the premature death of the "young Joshua," tables were removed from churches. Altars, statues, and the Mass soon emerged from the English catacombs.[35] The history of the reformed Service was transferred to the continent.

Activities on the continent during Mary's short reign were important, both doctrinally and politically, for their effect on subsequent revisions of the Communion Service.[36]

At first, the hardy English exiles rallied around friendly Frankfort. Friction soon arose between conservatives and more advanced reformers.[37] The former group demanded modified adherence to the 1552 Service. The advanced, or "Puritan" group, preferred a Service tantamount to Calvin's Geneva rite. The position of some at Frankfort was stated in 1554 in a letter to other English exiles at Zurich: "As touching the effect of the Book, we desire the execution thereof as much as you, so far as God's word doth commend it; but as for the unprofitable ceremonies, as well by His consent as by ours are not to be used." [38]

The Zurich exiles retorted that such alteration would "seem to condemn the chief authors thereof." It would allow the Roman Catholics to accuse "our doctrine of imperfection and us of mutability," and would cause the "godly to doubt in the truth wherein before they were persuaded, and to hinder their coming hither which before they had purposed." [39]

As "liturgically conservative" exiles converged on Frankfort, the Puritan group, led by John Knox, soon found themselves a minority. Finally, these enthusiasts for the "pure Word" retired to hospitable Geneva where they ultimately evolved their own liturgy along Calvinistic lines.[40]

Approximately one-fourth of all English exiles were in this Geneva faction. If a Protestant monarch regained the English throne, these stalwart men would have to be reckoned with. Among them were such influential English reformers as Sir William Stafford, John Bodley, Thomas Lever, James Pilkington, John Scory, Thomas Sampson, William Kethe, Thomas Bentham, Laurence Humphrey, Miles Coverdale, William Whittingham, Christopher Goodman, Anthony Gilby, and John Knox.[41]

Nor was this Geneva congregation devoid of influence on Frankfort. Time soon healed former wounds. By 1558 members of both groups were exchanging visits and apologies. A letter of Goodman to Martyr reflects the tempered zeal of Geneva leaders in their efforts to persuade those of conservative sympathies:

And as it is right never to spare our most bitter enemies the papists, so also according to our ability should we remove the ignorance of our brethren. This is the case whenever the truth, openly brought forth by this diligence and authority of learned men, is made manifest to the contemplation of all. . . .[42]

Goodman's letter indicates the three groups that an English monarch would have to deal with. There were "the papists," the "Coxians" of Frankfort, and the "Knoxians" of Geneva.

These latter two groups would have to be reckoned with in any liturgical revision. Knappen remarks that "at the moment the channel divided the important Protestants, but by far the great majority were on the Continent." [43] This continental majority wasted no time returning home when news of Mary's death travelled up the frozen rivers.[44] At Calvin's insistence, the Genevan group followed their brethren from Frankfort, Strasbourg, and Zurich to the shores of an England watching closely the actions of a new Queen.

GOVERNMENT POLICY

It seems that Elizabeth's real wishes will be forever a matter of historical conjecture. According to an account of the Spanish Ambassador, she was "resolved to restore religion as her father left it." [45] But the Coxians were resolved to restore religion as Edward VI had left it. Knoxians and others considered even the 1552 Communion Service too "papist."

With reformed sentiment so strong, Elizabeth would not have been able to restore—or retain—the Mass, even if this had been her wish.[46] If Lord Keeper Bacon's speech to Parliament in January, 1559, is indicative of her policy, it was one of moderation, of watching and waiting. She longed for uniformity in religion; and uniformity in religion strengthened unity in government. Bacon urged laws "for the according and uniting of these people of the realm into a uniform order of religion: . . . That nothing be advized or done anyway in continuance of time were likely to breed or nourish any kind of idolatry or superstition." But lest this look like an exclusion of a particular party, he also urged that "on the other side care is to be taken, that by no Licentious or loose handling any manner of Occasion be given, whereby any contempt or irreverent behaviour towards God or Godly things, or any spice of irreligion, might creep in or be conceived." [47]

Elizabeth was inimical to disciples of Calvin and Knox. For one thing she had a woman's love for finery. But what provoked her scorn the most was the "monstrous regiment" epithets that had emanated from Calvin's camp.[48] The great reformer vented his chagrin at her attitude to William Cecil:

The messenger to whom I gave in charge my commentaries upon Isaiah to be presented to the most serene queen, brought me word that my homage was not kindly received by her majesty, because she had been offended with me by reason of some writings published in this place.[49]

An interesting "device for alteration of religion" appeared in the serene Queen's first year. This document provided for a commission of Divines to compose a Service Book for the Queen's perusal.[50] The "device" foresaw opposition to a new Book from both Roman Catholics and Puritans.[51]

Another significant document of that time indicates a conservative government attitude toward revision. This document, a letter of Edmund Guest, refers to a new Prayer Book. Most probably this letter also referred to the commission mentioned in the "device." [52] If such is the case, Guest's letter indicates a governmental preference for a Service along the lines of 1549. At the same time it illustrates the difficulties involved in such a return to the recent past. Protestants who weathered Mary's reign in the British Isles as well as those who fled to safer ports advocated further change. There was to be no going back!

Guest's letter urged that "ceremonies once taken away, as evil used, should not be taken again." As for vestments:

Because it is thought sufficient to use but a surplice in baptizing, reading, preaching, and praying, therefore it is enough also for the celebrating of communion. For if we should use another garment herein, it should seem to teach us, that higher and better things be given by it than be given by the other services. . . .[53]

The letter vigorously opposed prayer for the deceased as indicative of Sacrifice, injurious to the doctrine of a unique Mediator, and implying purgatory:

That praying for the dead is not now used in the communion, because it doth seem to make for the sacrifice of the dead. And also, (because as it was used in the first book) it makes some of the faithful to be in heaven, and to need no mercy; and some of them to be in another place, and to lack help and mercy.[54]

As for the 1549 epiclesis, it was "disliked for two causes. The first, because it is taken to be so needful for the consecration, that the consecration is not thought to be without it. Which is not true: for petition is no part of consecration." [55] The second reason was "that it prays that the bread and wine may be Christ's body and blood; which makes for the popish transubstantiation: which is a doctrine that hath caused much idolatry." [56]

Finally, the letter expressed indifference as to posture for reception. But Communion should be received in the hands. "Christ gave the sacrament into the hands of his Apostles, 'Divide it,' saith he, 'among yourselves.' " As for standing or kneeling, it was "indifferent to every man's choice to follow the one way or the other; to teach men that it is lawful to receive either standing or kneeling." [57]

Guest's pleas to abandon 1549 usages may indicate by their very vehemence a government *preference* for 1549. But the vigor of his letter indicates also the difficulties Elizabeth would face in returning to earlier practices.

A similar letter of Parker and "others" to the monarch begs her to reconsider her plans for restoration of images. The fact that Parker and the unspecified "others" thought such expostulation necessary reveals a definite conservatism in Her Highness:

. . . we most humbly beseech your Majesty to consider, that besides weighty causes in policy, which we leave to the wisdom of your honourable councillors, the establishing of images by your authority shall not only utterly discredit our ministries, as builders of the things which we have destroyed, but also blemish the fame of your most godly brother, and such notable fathers as have given their lives for the testimony of God's truth, who by public law removed all images.[58]

With the attitude of men like Guest, Parker, and the "others," the Queen would be unable to return all the way to 1549. Despite an apparent predilection for that mellifluous—and in many ways moderate—Service, she *had* to consider the sentiments of the advanced reformers.[59]

THE "CELEBRATION OF THE LORD'S SUPPER"

Aware of conservative and advanced currents of thought within her realm, Elizabeth evolved a Communion Service that most citizens could abide by, at least for the present. Only Roman Catholics would be wholly displeased.[60] Advanced thought as reflected in the Geneva liturgy was too strong for a return to 1549 or before. Therefore, Elizabeth settled on the Lord's Supper of 1552.

But it was 1552 with three important changes. Two of these were indicated in the Act of Uniformity:

> And further be it enacted by the queen's highness, with the assent of the lords and commons, in this present Parliament assembled, and by authority of the same, that all and singular ministers, in any cathedral, or parish church, or other place within this realm of England, Wales, and the marches of the same, or other the queen's dominions, shall from, and after the feast of the Nativity of Saint John Baptist next coming, be bounden to say and use the Mattings, Evensong, celebration of the Lord's supper . . . in such order and form, as is mentioned in the said book, so authorized by Parliament in the said .v. and .vi. year of the reign of king Edward the sixt . . . and two Sentences only added in the delivery of the Sacrament to the communicants, and none other, or other wise. . . .
>
> PROVIDED always and be it enacted, that such ornaments of the Church, and of the ministers thereof, shall be retained and be in use as was in this Church of England, by authority of Parliament, in the second year of the reign of King Edward the vi. . . .[61]

Elizabeth restored the Communion formula of 1549, but in doing so she juxtaposed it to that of 1552. Those who wanted a formula for distribution that alluded to a presence of Christ within the elements would be satisfied. But so would those who preferred the "this" and "in remembrance" of 1552.

The juxtaposition of Cranmer's ambiguous 1549 formula and his more receptionist one of 1552 were recited as follows:

> Then shall the minister first receive the Communion in both kinds himself, and next deliver it to other ministers, if any be there present (that they may help the chief minister,) and after to the people in

their hands kneeling. And when he delivereth the bread he shall say,

The body of our Lord Jesus Christ, which was given for thee, preserve thy body and soul into everlasting life; and take and eat this in remembrance that Christ died for thee, and feed on him in thine heart by faith, with thanksgiving.

And the minister that delivereth the cup, shall say,

The blood of our Lord Jesus Christ, which was shed for thee, preserve thy body and soul into everlasting life; and drink this in remembrance that Christ's blood was shed for thee, and be thankful.[62]

The new "vestments rubric" appeared in the order for Morning and Evening Prayer.

And here is to be noted, that the minister at the time of the communion, and at all other times in his ministration, shall use such ornaments in the church as were in use by authority of parliament in the second year of the reign of king Edward .VI. according to the act of parliament set in the beginning of this book.[63]

Kneeling was prescribed in 1559 as in 1552, and this involved the third change in Elizabeth's Service. Despite the fact that kneeling was a great bone of contention to Puritans,[64] the notorious "Black Rubric" of 1552 was conspicuous by its absence.

With these three notable variations from 1552, England again had a reformed Communion Service. It was not all either conservatives or Puritans would have liked. But it contributed to the "settlement." Elizabeth had read the country's temper well as it had been expressed by James Pilkington from Frankfort: "We purpose to submit ourselves to such orders as shall be established by authority, being not of themselves wicked; so we would wish you willingly to do the same." [65]

The Communion Service of 1604

KING JAMES AND THE SCRIPTURAL BASIS FOR THE COMMUNION SERVICE

The principal doctrinal issue in the Communion Service strife of 1603 and 1604 was whether or not the Service adhered to Scripture. What should remain as it was should so remain because it adhered to Scripture. What should be abolished should be abolished because it did not adhere to Scripture. If some parts should be "explained" where corruptions of men had crept in, they should be explained instead of revised because of their essential adherence to Scripture.

For James I, adherence to Scripture was understood differently than it was by the Puritan party. In his Proclamation of Uniformity, he indicated his reluctance to make any changes because the doctrine was sincere and forms and rites "were justified out of the practice of the primitive church." [66]

James expressed conservative leanings in an early message to the Episcopal party. Archbishop Whitgift sent Dr. Thomas Nevill, Dean of Canterbury, to tender the clergy's respects and to learn "his Highness's pleasure" in ecclesiastical matters. He returned with a "welcome answer, to such as sent him, of his Highness's purpose, which was to uphold and maintain the government of the late queen, as she left it settled." [67]

In May, 1603, while admitting that some corruptions may have crept in, James expressed satisfaction that Church government and doctrine adhered to God's Word and the primitive Church:

> We are persuaded that both the constitution and doctrine thereof is agreeable to God's word, and near to the condition of the primitive church; yet forasmuch as experience doth shew daily that the Church militant is never so well constituted in any form of policy, but that the imperfections of men, who have the exercise thereof, do with time, though insensibly, bring in some corruptions. . . .[68]

Later, at Hampton Court, he would open that famous conference with a profession of satisfaction with his new kingdom. At that time, however, he revealed an aversion to things Scottish and Calvinistic: "Blessed be God's goodness, who hath brought me into the promised land, where religion is purely professed, where I sit amongst grave, learned, and reverend men, not as before, elsewhere, a king without a state . . . where beardless boys would brave us to the face." [69]

James was inimical to change in a land where religion was "agreeable to God's word." Matthew Hutton prayed almost prophetically: "The Lord, for his Christ's sake, bless his Majesty with his manifold graces: that he may maintain the Gospel in this Church, as his dear sister, most worthy Queen Elizabeth, did leave it. . . ." [70]

The King's attitude toward ceremonies was similar to that of Hooker. The latter desired the preservation of such externals as fostered "godliness," and the toleration or "cure" of minor inconveniences. Hooker was not limiting the Services to what was commanded explicitly in Scripture when he wrote:

> . . . in the external form of religion such things as are apparently or can be sufficiently proved, effectual and generally fit to set forward godliness, either as betokening the greatness of God, or as beseeming the dignity of religion, or as concurring with celestial impressions of the minds of men, may be reverently thought of, some few rare, casual and tolerable, or otherwise curable, inconveniences notwithstanding.[71]

In a similar vein, Lord Bacon urged the removal of the chaff but care in uprooting tolerable tares:

> For they need not doubt but your Majesty, with the advice of your council, will discern what things are intermingled like the tares amongst the wheat, which have their roots so enwrapped and entangled, as the one cannot be pulled up without endangering the other; and where are mingled but as the chaff and the corn, which need but a fan to sift and sever them.[72]

THE PURITANS AND THE SCRIPTURAL BASIS FOR THE COMMUNION SERVICE

There were those who thought the tares were rampant, and should be uprooted at once. These were the Puritans. Their earliest concerted effort after James's accession was the famous Millenary Petition for change in Church ceremonies and abuses.[73]

The Puritans did not think the Prayer Book adhered to Scripture. They were "groaning as under a common burden of human rites and ceremonies."

> We, to the number of more than a thousand, of your Majesty's subjects and ministers, all groaning as under a common burden of human rites and ceremonies, do, with one joint consent, humble ourselves at your Majesty's feet to be eased and relieved in this behalf.

The Puritan concept of adherence to Scripture differed from that of James. It was well expressed by William Perkins:

> [The Scriptures are] of sufficient credit in and by themselves, needing not the testimony of any creature, not subject to the censure of either men or angels, binding the consciences of all men or angels,

binding the consciences of all men at all times, and being the only foundation of our faith and the rule and canon of all truth.[74]

These Puritans thought it their duty to protest against unnecessary observances, and were of an acute and morbid sensitiveness as to things indifferent. They thought it sinful to use Services where they were required to bow at the name of Jesus, to observe the holidays of the Church, or to read uncanonical Scriptures.

Any ceremony not expressly taught in Scripture did not adhere to Scripture. Accordingly, they asked in the Millenary Petition that "the cap and surplice [be] not urged," and that "examination may go before communion."

One remark in the petition should be noted, since at the subsequent conference it drew attention to the Communion Service. This was the passing reference to absolution requesting that "divers terms of priests and absolution, and some other used, with the ring in marriage, and other such like in the Book, may be corrected."

There was some slight connection with the Lord's Supper when they petitioned that "the canonical scriptures only be read in the church."

Finally, the Puritans wrote that since "these with such other abuses yet remaining and practised in the church of England," they wished a conference or at least a chance to record their stand in writing. "If it shall please your Highness farther to hear us, or more at large by writing to be informed, or by conference among the learned to be resolved."

THE HAMPTON COURT CONFERENCE AND THE SCRIPTURAL BASIS FOR THE COMMUNION SERVICE

They got their conference. For three days in mid-January, 1604, the King met with Puritan and Episcopal representatives.[75]

On the first day, the King met with the Episcopal party. He inaugurated the conference with a sermon to the assembled clergy and divines, professing his prejudice in their favor: "I see yet no such cause to change, as to confirm, what I find well-settled already. . . . I assure you we have not called this assembly for any innovation."

Nevertheless, James got right to the point. He admitted "nothing can be so absolutely ordered, but that something may be added thereunto, and corruption in any state (as in the body of man) will insensibly grow either through time or persons." Therefore, "we have called you, bishops and deans, in severally by yourselves, not to be confronted by the contrary opponents; that if any thing shall be found meet to be redressed, it might be done without any visible altercation."

The King admitted he was disturbed by the word "absolution." He feared it was understood as Papal absolution; whereas absolution, except for excommunication, came from God.

As for absolution, I know not how it is used in our church, but have heard it likened to the pope's pardons. There be indeed two kinds thereof from God: One *general;* all prayers and preaching importing an absolution: The other *particular,* to special parties, having committed a scandal, and repenting. Otherwise where excommunication precedes not, in my judgment there needs no absolution.

When opportunity arose to discuss absolution, the Archbishop of Canterbury assured the King that the Communion Service clearly excluded all abuse and superstition.

Archbishop of Canterbury.—As for the point of Absolution, wherein your majesty desires satisfaction: it is clear from all abuse or superstition, as it is used in our Church of England, as will appear on the reading of both of the Confession and Absolution following it, in the beginning of the Communion-Book.

The King perused the Service and was satisfied. The Bishop of London, however, called attention to the Communion for the Sick. In this rite, the more private circumstances might easily give the impression of superstition. Nevertheless, the King was still satisfied the usage was apostolic and in the name of Christ. But he ordered the Bishops to consult whether "remission of sins" should not be added for "explanation-sake."

Here the king perused both, and returned.

His Majesty.—I like and approve them, finding it to be very true what you say.

Bishop of London.—It becometh us to deal plainly with your Majesty. There is also in the book a more particular and personal Absolution in *the Visitation of the Sick.*

Here the dean of the chapel turned unto it and read it.

Bishop of London.—Not only the Confessions of Augusta, Boheme, and Saxon, retain and allow it, but Mr. Calvin also doth approve both such a general and such a private (for so he terms it) Confession and Absolution.

His Majesty.—I exceedingly well approve it, being an apostolical and godly ordinance, given in the name of Christ, to one that desireth it, upon the clearing of his conscience.

The conclusion was this,—that the bishops should consult, whether unto the Rubric of the General Absolution, these words "Remission of sins," might not be added for explanation-sake.

On the second day the King met with the Puritan representatives, who requested "that the doctrine of the church might be preserved in purity, according to God's word."

Dr. Reynolds objected that in the Prayer Book the words "Jesus said to his disciples" were added to the pure Scriptures against their context:

Dr. Reynolds.—The next scruple against subscription, is, because it is twice set down in the Common-Prayer Book, Jesus said to his disciples, when by the text in the original, it is plain, that he spake to the Pharisees.

Reynolds had also objected to the reading of Apocrypha in Church; some chapters contained manifest errors repugnant to Scripture. The two Bishop-observers disagreed with the Puritans on this point. But James settled it as follows:

His Majesty.—To take an even order betwixt both: I would not have all canonical books read in the church: nor any chapter out of the Apocrypha, wherein any error is contained. Wherefore, let Dr. Reynolds note those chapters in the Apocrypha-books wherein those offences are, and bring them to the Archbishop of Canterbury against Wednesday next. . . .

It was the Episcopal representatives themselves who brought up kneeling. The Bishop of Winchester claimed it was a significant, lawful ceremony. The Dean of the Chapel added that the Jews had added ceremonies to the Passover; and Christ had used these additions at the Last Supper. Therefore Christ had approved the institution and retention of such signs.

On the third day the Bishops presented their minimal "explanations" to the assembled gathering. There were no real changes. The Puritans, whether out of conviction or out of fear, accepted the inevitable and promised fealty to the King. They did however request the King to permit certain Ministers in Lancashire to continue without surplice. When the King granted this, Mr. Knewstubs requested the same for Suffolk. At this the King lashed out at both the Doctor and the "Scotch." "Sir, you show yourself an uncharitable man. We have here taken pains for unity and uniformity; and you, for sooth, must prefer the credits of a few private men before the peace of the church. This is just the Scotch argument." James warned that the Highlanders argued that Ministers would be discredited if they did what was not pleasing to them. He concluded: "Let them either conform themselves shortly, or they shall hear of it."

Fuller's account terminates in a Puritan-Episcopal exchange on that old bone of contention: kneeling.

Lord Cecil.—The indecency of *ambling* communions is very offensive, and hath driven many from the church.

Bishop of London.—And Mr. Chaderton, I could tell you of *sitting* communions in Emmanuel College.

Mr. Chaderton.—It is so, because of the seats so placed as they be; and yet we have some kneeling also in our chapel.

His Majesty.—No more hereof for the present, seeing they have jointly promised hereafter to be quiet and obedient.

Whereat he rose up to depart into an inner chamber.

THE COMMUNION SERVICE OF 1604

The Communion Service of 1604 was still that of 1559. The minuscule changes in the Prayer Book were termed by James "some declaration and enlargement by way of explanation." [76]

The only portion of the King's letter to Canterbury concerning the "declaration and enlargement" that pertained in any way to the Communion Service was the following:

In the rubricke before Absolution these wordes followinge are to be placed, the Absolution or Remission of Synnes to be pronounced by the minister alone.

John X.11. being the Gospel "Dominica secunda post Pasch." these wordes (Christe sayed) to be printed in letters differing from the text: and these words to be left out, videlicet, *to his disciples.*

Matth. XXII.1. "Dominica vicesima post Trinitat." These words (*Jesus said*) to be printed in letters differing from the text; and these words to be left out, videlicet, *unto his disciples.*[77]

There would henceforth be less danger of false interpretations of the word "absolution." It meant "remission of synnes" and was not to be construed in the alleged Roman sense of priestly absolution over and above the unique mediation of Christ. It was not "given" but "pronounced" by the Minister.

In his *Proclamation for Uniformity*, James explained why ceremonies that had aroused "mighty and vehement informations" remained in use. These forms and rites were justified by the practice of the *primitive Church*. With this explanation, the proceedings concerning the Prayer Book concluded fittingly enough with a final indication of James's enlarged sense of adherence to Scripture.

For we found mighty and vehement informations supported with so weak and slender proofs, as it appeared unto us and our council, that there was no cause, why any change should have been at all in that, which was most impugned, the Book of Common Prayer, containing the form of the public service of God here established; neither in the doctrine, which appeared to be sincere, nor in the forms and rites, which were justified out of the practice of the primitive church.[78]

In a private letter James dismissed the "slender proofs" in a less regal style:

They fled me so from argument to argument, without ever answering me directly, *ut est eorum moris,* as I was forced at last to say unto thaime; that if any of thaime had been in a college disputing with thair scholars, if any of thair disciples had answered them in that sort, they would have fetched him up in a place of reply; and so should the rod have plyed upon the poor boyes buttocks.[79]

Conclusion

The Jacobean Prayer Book and that of Elizabeth were, as far as the Communion Service was concerned, the same.

In three instances Elizabeth had returned to 1549. She restored the Ornaments rubric of that year. She juxtaposed the formula for distribution of 1549 with that of 1552. And she omitted the "Black Rubric."

With these three significant exceptions, the Elizabethan and Jacobean Services were the same as 1552.

But strong currents were flowing in the British Isles, many of them in diverse directions. The Puritans were by no means satisfied that the Service "adhered to Scripture" in their understanding of these words. And within three decades the Scottish Episcopal party would develop a school of divines who desired a return to a more Sacrificial and Real Presence sense.

When these two contrary currents flowed together, the result would be a flood. Blood would flow in England. And one catalyst for the flood would be a Communion Service, the Scottish Communion Service of 1637.

CHAPTER IV

The Communion Services of 1637 and 1662

Four important revisions appeared in the next century and a half. The stately rhythms of Thomas Cranmer were adapted and molded by a varied stream of theologians as the day inexorably approached when the colonists in the New World would evolve their own Communion Service.

A short-lived Scottish Communion Office of 1637 was the product of scholarly northern Bishops and the mighty William Laud. This Service returned to ancient forms and the Communion Service of 1549. Although its life was short, its influence has been immense in Anglican Eucharistic development.

All Anglican Services were outlawed during the mid-century interregnum, but when the Restoration occurred, Prayer Book revision was part of the Restoration Settlement. The Laudian party wished a rite resembling 1549 and 1637, but they were prevented from making extensive changes by the political tone of the Settlement. Nevertheless, the Laudians did manage to restore some emphasis on representative Sacrifice and a perduring Real Presence.

An interesting chapter in English history began when William of Orange ascended the historic throne in 1688. Some refused the oath to such a monarch. These recusants were known as Nonjurors, a relatively small group whose influence on Anglican Eucharistic development belied the paucity of their numbers. In 1718 they published their own Communion Service, which was in the tradition of the ancient liturgies, 1549, and 1637. Finally, in 1764, the Scottish Nonjurors produced a Communion Service along similar lines. It was the Canon of this Office that Samuel Seabury, first Bishop of the Protestant Episcopal Church, promised to urge in the United States.

It was through these varied channels—1637 in Scotland, 1662 in England, 1718 among the Nonjurors, and 1764 among the Scottish Nonjurors—that the currents were flowing toward an eventual native American Service. We shall study the first two in this chapter. But first the Scottish Service of 1637.

The Communion Service of 1637

During the turbulent period preceding the 1637 Prayer Book, there were two principal Communion Services in the highlands. One was the Lord's Supper from the Book of Common Prayer; the other the *Maner of the Lordes Supper* that had made the trip from Geneva to Edinburgh.[1]

King James I was reluctant to impose a Service of English vintage on his northern subjects. He would have preferred a uniform English rite, but wisely limited his religious reforms to the promulgation of Five Articles at Perth.[2] The Book of Common Prayer was used, at least in part, in the royal chapel, in some cathedrals, and in university chapels.[3]

A seventeenth-century historian, David Calderwood, referred to the imposition of the English liturgy on St. Andrew's College. His remark is interesting because of its reference to a young "Doctor Wedderburn" who was the chief architect of the 1637 Communion Service:

> Upon the 15th of January, Mr. Robert Howie, Principal of the New College of St. Androes, Doctor Wedderburn and Doctor Melvine, were directed by a letter from Doctor Young in the king's name, to use the English Liturgie morning and evening in the New Colledge, where all the students were present at morning and evening prayers. . . .[4]

According to a modern historian, Trevor-Roper, James hoped to secure "the loyalty of the Scots by the imposition of an appropriate form of worship," but "his canny timidity had prevented him from imposing it with a flourish or proceeding with it too fast." [5] James died with disparate forms of worship in use in Scotland. Responsibility for a new liturgy devolved on Charles I.

The complex history of the 1637 Prayer Book began at the latest in 1616. Around that year William Cowper, Bishop of Galloway, composed a draft liturgy for Scotland.[6] Donaldson believes that "Cowper's draft represented a not unreasonable compromise,

which in favourable circumstances might have had a fair chance
of general acceptance in Scotland. The king's other moves, however, had ensured . . . grave opposition to any alterations in the
church's services." Cowper's liturgy was shelved until 1629.

In that year John Maxwell, then a Minister in Edinburgh and
later Bishop of Ross, brought the Cowper draft to Charles at the
King's own request.[7]

Charles referred Maxwell to William Laud. The latter frowned
on this Scottish composition: "I told him I was clear of opinion,
that if his Majesty would have a Liturgy settled there, it were best
to take the English Liturgy without any variation, that so the same
Service-book might be established in all his Majesty's domin-
ions. . . ."[8]

Maxwell demurred at this:

To this he replied, that he was of a contrary opinion; and that not
he only, but the bishops of that kingdom, thought their countrymen
would be much better satisfied, if a Liturgy were framed by their own
clergy, than to have the English Liturgy put upon them; yet he added
that it might be according to the form of our English Service-book.[9]

Laud promised to defer any decision until a consultation with
His Majesty. To Charles he represented his case. "His Majesty
avowed the sending of Dr. Maxwell to me . . . but then he inclined to my opinion, to have the English Service without any
alteration to be established there." [10]

Laud continued to advocate the imposition of the English
Services on Scotland. But apparently, in 1633 or 1634, the Scottish
Bishops prevailed on Charles to change his decision. Laud tes-
tified as follows:

Afterwards, the Scottish bishops still pressing his Majesty, at a
Liturgy framed by themselves, and in some things different from ours,
would relish better with their countrymen, they at last prevailed with
his Majesty to have it so, and carried against me, notwithstanding all
I could say or do to the contrary.[11]

Charles and Laud specified that the Services should be "as
near that of England as might be." [12] In September, 1634, Maxwell journeyed south for more precise instructions; perhaps because the Scottish felt compelled to protest afresh that considerable
deviation from the Book of England would be necessary and per-

haps to ask for guidance as to the precise scope of the changes which they would be permitted to make.[13]

The outcome of Maxwell's visit was a copy of the English Book of Common Prayer, signed by the King in September, 1634, with certain alterations and a number of instructions and suggestions.[14] This annotated copy was to provide the basis for the Scottish revision; the changes were few and the Communion Service was practically untouched. Gordon Donaldson describes the instructions of Charles caustically:

> On the whole, the changes expressed in this book show every sign of having emanated from the king personally, and seem to reflect the views of a somewhat small-minded and sacerdotally inclined layman, rather than of a churchman interested in doctrine and other larger issues. They also suggest that his majesty intended the Scots to have something very near indeed to the Book of England.[15]

Within six months the Scots had produced a liturgy. Laud reported that "the Scottish Bishops were commanded by his Majesty to let me see, from time to time, what they did in that Servicebook, they had good reason (As I conceive) to give me 'some account of their diligence.' "[16] So the Bishops sent their faithful courier, John Maxwell, south once again to report to Laud and His Majesty.

Apparently, the Highlanders had gone somewhat beyond the authorized changes, since they remarked that it would take some time to reach a full conformity with England.[17] Nevertheless, Charles was satisfied. He wrote in May, 1635: "We have seen and approved of the liturgy sent by you to us . . . with these corrections and instructions which we have signed and sent unto you. . . . We recommend that all be forthwith printed."[18]

The Scots labored over these "corrections and instructions" until September. Finally, on September 19, 1635, Laud wrote Maxwell:

> I have acquainted his Majesty in what forwardness your Liturgy there is, and with what approbation it is like to come forth. And by the King's command I have sent for Yonge, the printer, the better to prepare him to make ready a black-letter and to bethink himself to send to his servants at Edinburgh, that so . . . all things might be in better readiness. . . .[19]

It appeared to English and Scottish alike that the northern Church finally had its own Prayer Book. But Laud's command to the printer was premature. The liturgy which Charles and Laud had approved in September, 1635, never saw the light of day.

In February, 1636, an event took place that was to have weighty impact on the Communion Service of 1637 and on the imminent Civil War itself. That event was the elevation of James Wedderburn to the See of Dunblane.

Wedderburn was a "Scottish Canterburian" in favor with Laud and King Charles. In the 1635 letter to Maxwell, Laud wrote: "I thank you for your care of Dr. Wedderburn. . . . I pray my love to him, and tell him I would not have stickle at anything, for the King will not leave him long at Dunblane. . . ." [20]

A Scottish scholar, James Cooper, testified that Wedderburn was "a man of antique probity and faith, and for his excellent learning a great ornament to his fatherland." [21] Wedderburn believed that 1635 was the hour of decision for Scotland, the hour to make the Prayer Book as perfect as possible.

That the Scottish might have a liturgy "as perfect as they could," Wedderburn sent some "certain notes" to Laud concerning further improvement. In April, Laud acknowledged the reception of these important "certain notes":

I received likewise from you . . . certain notes to be considered of, that all, or at least so many of them as his Majesty should approve, might be made use of in your Liturgy, which is now in printing. And though my business hath of late lain very heavy upon me, yet I presently acquainted his Majesty with what you had written. After this I, and Bishop Wren, (my Lord Treasurer being now otherwise busied) by his Majesty's appointment sat down seriously, and considered of them all; and then I tendered them again to the King, with our animadversions upon them. . . . [22]

The King approved the majority of Wedderburn's suggestions. Once again a Prayer Book with written alterations was sent north. Laud acted as scribe: "So many of them as his Majesty approved, I have written into a Service Book of ours, and sent you the book with his Majesty's hand to it, to warrant all your alterations made therein." [23]

But this meant the Scots had two English Prayer Books, each with its own handwritten changes and suggestions authorized by the King and Laud. So Laud decreed that the later copy was to take preference:

So in the printing of your Liturgy, you are to follow the book which my Lord Ross brought, and the additions which are made to the book I now send. But if you find the book of my Lord Ross's and this, to differ in anything that is material, there you are to follow this later book I now send. . . .[24]

Laud consoled Wedderburn because some of his proposed alterations were rejected: "I shall not need to write largely to you, what the reasons were, why all of yours were not admitted; for your judgment and modesty is such, that you will easily conceive some reason was apprehended for it." [25]

The Northerners made the final revision quickly. Laud sincerely approved. Maxwell made a final trip to Court in August, 1636, with the draft containing Wedderburn's changes. King Charles was satisfied. He ordered the addition of a Preface, signed by himself, and a Proclamation.[26] He decreed that in the Calendar the Scots should keep the English saints, and add some Scottish saints as well. A few lessons from the "Apocrypha" were to be added.

On October 18, the King issued a missive to the Scottish Council that would have thundering repercussions. He ordered them to issue a proclamation commanding the use of the new liturgy, which was still *unprinted* and an *unknown quantity* to the nation. On December 20, Council issued its fateful proclamation commanding the use of the still unknown Prayer Book.

Despite its inherent virtues, the 1637 Prayer Book never had a fair trial. In its first and only appearance it provoked a riot. A harridan named "Jenny Geddes" is supposed to have thrown a chair that precipitated a flood of violence and bloodshed. The Scottish scholar Burnet remarks: "Its first and only reception in St. Giles on 23 July 1637, was not a spontaneous outburst by 'Jenny Geddes' but a well-organized demonstration led by a number of 'rascally' Jenny Geddesses hired by nobles for the purpose." [27]

Burnet lists four causes for this organized outbreak and its lamentable consequences:

First, there was the King's arrogant order in the Canons that the Service "was the only Form which We, having taken the counsel of our clergy, think fit to be used in God's public worship in this Our Kingdom." [28]

Second, there was Scottish chauvinism. Submission to Anglican usages would be submission of nationality.

Third, the Services were issued without consultation of the Assembly, against the will of Parliament, and without the consent of the whole Church.

Finally, there was a latent financial reason. The King had recalled for benefit of the clergy certain illegitimate land grants and bribes with which his father had enriched many nobles. In St. Giles these dispossessed citizens took their revenge.[29]

Burnet seems to overlook another cause of the rebellion. And that was the issue of Episcopacy. The Prayer Book was the product of Episcopacy, English and Scottish alike. The issue was less liturgy or no liturgy than it was Episcopacy or no Episcopacy.

Laud and Wedderburn were most prominent in the final revision. But responsibility for the book rested ultimately with the whole Episcopate. The liturgy was doomed not on account of what it was, but on account of whose it was. This issue transcended English-Scottish rivalries. This was a life and death struggle between two incompatible concepts of Church order.[30]

Despite its violent rejection, the Scottish Prayer Book was to exercise influence beyond the dreams of its compilers. As Parsons and Jones, the historians of the American rite, state, "the ill-fated Scottish Prayer Book of 1637, though utterly rejected at the time in the country for which it was issued, has had great influence on subsequent revisions." [31]

In brief, the Service of 1637 was the product of Canterburianism. The primary impetus for its considerable innovations came from the scholarly Wedderburn. But Laud approved with a readiness exceeding his muted acceptance of pre-Wedderburn drafts. It reflects the theology of these two men most responsible for its production, a theology that connected the Eucharistic elements with Real Presence and Sacrifice.

WILLIAM LAUD

Laud's attitude toward the 1637 Communion Service could be summarized by saying he was not the author, but he would be proud if he were. He defended the Eucharistic doctrine in the new Service as reflecting current "high" Churchmanship, of which he was the towering figure.

He regretted the demise of the Service and feared Scotland would never again see the like. "The Bishops were deceived in their expectation of a peaceable admission of that Service-book; the King lost the honour and safety of that settlement; and that kingdom such a form of God's service, as I fear they will never come near again." [32]

In the presence of his enemies, he expressed contentment with the abortive Prayer Book. "I like the book exceeding well, and hope I shall be able to maintain anything that is in it. . . ." [33]

Even in denying his own authorship, he expressed willingness to bear the burden of it: "Though this be no more 'Canterbury's work' than the Canons were, yet, by their good will, I shall bear the burden of all." [34]

Although he found no fault with the English Lord's Supper, Laud went so far as to compare the Scottish Communion Service favorably with that of England:

And though I shall not find fault with the order of the prayers as they stand in the Communion-book of England (for, God be thanked, 'tis well;) yet, if a comparison must be made, I do think the order of the prayers, as now they stand in the Scottish Liturgy, to be the better, and more agreeable to use in the primitive Church; and I believe, they which are learned will acknowledge it.[35]

His enemies accused him of adopting practices from the Roman Mass and rituals. His answer was a forthright admission of this. His statement is important because it elucidates his Eucharistic doctrine. He wanted the Services to adhere to primitive Church practice. If certain aspects of the Mass attained this ideal, he was most willing to adopt them:

Now all reformation that is good and orderly takes away nothing from the old, but that which is faulty and erroneous. If anything be good, it leaves that standing. So that if these changes from the Book of England be good, 'tis no matter whence they be taken. For every line in the Mass-book, or other popish rituals, are not all evil and corruptions. There are many good prayers in them; nor is anything evil in them, only because 'tis there.[36]

Laud and Sacrifice

Laud's doctrine on Sacrifice is stated clearly in his conference with Mr. Fisher, a Jesuit. He defended the unicity of Christ's Sacrifice. But Scripture revealed Christ's command for a sacramental memorial of that Sacrifice "till His coming again."

Laud enumerated three Sacrifices "at and in the Eucharist." The first was by the priest. This was the commemorative Sacrifice of Christ's death, which was "represented" in the elements of broken bread and wine poured out. The second was the Sacrifice of "praise and thanksgiving" for the benefits of Christ's death. This was offered jointly by priest and people. The third Sacrifice was that of soul and body, and this Sacrifice was offered "by every particular man for himself."

Laud's doctrine of the unicity of Christ's Sacrifice and the threefold Sacrifice of the Mass is clearly stated in the following paragraph:

. . . for, as Christ offered up Himself once for all, a full and all-sufficient sacrifice for the sin of the whole world, so did He institute and command a memory of this sacrifice in a sacrament, even till His coming again. For, at and in the Eucharist, we offer up to God three sacrifices: One by the priest only; that is the commemorative sacrifice of Christ's death, represented in bread broke and wine poured out. Another by the priest and the people jointly; and that is, the sacrifice of praise and thanksgiving for all the benefits and graces we receive by the precious death of Christ. The third, by every particular man for himself only; and that is, the sacrifice of every man's body and soul, to serve Him in both all the rest of his life, for this blessing thus bestowed on him.[37]

He added that divided Christendom agreed on these three Sacrifices. "These dissenting Churches agree, that in the Eucharist there is a sacrifice of duty, and a sacrifice of praise, and a sacrifice of commemoration of Christ." Despite his emphasis on the elements for the Sacrifice of commemoration and representation, Laud denied that the Body and Blood of Christ were offered. He considered identification of the elements with Christ a Roman superstition: "It is safest for a man to believe the commemorative, the praising, and the performing sacrifice, and to offer them duly to God, and leave the Church of Rome in that particular to her superstition." [38]

In the *History of the Troubles,* there is an accusation leveled against Laud of teaching an oblation of the Body and Blood of Christ:

The Book of England abolishes all that may import the oblation of an unbloody sacrifice; but we have, besides the preparatory oblation of the elements, which is neither to be found in the Book of England now, nor in King Edward's Book of old, the oblation of the body and blood of Christ, which Bellarmin calls, *Sacrificium laudis, quis Deus per illud magnopere laudatur.*[39]

In reply, Laud repeated his position of the conference with Fisher. Despite the importance he restored to the elements, he taught a "commemoration and representation" was the oblation, not the Body and Blood of Christ.

And these words, "We entirely desire Thy fatherly goodnes, mercifully to accept this our sacrifice of praise, and thanksgiving, &c." are both in the Book of England, and in that which was prepared for Scotland. And if "Bellarmin do call the oblation of the body and blood of Christ, *sacrificium* of praise," sure he doth well in it; (for so it is) if Bellarmin mean no more, by the oblation of the Body and the Blood of Christ, than a commemoration and a representation of that great sacrifice offered up by Christ himself; as Bishop Jewel very learnedly and fully acknowledges. But if Bellarmin go further than this, and by "the oblation of the body and the blood of Christ," mean, that the priest offers up that, which Christ himself did, and not a commemoration of it only, he is erroneous in that, and can never make it good.[40]

Laud did not have at hand the exact words of Bellarmine.[41] If he had, he would have disagreed. For Bellarmine in the statement quoted taught explicitly that Christ was offered. It was the position of which Laud had said, "he is erroneous in that, and can never make it good."

Bellarmine's statement which taught more than an oblation of commemoration and representation was as follows:

It is false to understand the words "sacrifice of praise" of which there is mention in the Canon as spiritual sacrifice which consists in praise and thanksgiving; those words signify a sacrifice of the true Body of the Lord, which is called sacrifice of praise, because God is greatly praised through it and thanks are given to him for his very great benefits to us.[42]

Laud concurred with Jewel's position. Jewel denied a corporal Presence of Christ in the Sacrifice. The Sacrifice was a representation and commemoration. The position which "Bishop Jewel very learnedly and fully acknowledges" was as follows:

The ministration of the Holy Communion is sometimes of the ancient Fathers called an unbloody sacrifice, not in respect of any corporal or fleshly presence, that is imagined to be there without bloodshedding but for that it representeth and reporteth unto our minds that One and Everlasting Sacrifice that Christ made in His Body upon the Cross. . . .[43]

Nevertheless, Laud attributed importance to the elements. His enemies seized on this renewed emphasis in their accusation that his preparatory oblation departed from Anglican practice. Laud simply agreed to the charge: "As for the oblation of the elements, that's fit and proper; and I am sorry, for my part, that it is not in the Book of England." [44]

Laud denied that commemoration of the Saints in the early Church detracted from the unicity of Christ's mediation. He considered Saints "mediators of intercession."

And when the Church prayed to God for anything, she desired to be heard for the mercies and the merits of Christ, not for the merits of any saints whatsoever. For I much doubt this were to make the saints more than "mediators of intercession". . . .[45]

Laud and Real Presence

In true Anglican tradition, Laud vehemently ridiculed Transubstantiation. He considered it an accretion, and linked it with Communion in one species as not taught by the primitive Church:

For Transubstantiation, first: that was never heard of in the primitive Church, nor till the Council of Lateran, nor can it be proved out of Scripture; and, taken properly, cannot stand with the grounds of Christian religion. As for Communion in One Kind, Christ's institution is clear against that; and not only the primitive Church, but the whole Church of Christ, kept it so till within less than four hundred years.[46]

Not only was Transubstantiation an accretion, it was a doctrine that even learned Roman Catholics found inexplicable:

For the primitive Church never . . . dream of a Transubstantiation for which the learned of the Roman party dare not understand properly, for a change of one substance into another, for then they must grant that Christ's real and true body is made of the bread, and the bread changed into it, which is properly transubstantiation; nor yet can they express it in a creditable way. . . .[47]

Despite his denial of Transubstantiation, Laud defended a "true and real" Presence as the doctrine of all Protestants:

And for the Church of England, nothing is more plain, than that it believes and teaches the true and real presence of Christ in the Eucharist. . . . So Protestants of all sorts maintain a true and real presence of Christ in the Eucharist; and then, where is any known or damnable heresy here? [48]

The Marian martyrs professed a "true and real" Presence. They were martyred for separating this Presence from Transubstantiation. He added that all ancient Christians believed the true and real Presence, but only superstitious moderns believed Transubstantiation. Laud even expressed doubts that *anyone* really believed Transubstantiation:

And as for the learned of those zealous men that died in this cause in Queen Mary's days, they denied not the real presence simply taken, but as their opposites forced transubstantiation upon them, as if that and the real presence had been all one. Whereas, all the ancient Christians ever believed the one, and none but modern and superstitious Christians believe the other—if they do believe it; for I, for my part, doubt they do not.[49]

Laud expressed the traditional Anglican belief that the worthy recipient by faith partook spiritually of Christ's Body and Blood. "For all sides agree in the faith of the Church of England, That in the most Blessed Sacrament, the worthy receiver is, by his faith, made spiritually partaker of the 'true and real Body and Blood of Christ, truly and really,' and all the benefits of His passion." [50]

Laud's enemies accused him of teaching corporal Presence in the 1637 Communion Service because of the restored epiclesis. His opponents buttressed their contention by reference to Bucer's criticism of the 1549 epiclesis.[51] They also used the translation of *fiat nobis* against him. Ironically this was the very translation with which Cranmer had taken such pains in 1549 to obviate the interpretation now used by the enemies of his successor at Canterbury.[52] The charge was as follows:

> The corporal presence of Christ's body in the Sacrament, is also to be found here. For the words of the Mass-book, serving to that purpose, are sharply censured by Bucer in King Edward's Liturgy, and are not to be found in the Book of England, are taken in here. Almighty God is in-called, that of His Almighty goodness he may vouchsafe so to bless and sanctify with His word and His Spirit these gifts of bread and wine, that they may be unto us the Body and Blood of Christ. The change here, is made a work of God's omnipotency. The words of the Mass, *ut fiant nobis,* are translated in King Edward's Book, "that they may be unto us." [53]

Laud vehemently denied the teaching of corporal Presence either in 1549 or 1637:

> They say, "the corporal presence of Christ's body in the Sacrament, is found in this Service-book." But they must pardon me; I know it is not there. I cannot be myself of a contrary judgment, and yet suffer that to pass. But let's see their proof. "The words of the Mass-book serving to that purpose, which are sharply censured by Bucer in King Edward's liturgy and are not to be found in the Book of England, yet are taken into this Service-book." I know no words tending to this purpose in King Edwd's Liturgy, fit for Bucer to censure sharply; and therefore not tending to that purpose: for did they tend to that, they could not be censured too sharply.[54]

Laud definitely held a consecration of the elements, but one that did not effect corporal Presence. In his doctrine, the epiclesis invoked God's omnipotence on the bread and wine that *in use* they would be the Body and Blood of Christ. But the reception was a spiritual one by faith.

> For less than Omnipotence cannot change those elements, either in nature or use, to so high a service as they are put in that great Sacrament. And therefore the invocating of God's Almighty goodness to effect this by them, is no proof at all of intending the "corporal presence of Christ in this Sacrament." 'Tis true, this passage is not in the Service-book of England; but I wish with all my heart it were.[55]

Laud's discussion of *ut fiat nobis* demonstrated his denial of corporal Presence, and his belief in a spiritual Presence *in use* to the worthy recipient. He even denied that the *ut fiat nobis* of the

Roman Mass involved Transubstantiation or corporal Presence.

Secondly, "these words", they say, "intend the corporal presence of Christ in the Sacrament, because the words in the Mass are, *ut fiant nobis,* "that they may be unto us the Body and the Blood of Christ." Now for the good of Christendom, I would with all my heart, that these words, *ut fiant nobis,*—that these elements might be, "to us," worthy receivers, the blessed Body and Blood of our Saviour,—were the wordst error in the Mass. For then I would hope, that this great controversy, which to all men that are out of the Church, is the shame, and among all that are within the Church, is the division of Christendom, might have some good accommodation. For if it be only, *ut fiant nobis,* that they may be to us, the Body and the Blood of Christ; it implies clearly, that they "are to us", but are not transubstantiated in themselves, into the Body and Blood of Christ, nor that there is any corporal presence, in, or under the elements.[56]

He continued in the same vein, adding that the *fiat nobis* of the Mass "cannot well be understood otherwise, than to imply not the corporal substance, but the real, and yet the spiritual use of them. And so the words, *ut fiant nobis,* import quite contrary to that which they are brought to prove." [57]

His accusers then alleged that he taught corporal Presence by his *omission* of the second part of the 1559 formula for distribution. They charged that "on the other side, the expressions of the Book of England, at the delivery of the elements; of feeding on Christ by faith; and of eating and drinking in remembrance that Christ died for thee, are utterly deleted." [58]

Laud reiterated his denial of corporal Presence: "It is altogether false, either that this omission was intended to help make good 'a corporal presence,' or that a 'corporal presence' can by any good consequence [be] proved out of it." [59]

Laud's defense of the omission demonstrated his doctrine of a spiritual reception of Christ by faith. He ridiculed the allegation that the omission propounded corporal Presence:

For the first, "of feeding on Christ by faith," if that omission be thought to advantage anything toward a "corporal presence;" surely, neither the "Scottish bishops," nor myself, were so simple to leave it out here, and keep these words in immediately after: "which have duly received these holy mysteries, with the spiritual food of the most precious Body and Blood of Thy Son." For "the feeding on Christ by faith," and the "spiritual food of the Body and Blood of Christ," are all one; and 'tis hard that the asserting of a "spiritual food," should be made the proof of a "corporal presence;" or, that the omitting of it in one place, should be of greater force than affirming it in another.[60]

The Archbishop was accused of teaching "the bodily presence of Christ very agreeable to the doctrine taught by his sectaries." He replied by further repudiation of corporal Presence: "Among these 'sectaries' which they will needs call mine, they say 'there are, which teach them, that Christ is received in the sacrament *corporaliter*, both *objective* and *subjective*.' For this opinion . . . I for my part do utterly condemn it." [61]

Consistent with his doctrine of a Spiritual Presence, Laud did not believe adoration was due the consecrated elements. His opponents accused him of advocating elevation and adoration by the manual acts of the new Service and by the prescription for a kneeling Confession. The accusation was as follows:

That he may the more conveniently lift up the bread and wine over his head, to be seen and adored of the people; who, in the Rubric of General Confession a little before, are directed to kneel humbly on their knees, that the priest's elevation, so magnified in the Mass, and the people's adoration may go together.[62]

Laud denied any directions for elevation of the Host or kneeling adoration:

Good God! whither tends this malice? There is not a word in the book of this neither: not of "lifting the bread and wine over his head;" much less is there anything, "to have it adored by the people." And as there is nothing in the book, so nothing hath ever been said, or done by me, that tends this way. . . . But that which follows, namely, "that the priest's elevation and the people's adoration may go together," is utterly false. There is not one word of it in the rubric, nor ever was there one thought of it in myself, or (as I verily believe) in any of the compilers of that book. And 'tis well known, that through the whole Church of England, the form is to receive the blessed Sacrament kneeling; and yet without any "adoration" at all "of the bread and wine." [63]

At the high-water mark of his influence, Laud had encouraged frequent Communion. In a letter to the Vice-Chancellor of Oxford he expressed the opinion, in direct opposition to Puritan tenets, that celebration in the chancel was more conducive to frequent reception than celebration in the body of the church:

The communion was celebrated in the body of the church, and not in the chancel, which though it be permitted in the Church of England in some cases of necessity, where there is a multitude of people; yet very indecent it is, and unfitting in that place, where so few (the more the pity) use to communicate at these solemn times. But this abuse I caused to be rectified in Dr. Duppa's time, and I hope neither you nor your successors will suffer it to return again into the former indecency.[64]

Laud's dogged defense of the 1637 Service and the doctrine reflected in its pages was manly and courageous. It helped cost him his life. This is especially remarkable because the final draft of the Service was less the work of Laud than of his northern protégé, James Wedderburn of Dunblane.

JAMES WEDDERBURN

Unfortunately, no published works of Wedderburn are extant. His doctrine must be derived from two passages in Laud's *Works,* and the 1637 Communion Service.

One paragraph of his "certain notes" to Laud about the 1637 revision is extant and is quoted by the Archbishop in his *History of the Troubles.* Wedderburn had recommended elimination of the receptionist 1552 formula for distribution. He wanted the "Body of our Lord Jesus Christ" formula of 1549 to stand alone. Since this is his sole extant paragraph it is quoted completely:

The Body of our Lord Jesus Christ, which was given for thee, preserve thy body and soul unto everlasting life: and so, the Blood of, &c: whereunto every receiver answered, Amen. There is no more in King Edw. VI his first book. And if there be no more in ours, the action will be much the shorter. Besides, the words which are added since, "Take, eat, in remembrance, &c," may seem to relish somewhat of the Zuinglian tenet, That the Sacrament is a bare sign taken in remembrance of Christ's passion.[65]

This quotation, as well as Laud's letter to Wedderburn, indicate the Scottish scholar's predilection for the 1549 Service. However, his preference stemmed from more than mere antiquarian leanings. Wedderburn, like Laud, considered the elements more than bare signs. The Sacrament was more than "a bare sign taken in remembrance of Christ's passion." It was the Body and Blood of Christ.

Laud's letter to Wedderburn bears this out. After conceding the Dunblane Bishop's docility, Laud wrote that he would explain why some of Wedderburn's suggestions were not followed. The explanation unfortunately does not quote Wedderburn's own words. But it indicates clearly that the latter connected the elements intimately with Sacrifice and the real Presence of Christ.[66]

Wedderburn had suggested new Offertory verses from the Old Testament. These were connected with an *offering of elements of the soil* to God.[67] Laud agreed. But he and the King insisted that ten of the English sentences be preserved.

It seems from Laud's letter that Wedderburn suggested naming each prayer or action in a preceding rubric. Laud approved this idea and began the process himself with the suggestion that Wedderburn complete it:

I would have every prayer or other action through the whole Communion named in the rubric before it, that it may be known to the people what it is, as I have begun to do in the Prayer of Consecration, and in the Memorial, or Prayer of Oblation. *Fac similiter.*

Wedderburn wished to restore the 1549 prayers between Consecration and Communion to their pre-1552 order. Laud agreed for the Oblation, *Pater Noster,* and Humble Access. But he and the King balked at rearranging the others:

We do fully approve the Collect of Consecration and Oblation should precede, and the Lord's Prayer follow, next, and be said before the Communion, in that order which you have expressed. But for the Invitation, Confession, Absolution, Sentences, Preface, and Doxology, we think they stand best as they are now placed in our Liturgy; and as for the Prayer of humble access to the Holy Communion, that will stand very well next before the participation.

Wedderburn desired a marginal rubric for manual acts. Again, Laud agreed. There was some dispute about the exact timing for these acts. Wedderburn preferred their insertion at the words "Do this in commemoration of me." Laud ordered them inscribed at the words of Consecration:

I have ordered a rubric in the margin of this book, according as you desire, to direct him that celebrates, when to take the sacrament into his hands. Namely, to take, and break, and lay hands on the chalice, as he speaks the words. . . . And for the objection, that we should not do it, till we express our warrant so to do, which you conceive is in these words, "Do this," &c; I answer, first, that those words, "Do this," &c; are rather our warrant for the participation or communication, than the consecration.

It seems that Wedderburn wanted to go even further. Laud's tactful response was that the new liturgy would do very well.

. . . God be thanked this will do very well, and I hope breed up a great deal of devout and religious piety in that kingdom. Yet I pray, for my further satisfaction, at your best leisure draw up all those particulars, which you think might make the Liturgy perfect, whether the times will bear them, or not.

Laud's letter closed with a final admonition to the effect that His Majesty "having viewed all these additions, hopes there will be no need of change of anything, and will be best pleased with little or rather no [further] alteration."

In brief, Wedderburn urged a Service approaching that of 1549. His view of the bread and wine approached the medieval doctrine of Real Presence and Sacrifice. In this he was at one with his patron, the then Archbishop of Canterbury.

THE LORD'S SUPPER OR HOLY COMMUNION

In Grisbrooke's phrase, there was to the Puritans a "sinister vagueness" to the 1637 ornaments rubric.[68] This directive suggested further changes in the Communion Service. The rubric read as follows:

And here is to be noted, that the Presbyter or Minister at the time of the Communion, and at other times in his ministration, shall use such ornaments in the Church, as are prescribed, or shall be, by His Majesty or his successors, according to the Act of Parliament provided in that behalf.[69]

In the Communion Service itself, except for verbal changes, the three rubrics for penitential preparation were the same as the English Service. One verbal change, the substitution of "Presbyter" for Minister or Priest, was an attempt to mollify the Puritans.[70] Another change, the substitution of "Church" for congregation, appeared an affront to Puritan sensibilities.

The fourth rubric was considerably different from that of England. And it reflects the different emphasis of the Scottish Communion Office. This emphasis indicated an intimate connection of the elements with Real Presence and Sacrifice. In addition to a fair white linen cloth, the holy Table in 1637 would have a "carpet" and "other decent furniture meet for the high mysteries there to be celebrated." The Table would stand in a position suggestive of Sacrifice, that is "at the uppermost part of the Chancel or Church." Further indication of its altar-like position was the directive for the Presbyter to stand at the northside "or end" thereof. And the Lord's Prayer and Collect were for *preparation.* The Scottish rubric is compared with the English below.[71] Important changes are italicized.

ENGLISH	SCOTTISH
The Table having at the Communion time a fair white linen cloth upon it, shall stand in the body of the Church, or in the Chancel, where Morning prayer and Evening prayer be appointed to be said. And the Priest, standing at the northside of the Table, shall say the Lord's prayer with this collect following.	The holy Table, having at the Communion time *a carpet and* a fair white linen cloth upon it, *with other decent furniture meet for the high mysteries there to be celebrated, shall stand at the uppermost part of the Chancel or Church,* where the Presbyter, standing at the northside *or end,* thereof, shall say the Lord's Prayer with this Collect following *for due preparation.*

The Lord's Prayer and Collect for Purity were unchanged.

In the rubric preceding the penitential litany, the Presbyter was ordered to turn toward the people. The latter were to ask God's mercy for their transgression "either according to the letter, or to the mystical importance of the said Commandment." This addition was probably intended to obviate fundamentalistic morality. The English and Scottish rubrics are compared below:

ENGLISH	SCOTTISH
Then shall the Priest rehearse distinctly all the .x. Commandments: and the people kneeling, shall after every Commandment	Then shall the Presbyter, turning to the People, rehearse distinctly all the TEN COMMANDMENTS: the People all

ENGLISH

ask God's mercy for their transgression of the same, after this
sort.

SCOTTISH

the while kneeling, and asking
God's mercy for the transgression
of every duty therein, either according to the letter, or to the
mystical importance of the said
Commandment.

The 1637 Litany proceeded as in the past.

There was perhaps an unfortunate change in the Collects. In
1637 the Collects for the King *preceded* the Collect of the day.[72]
There was also an interesting change in wording of the first Collect.
The petition for the whole congregation was clarified to read for
"thy holy Catholic Church." It contained the first explicit reference
to the Church of Scotland as a particular Church within the "holy
Catholic Church."

The Epistle and Gospel rubrics resembled the 1549 Service
and the Mass. There was a prescription to indicate the exact beginning verse of Scripture. The people were to respond "Glory be
to thee, O Lord" after the announcement of the Gospel and
"Thanks be to thee, O Lord" at its conclusion. The Creed was to
be said "or sung" while the people stood.

There was another phrase that may have appeared "sinister"
to the Puritans. That was the prescription that after the Creed, "if
there be no sermon, shall follow one of the Homilies which shall
hereafter be set forth by common authority."

The Offertory rubrics, like the ornaments and altar rubrics,
indicated the changed complexion of the new Service. The words
"offertory" and "offering" were restored. There was every indication from the directive rubric that the people would actively participate in the offering. The two "Offertory" rubrics are compared
below:

ENGLISH

After such sermon, homily
or exhortation the Curate shall
declare unto the people whether
there be any holy days or fasting
days the week following: and earnestly exhort them to remember
the poor, saying one or more of

SCOTTISH

After the Creed, if there be
no Sermon, shall follow one of
the Homilies which shall hereafter be set forth by common authority. After such Sermon, Homily, or Exhortation, the Presbyter
or Curate shall declare unto the

ENGLISH

these sentences following, as he thinketh most convenient by his discretion.

SCOTTISH

People whether there be any Holy days, or Fasting-days the week following, and earnestly exhort them to remember the poor, saying (*for the Offertory*) one or more of these Sentences following, as he thinketh most convenient by his discretion, *according to the length or shortness of the time that the people are offering.*

The new Offertory sentences, submitted by Wedderburn and approved by Laud, are significant for the Eucharistic doctrine of the Service. These five additions, all from the Old Testament, pertain to a sacrificial offering of elements of the soil to God. The following are Wedderburn's selections:

And in process of time it came to pass, that Cain brought of the fruit of the ground an offering unto the Lord: and Abel, he also brought of the firstlings of his flock, and of the fat thereof. And the Lord had respect unto Abel, and to his offering: but unto Cain and to his offering he had not respect. Gen. iv. 3, 4, 5.

Speak unto the children of Israel, that they bring me an offering: of every man that giveth it willingly with his heart, ye shall take my offering. Exod. xxv. 2.

Ye shall not appear before the Lord empty: every man shall give as he is able, according to the blessing of the Lord your God which he hath given you. Deut. xvi. 16.

David blessed the Lord before all the congregation: and said, Blessed be thou, O Lord God, for ever and ever. Thine, O Lord, is the greatness, and the glory, and the victory, and the majesty: for all that is in the heaven and in the earth, is thine: thine is the kingdom, O Lord, and thou are exalted as head above all. Both riches and honour come of thee, and of thine own do we give unto thee. I know also, my God, that thou triest the heart, and hast pleasure in uprightness. As for me, in the uprightness of my heart I have willingly offered all these things. And now have I seen with joy thy people, which are present here, to offer willingly unto thee. 1 Chron. xxix. 10, etc.

Give unto the Lord the glory due unto his Name: bring an offering, and come into his courts. Psal. xcvi. 8.

Laud's omission of some English verses and retention of others is also significant. Those retained, for the most part, indicate an obligation to support the Minister who sacrifices. Those indicating an offering of alms to the poor are omitted.

The two following verses exemplify the sentences retained from the English Service by Laud:

Who goeth a warfare any time at his own charges? who planteth a vineyard, and eateth not of the fruit thereof? or who feedeth a flock, and eateth not of the milk of the flock? 1 Cor. ix. 7.

If we have sown unto you spiritual things, is it a great thing if we shall reap your carnal things? 1 Cor. ix. 11.

The two following verses exemplify the sentences Laud omitted:

Whoso hath this world's good, and seeth his brother have need, and shutteth up his compassion from him, how dwelleth the love of God in him? 1. John iii.

Give almose of thy goods, and turn never thy face from any poor man, and then the face of the Lord shall not be turned away from thee. Toby iv.

As already indicated in the Offertory sentences, the Offertory was no longer "the devotion of the people" for the "poor men's box." Nor were certain "offering days" appointed for support of the Curate. In 1637 the Presbyter was to pronounce some *or all* of the Sentences. This time the people's devotion was *offered;* their offerings were "oblations." The Presbyter was directed to "humbly present it before the Lord, and set it upon the holy Table." These oblations were connected with the Eucharistic elements by the final sentence of the rubric: "And the Presbyter shall then offer up and place the bread and wine prepared for the Sacrament upon the Lord's Table, that it may be ready for that service." The two rubrics are compared below:

ENGLISH	SCOTTISH
Then shall the Churchwardens, or some other by them appointed, gather the devotion of the people, and put the same into the poor men's box: and upon the offering days appointed, every man and woman shall pay to the Curate the due and accustomed	While the Presbyter distinctly pronounceth *some or all* of these sentences *for the Offertory,* the Deacon or (if no such be present) one of the Churchwardens shall receive the devotions of the People there present in a bason provided for that purpose. And *when*

ENGLISH

offerings: after which done, the
Priest shall say.

SCOTTISH

all have offered, he shall reverently
bring the said bason with the ob-
lations therein, and deliver it to
the Presbyter, who shall humbly
present it before the Lord, and
set it upon the holy Table. And
the Presbyter shall then offer up
and place the bread and wine pre-
pared for the Sacrament upon the
Lord's Table, that it may be ready
for that service. And then he shall
say,

The prayer for the Church militant followed. There were
three important additions in 1637. There was a petition for the
congregation "here assembled" to "celebrate the commemoration
of Christ's death and Sacrifice." Second, there was a commemoration of the faithful departed. Finally, there was praise and thanksgiving for the example of the Saints, with the restoration of Cranmer's original reference to the general Resurrection and Mystical
Body. The two prayers are compared below with additions italicized:

ENGLISH

Let us pray for the whole
state of Christ's Church militant
here in earth.*

SCOTTISH

Let us pray for the whole state of
Christ's Church militant here in
earth.†

Almighty and everliving
God, which by thy holy Apostle
has taught us to make prayers and
supplications, and to give thanks
for all men: we humbly beseech
thee most mercifully to accept our
almose and to receive these our

Almighty and everliving
God, which by thy holy Apostle
hast taught us to make prayers
and supplications, and to give
thanks for all men: We humbly
beseech thee most mercifully (*to*
accept our alms, and) to receive

---

* Marginal rubric: "If there be none alms given unto the poor,
then shall the words of accepting our alms be left out unsaid."

† Marginal rubric: "If there be no alms given to the poor, then
shall the words (*of accepting our alms*) be left out unsaid."

ENGLISH	SCOTTISH
prayers which we offer unto thy divine Majesty: beseeching thee to inspire continually the universal Church with the spirit of truth, unity and concord: And grant that all they that do confess thy holy name, may agree in the truth of thy holy word, and live in unity and godly love. We beseech thee also to save and defend all Christian Kings, Princes, and Governours, and specially thy servant Elizabeth our Queen, that under her we may be godly and quietly governed: and grant unto her whole council, and to all that be put in authority under her, that they may truly and indifferently minister justice, to the punishment of wickedness and vice, and to the maintenance of God's true religion and virtue. Give grace (O heavenly Father) to all Bishops, pastors and Curates, that they may both by their life and doctrine set forth thy true and lively word, and rightly and duly administer thy holy Sacraments: and to all thy people give thy heavenly grace, and especially to this congregation here present, that with meek heart and due reverence they may hear and receive thy holy word, truly serving thee in holiness and righteousness all the days of their life. And we most humbly beseech thee of thy good-	these our prayers, which we offer unto thy Divine Majesty, beseeching thee to inspire continually the universal Church with the spirit of truth, unity, and concord. And grant that all they that do confess thy holy Name may agree in the truth of thy holy word, and live in unity and godly love. We beseech thee also to save and defend all Christian Kings, Princes, and Governors, and specially thy servant *Charles* our King, that under him we may be godly and quietly governed: and grant unto his whole Council, and to all that be put in authority under him, that they may truly and indifferently minister justice, to the punishment of wickedness and vice and to the maintenance of God's true religion and virtue. Give grace, O heavenly Father, to all Bishops, Presbyters, and Curates, that they may both by their life and doctrine set forth thy true and lively word, and rightly and duly administer thy holy sacraments: and to all thy people give thy heavenly grace, that with meek heart and due reverence they may hear and receive thy holy word, truly serving thee in holiness and righteousness all the days of their life.* [*And we commend especially unto thy merciful goodness, the congregation which*

---

* Marginal rubric: *"When there is no Communion, these words thus inclosed [ ] are to be left out."*

ENGLISH	SCOTTISH
ness (O Lord) to comfort and succour all them which in this transitory life be in trouble, sorrow, need, sickness, or any other adversity: Grant this, O Father, for Jesus Christ's sake our only mediator and advocate. Amen.	*is here assembled in thy Name, to celebrate the commemoration of the most precious death and sacrifice of thy Son and our Saviour Jesus Christ.*] And we most humbly beseech thee of thy goodness, O Lord, to comfort and succour all them which in this transitory life be in trouble, sorrow, need, sickness or any other adversity. And *we also bless thy holy Name for all those thy servants, who, having finished their course in faith, do now rest from their labours. And we yield unto thee most high praise and hearty thanks for the wonderful grace and virtue declared in all thy saints, who have been the choice vessels of thy grace and the lights of the world in their several generations: most humbly beseeching thee, that we may have grace to follow the example of their stedfastness in thy faith, and obedience to thy holy commandments; that at the day of the general resurrection, we, and all they which are of the mystical body of thy Son, may be set on his right hand, and hear that his most joyful voice, Come, ye blessed of my Father, inherit the kingdom prepared for you from the foundation of the world.* Grant this, O Father, for Jesus Christ's sake, our only Mediator and Advocate. Amen.

There were two changes in the first exhortation. One change made Christ's Sacrifice explicit and recalled the institution obliging us "to celebrate and receive the holy Communion together in the remembrance of his death and sacrifice." The second change referred not to "this holy Communion with other" but "this holy Sacrament."

There was no alteration in the other two exhortations. The Invitation and General Confession were likewise unchanged. In the rubric preceding the Confession, there was a prescription that "the Presbyter himself, or the Deacon" make the Confession in the name of all. Unlike the English Service, there was no provision for recitation "either by one of them [the communicants], or else by one of the ministers, or by the Priest himself."

Laud's belief in the priestly power of the keys is reflected in the rubric for the Absolution. It is compared with the English below:

ENGLISH	SCOTTISH
Then shall the Priest or the bishop, being present, stand up, and turning himself to the people, say thus.	Then shall the Presbyter, or the Bishop (being present) stand up, and, turning himself to the people, *pronounce the Absolution,* as followeth.

The Absolution, Comfortable Words, Preface, and *Sanctus* were unchanged in 1637.

But the Consecration rubrics and the prayer itself emphasize Sacrifice and Real Presence. Once again the elements are intimately connected with the Sacrifice and Real Presence.

In the new introductory rubric the Presbyter is to say "the Prayer of Consecration," and not just "as followeth." He is to stand "at such a part of the holy Table, where he may with the more ease and decency use both his hands."

Manual acts rubrics instruct the Presbyter to "take the paten in his hands" at the words "took bread." He is to "take the chalice in his hand, and lay his hand upon so much, be it in chalice or flagons, as he intends to consecrate" at the words "took the cup."

In the Consecratory prayer, Christ is said to have instituted a memory of His death *and Sacrifice.* The 1549 epiclesis was restored with its fateful "that they may be unto us." An almost inconspicuous addition of three words after the epiclesis identified the elements with Christ's Body and Blood. The three short words, "of the same," reminded the communicants that the "creatures of bread and wine" through the invocation of God's omnipotence become the Body and Blood of Christ.

The two prayers are compared below:

ENGLISH

Then the Priest standing up, shall say as followeth:

ALMIGHTY God our heavenly Father, which of thy tender mercy didst give thine only Son Jesus Christ, to suffer death upon the cross for our redemption, who made there (by his one oblation of himself once offered) a full, perfect and sufficient Sacrifice, Oblation, and Satisfaction for the sins of the whole world: and did institute, and in his holy Gospel command us to continue, a perpetual memory of that his precious death, until his coming again. Hear us, O merciful Father, we beseech thee: and grant that we receiving these thy creatures of bread and wine, according to thy Son our Saviour Jesu Christ's holy Institution, in remembrance of his death and Passion, may be partakers of his most blessed body and blood: who, in the same night that he was betrayed, took bread, and, when he had given thanks, he brake it, and gave it to his Disciples, saying: Take, eat, this is my body which is given for you. Do this in remembrance of me. Likewise after supper he took the cup, and when he had given thanks, he gave it to them, saying: Drink ye all of this, for this is my

SCOTTISH

Then the Presbyter, standing up, shall say the *Prayer of Consecration,* as followeth. But then, during the *time of Consecration,* he shall *stand at such a part of the holy Table, where he may with the more ease and decency use both his hands.*

Almighty God, our heavenly Father, which of thy tender mercy didst give thy only Son Jesus Christ to suffer death upon the cross for our redemption; who made there (by his one oblation of himself once offered) a full, perfect, and sufficient sacrifice, oblation, and satisfaction for the sins of the whole world, and did institute, and in his holy gospel command us to continue, a perpetual memory of that his precious death *and sacrifice,* until his coming again: Hear us, O merciful Father, we most humbly beseech thee, and *of thy Almighty goodness vouchsafe so to bless and sanctify with thy word and Holy Spirit these thy gifts and creatures of bread and wine, that they may be unto us the body and blood of thy most dearly beloved Son;* so that we, receiving them according to thy Son our Saviour Jesus Christ's holy institution, in remembrance of his death and

ENGLISH	SCOTTISH
blood of the New Testament, which is shed for you and for many, for remission of sins: do this as oft as ye shall drink it in remembrance of me.	passion, may be partakers *of the same* his most precious body and blood: Who, in the night that he was betrayed, *took bread,** and when he had given thanks, he brake it, and gave it to his disciples, saying, Take, eat, this is my body, which is given for you; do this in remembrance of me. Likewise, after supper, he *took the cup,†* and when he had given thanks, he gave it to them, saying, Drink ye all of this, for this is my blood of the new testament, which is shed for you, and for many, for the remission of sins: do this, as oft as ye shall drink it, in remembrance of me.

As Wedderburn had requested, the Oblation, Lord's Prayer, and Prayer of Humble Access were restored to their place between Consecration and Communion.

There were further changes in the Oblation. A commemoration of the Institution connected the elements with the celebration of a Memorial. There was a commemoration of the passion, resurrection, and ascension. There was a return of the words "the most precious body and blood of thy Son Jesus Christ," and Cranmer's "made one body with him, that he may dwell in them, and they in him."

The 1637 Oblation is compared with its English counterpart which since 1552 had *followed* the Communion:

ENGLISH	SCOTTISH
After shall be said as fol-	Immediately after shall be

---

* Marginal rubric: *"At these words* [took bread] *the Presbyter that officiates is to take the paten in his hand."*

† Marginal rubric: *"At these words* [took the cup] *he is to take the chalice in his hand, and lay his hand upon so much, be it in chalice or flagons, as he intends to consecrate."*

ENGLISH

loweth.

O LORD and heavenly Father, we thy humble servants entirely desire thy fatherly goodness, mercifully to accept this our Sacrifice of praise and thanksgiving: most humbly beseeching thee to grant, that by the merits and death of thy Son Jesus Christ, and through faith in his blood, we and all thy whole church, may obtain remission of our sins, and all other benefits of his passion. And here we offer and present unto thee, O Lord, our selves, our souls, and bodies, to be a reasonable, holy, and lively Sacrifice unto thee, humbly beseeching thee, that all we which be partakers of this holy Communion, may be fulfilled with thy grace, and heavenly benediction. And although we be unworthy, through our manifold sins, to offer unto thee any sacrifice: yet we beseech thee to accept this our bounden duty and service, not weighing our merits, but pardoning our offences, through Jesus Christ our Lord: by whom and with whom, in the unity of the Holy Ghost, all honour and glory be unto thee, O Father Almighty, world without end. Amen.

SCOTTISH

said this *Memorial* or *Prayer of Oblation,* as followeth.

Wherefore, O Lord and heavenly Father, *according to the institution of thy dearly-beloved Son,* our Saviour Jesus Christ we thy humble servants do *celebrate and make here before thy Divine Majesty, with these thy holy gifts, the memorial which thy Son hath willed us to make; having in remembrance his blessed passion, mighty resurrection, and glorious ascension;* rendering unto thee most hearty thanks for the innumerable benefits procured unto us by the same. And we entirely desire thy Fatherly goodness mercifully to accept this our sacrifice of praise and thanksgiving, most humbly beseeching thee to grant, that by the merits and death of thy Son Jesus Christ, and through faith in his blood, we and all thy whole Church may obtain remission of our sins and all other benefits of his passion. And here we offer and present unto thee, O Lord, ourselves, our souls and bodies, to be a reasonable, holy, and lively sacrifice unto thee; humbly beseeching thee, that whosoever shall be partakers of this holy Communion, may *worthily receive the most precious body and blood of thy Son Jesus Christ,* and be fulfilled with thy grace and heavenly benediction, and *made one body with him, that he may dwell in them, and they in him.* And although we be unwor-

ENGLISH   SCOTTISH

thy, through our manifold sins, to
offer unto thee any sacrifice: yet
we beseech thee to accept this our
bounden duty and service, not
weighing our merits, but pardoning our offences, through Jesus
Christ our Lord: by whom and
with whom, in the unity of the
Holy Ghost, all honour and glory
be unto thee, O Father Almighty
world without end. Amen.

The Our Father concluded with the doxology so pleasing to
the Puritans.

The Prayer of Humble Access was unchanged.

The rubric for the Communion twice referred to the principal
Presbyter "that celebrateth." It prescribed a distribution "in due
order" instead of "in their hands."

The receptionist 1552 Communion formula, combined with
that of 1549 by Elizabeth, was omitted in the "true and real"
Presence context of 1637. The English and Scottish Communions
are compared below:

ENGLISH   SCOTTISH

Then shall the minister first
receive the Communion in both
kinds himself, and next deliver it
to other ministers, if any be there
present (that they may help the
chief minister,) and after to the
people in their hands kneeling.
And when he delivereth the bread
he shall say,

The body of our Lord Jesus
Christ, which was given for thee,
preserve thy body and soul into
everlasting life: and take and eat
this in remembrance that Christ
died for thee, and feed on him in
thine heart by faith, with thanksgiving.

Then shall the Bishop, if he
be present, or else the Presbyter
that celebrateth, first receive the
Communion in both kinds himself, and next deliver it to other
Bishops, Presbyters, and Deacons
(if any be there present), that
they may help him *that celebrateth;* and after to the people *in due
order,* all humbly kneeling. And
when he receiveth himself, or delivereth the bread to others, he
shall say this benediction:

The body of our Lord Jesus
Christ which was given for thee,
preserve thy body and soul unto
everlasting life.

ENGLISH

And the minister that delivereth the cup, shall say,

The blood of our Lord Jesus Christ, which was shed for thee, preserve thy body and soul into everlasting life: and drink this in remembrance that Christ's blood was shed for thee, and be thankful.

SCOTTISH

Here the party receiving shall say, Amen.

And the Presbyter or Minister that receiveth the cup himself, or delivereth it to others, shall say this benediction.

The blood of our Lord Jesus Christ, which was shed for thee, preserve thy body and soul unto everlasting life.

Here the party receiving shall say, Amen.

The 1637 prayer of thanksgiving was the same as the second English prayer after Communion. However, a preceding rubric in the Scottish Service indicated enhanced sacredness of the elements. The Presbyter was to cover with cloth or corporal "that which remaineth of the consecrated elements."

The *Gloria* and sonorous terminal blessing were unchanged. There was a new provision in 1637 for the money which "was offered."

After the Divine Service ended, that which was offered shall be divided in the presence of the Presbyter and the Churchwardens: whereof one half shall be to the use of the Presbyter to provide him books of holy divinity; the other half shall be faithfully kept and employed in some pious or charitable use, for the decent furnishing of that church, or the public relief of the poor, at the discretion of the Presbyter and Churchwardens.

The Collects and rubrics for a truncated Service were the same in both kingdoms. Rubrics for the number of communicants, and for the clergy, were also unchanged.

But the rubric for the bread and wine was considerably different. In 1637 there was emphasis on the elements and the power of Consecration. Wafer bread was "lawful." If any consecrated bread remained after the Service, it was not to be carried out of Church, but reverently consumed. To forestall the consecration of too many wafers (or too much bread) the Presbyter was to consecrate "with the least." If more bread or wine was needed, he was to repeat the "words of Consecration" over the necessary element. Because of the doctrinal importance of this rubric, it is compared below with the receptionist English rubric:

ENGLISH	SCOTTISH
And to take away the superstition which any person hath, or might have, in the bread and wine, it shall suffice that the bread be such, as is usual to be eaten at the Table with other meats, but the best and purest wheat bread, that conveniently may be gotten. And if any of the bread or wine remain, the Curate shall have it to his own use.	And to take away the superstition, which any person hath or might have in the bread and wine, (*though it be lawful to have wafer bread*) it shall suffice that the bread be such as is usual: yet the best and purest wheat bread that conveniently may be gotten. *And if any of the bread and wine remain which is consecrated, it shall be reverently eaten and drunk by such of the communicants only, as the Presbyter which celebrates shall take unto him; but it shall not be carried out of the church. And to the end there may be little left, he that officiates is required to consecrate with the least, and then if there be want, the words of the consecration may be repeated again, over more either bread or wine: the Presbyter beginning at these words in the Prayer of Consecration* (*Our Saviour, in the night that he was betrayed, took, etc.*)

There was again a rubric directing that Churchwardens and Curate provide the elements. Since the "duty" of offering money was now an "offering" and "oblation," there were no references to support of the parish.

Parishioners were still to communicate at least three times a year, including "Pasch," or Easter.

The 1637 Communion Service illustrates the two Eucharistic traditions within Anglicanism, namely, the Catholic tradition of

1549 and the Evangelical tradition of 1552. In 1637 there was a brief moment in which the Catholic tradition was reflected in Scotland, the Evangelical in England. To this day, Scottish Services have proceeded along the lines of the Catholic tradition. But in 1662, twenty-five turbulent years after the attenuated life of the 1637 Mass, the Church of England produced a Communion Service that reflected both Catholic and Evangelical traditions.

The Communion Service of 1662

On January 3, 1645, Parliament ordained that "the said *Book of Common Prayer* be abolished, and the *Directory* for the Public Worship of God hereafter mentioned be established and observed, in all the Churches within this kingdom." [73] The Prayer Book, under heavy fire since 1637,[74] was now outlawed. The *Directory* was the official form of worship during the Puritan ascendency.[75]

But the Commonwealth did not last for long. On May 1, 1660, Charles II issued his *Declaration,* dated from Breda. The King declared liberty of conscience "and that no man shall be disquieted or called in question for differences of opinion in matters of religion which do not disturb the peace of the kingdom; and that we shall be ready to consent to such an Act of Parliament . . . shall be offered to us." [76]

Once again the Puritans went to a Stuart to request a Conference. They petitioned Charles:

Forasmuch as the Book of Common Prayer is in some things justly offensive, and needs amendment, we most humbly pray, that some learned, godly, and moderate Divines of both persuasions may be employed to compile such a form as is before described, as much as may be in scripture words; or at least to revise and reform the old, together with an addition of other various forms in scripture phrase, to be used at the minister's choice.[77]

The King agreed. On March 25, 1661, he issued a warrant for a Conference at the Bishop of London's lodgings in the Savoy: "To advise upon and review the said Book of Common Prayer, comparing the same with the most ancient Liturgies which have been used in the Church, in the primitive and purest times." However, in a significant phrase the King declared his predilection for the traditional Prayer Book and indicated in advance how slight would be the changes made in the Services: "but avoiding, as much as may be, all unnecessary alterations of the forms and Liturgy wherewith the people are already acquainted, and have so long received in the Church of England." [78]

As at Hampton Court, the Puritans gained little from the Conference. Although they proposed an exhaustive list of "Exceptions," the Bishops saw fit to allow only seventeen minor "Concessions." [79]

It is noteworthy that the Puritans had requested a manual acts rubric, and the Bishops had conceded the same. It was agreed that "the manner of consecrating the elements be made more explicit and express, and to that purpose those words be put into the rubr., 'then shall he put his hand upon the bread and break it,' 'then shall he put his hand into the cup.' " [80]

The King had kept his promise in calling the Savoy Conference. He also invoked Convocation "to review or cause a review . . . of the *Book of Common Prayer*." [81] Convocation produced a Prayer Book in which the Communion Service remained substantially intact. The Prayer Book was approved on December 20, 1661. [82]

On May 19, 1662, after considerable debate, the Act of Uniformity with the new Prayer Book annexed became law. It was enacted:

. . . by the King's most excellent Majesty, by the Advice and with the Consent of the Lords Spiritual and Temporal, and of the Comons in this present Parliament assembled, and by the authority of the same, That all and singular Ministers . . . shall be bound to say and use the Morning-Prayer, Evening-Prayer, Celebracon and Administracon of both Sacraments, and all other the Publique and Comon Prayer, in such Order and Form as is menconed in *the said Booke annexed and joyned to this present Act.*[83]

Accordingly, on St. Bartholomew's Day, August 24, 1662, a new Communion Service was celebrated in England. It has been the official Communion Service of that country ever since.

JOHN COSIN

John Cosin of Durham, a leading Laudian during the Puritan ascendency, had long "interested himself in ritual matters." [84] He was *persona non grata* during the interregnum and in 1643 went into exile on the continent.[85]

Cosin had already drawn up several collections of notes for Prayer Book revision. His interest continued unabated during exile, and shortly after his return in 1660 he committed to paper a list of "Particulars" for revision.[86]

When leading Divines of both persuasions were chosen for the Savoy Conference, Cosin was selected as one of the Episcopal representatives.[87] Although exclusively concerned with Prayer Book revision, this conference was part of the Restoration Settlement. As such, it was managed by politicians rather than scholars such as Cosin.[88] Despite his Laudian outlook, Cosin was one of the most sympathetic of the Bishops to Presbyterian sentiment. Nevertheless, government policy was for little or no revision, and Cosin had to submit to that policy.[89] The 1604 Prayer Book had taken on the martyr's halo; it was cherished for its proscription during the Commonwealth. It had also become an instrument of the government for unity and uniformity. Accordingly, Cosin and other Laudians left the conference in a quandary. If so few concessions could be granted the Presbyterians because of the policy of preservation of 1604, the Laudian proposals would be thwarted by the same policy.[90]

The large proposals Cosin had envisaged would not be possible, but he was able to cut his losings as much as he could. He was still in a prominent position to guide at least *some* Laudian proposals into the Communion Service. During preliminary stages of the Convocation revision meetings, he was secretary to the Bishops. Later when Convocation selected a committee of revision he was a member. Most of the corrections decided on were in his handwriting or that of his faithful chaplain, William Sancroft.[91]

But since the committee of revision was overwhelmingly for a Prayer Book *status quo,* Cosin was hampered. He and Matthew Wren were the only two of the eight prelates in favor of revision.[92] And even Wren was more conservative than Cosin.[93]

Despite these obstacles, Cosin successfully advocated some important adjustments in the Communion Service. The changes he championed reflected his Laudian doctrine of Sacrifice and Real Presence.

Cosin and Sacrifice

Cosin considered the Lord's Supper a Sacrifice that "signified" the Sacrifice of Christ. It was an analogical Sacrifice, a Sacrifice "formally and truly" but "not in strictness and rigour of speech." He wrote that "it may analogically be called a sacrifice . . . yet formally and truly it may be called a sacrifice also, in the very natural signification of a sacrifice, for aught I know any harm should come on't." After this remark, Cosin wrote in the margin: "Not in strictness and rigour of speech; for so was there never sacrifice, nor never shall be any, but Christ's alone." [94]

The Bishop explained that the Lord's Supper was an oblation of Christ's unique death; it was a representative Sacrifice of Christ's Sacrifice; it was a commemoration of the same:

> This is a plain oblation of Christ's death once offered, and a representative sacrifice of it, for the sins, and for the benefit of the whole world, of the whole Church. . . . And if the authority of the ancient Church may prevail with us, as it ought to do, there is nothing more manifest than that it always taught as much. And it is no absurdity to say, here is an oblation made for all, when it is not only commemorated to have been once offered, but solemn prayers are here also added, and request made, that it may be effectual to all.[95]

Christ's Sacrifice was "once offered" on the cross. But the Lord's Supper was a sacrifice "in recognition and memory of Christ's own sacrifice."

> And indeed, the Sacrament of the Eucharist carries the name of a sacrifice, and the table whereon it is celebrated an altar of oblation, in a far higher sense than any of their former sacrifices did, which were but the types and figures of those services that are performed in recognition and memory of Christ's own sacrifice, once offered upon the altar of His Cross.[96]

Cosin denied the Sacrifice was a naked commemoration. "We do not hold this celebration to be so naked a commemoration of Christ's Body given to death, and of His Blood shed for us, but that the same Body and Blood is present there in this commemoration . . . to all that faithfully receive it." [97]

Although Cosin taught "this commemorative sacrifice to be

propitiatory," [98] he denied that this meant a daily killing of Christ. Christ died but once; it was blasphemous to say He was killed in the Mass.

But a true, real proper, and propitiatory sacrificing of Christ, *toties quoties* as this Sacrament is celebrated, which is the popish doctrine, and which cannot be done without killing of Christ so often again, we hold not; believing it to be a false and blasphemous doctrine; founding ourselves upon the apostles doctrine, that Christ was sacrificed but once, and that he dieth no more.[99]

The English Church abrogated the "Roman" doctrine of a "proper and true" Sacrifice. Christ was not offered in the Eucharist in the same way that He offered Himself on Calvary:

And therefore Christ can be no more offered, as the doctors and priests of the Roman party fancy Him to be, and vainly think that every time they say mass, they offer up and sacrifice Christ anew, as properly and truly as He offered up Himself in His sacrifice upon the cross.[100]

By a "proper" Sacrifice Cosin meant a Sacrifice involving killing of a victim. He alleged the Roman Mass taught a daily killing of Christ: "So that without shedding of His blood, and killing Him over again, no proper sacrifice can be made of Him; which yet in their masses the Roman priests pretend every day to do." [101]

At the consecration of Bishop White, Cosin stressed the necessity of applying the Sacrifice *of Christ*:

They [are] sent by Him, to mediate and to pray for the people, to be ministers of the reconciliation, as St. Paul speaks, and in a manner, to be sacrificers too, representers at the Altar here, and appliers of the Sacrifice once made for all; without which last act, the first will do us no good.[102]

This application of Christ's Sacrifice (once offered) extended itself to both living and dead: "The virtue of this sacrifice (which is here in this prayer of oblation commemorated and represented) doth not only extend itself to them that are present, but likewise to them that are absent, and them that be already departed. . . ." [103] It was a Sacrifice "for the sins, and for the benefit, of the whole world, of the whole Church; that both those which are here on earth, and those that rest in the sleep of peace, being departed in the faith of Christ, may find the effect and virtue of it." [104]

Nevertheless, Cosin denied purgatory as "a very vain collection." To conclude "as the new Roman Catholics do, that therefore their souls are in purgatory and pain, is a very vain collection." [105] Although Greek and Latin liturgies prayed for the dead, "of bringing them out of purgatory, or relieving them in their pains there, they say nothing at all, for they knew of no such matter, neither did the Church of old teach the people to believe it." [106]

Cosin advocated a daily Lord's Supper. He alleged that the proper prefaces for octaves were "a plain proof that our Church intends to have the Communion celebrated every day." [107] He likewise interpreted the rubrics after the Communion Service as proof that "the mind of the Church of England ever was and is to have a Communion and commemorative sacrifice of Christ's death every day." [108] This was the practice of the primitive Church: "In the primitive Church, while Christians continued in their strength of faith and devotion, they did every day communicate, as we read in the Acts of the Apostles. . . ." [109]

Yet he opposed private Masses. The words about "gasers and lookers on" in the most recently composed exhortation was an invective "against the lewd and irreligious custom of the people then nursed up in popery, to be present at the Communion, and to let the priest communicate for them all: from whence arose the abuse of private masses; a practice so repugnant to the use of the ancient Church." [110]

Cosin and Real Presence

Cosin wrote at length against Transubstantiation. He believed it possible through God's omnipotence, but opposed to sense testimony, Scripture, and ancient approbation:

God in His almightiness might be able to turn the substance of bread into some other substance, yet none will believe He doth it, as long as it appears to our senses that the substance of the bread doth still remain whole and entire. Certain it is that hitherto we read of no such thing done in the Old or New Testament . . . and hath been but lately approved by the pope's authority in the councils of Lateran and Trent.[111]

Since Cosin was representative of the research into the early Church undertaken by the Caroline Divines, it is well to quote in full the conclusion to his studies on Transubstantiation:

Any considering person may easily see, that transubstantiation is a mere novelty, not warranted either by Scripture or antiquity, invented about the middle of the twelfth century out of some misunderstood sayings of some of the fathers, confirmed by no ecclesiastical or papal decree before the year 1215, afterwards received only here and there in the Roman Church, debated in the schools by many disputes, liable to many very bad consequences, rejected (for there was never those wanting that opposed it) by many great and pious men: until it was maintained in the sacrilegious council of Constance, and at last, in the year 1551, confirmed in the council of Trent, by a few Latin Bishops, slaves to the Roman see, imposed upon all under pain of an anathema to be feared by command of the pope. So that we have no reason to embrace it, until it shall be demonstrated that, except the substance of the bread be changed into the very Body of Christ, His words cannot possibly be true, nor His Body present; which will never be done.[112]

Yet Protestant Divines did not deny "a true and well-understood real presence and communication of the Body and Blood of Christ in the blessed sacrament; whereas, on the contrary, they do professedly own it in terms as express as any can be used." [113]

He argued that the words in the Communion Service about eating Christ's Flesh and drinking His Blood reflected the doctrine of the English Church: "Our Church believeth and teacheth of the presence of Christ's Body and Blood in the Sacrament." [114]

Cosin believed that Christ was present *in use* to the faithful communicants. But he seemed hesitant throughout his writings as to the sacredness of the elements *after use*. His long-standing uncertainty is illustrated in his later *Notes and Collections,* a work to which he contributed as late as 1656.[115] Speaking of the rubric about the elements that remained after the Service, Cosin wrote:

Which is to be understood of that bread and wine, that the churchwardens provided, and carried into the vestry, not of that which the priest consecrated for the Sacrament; for of this, if he be careful, as he ought to be, to consecrate no more than will suffice to be distributed unto the communicants, none will remain.[116]

After the above paragraph, Cosin commented in a marginal note as follows:

(Yet if for lack of care they consecrate more than they distribute, why may not the curates have it to their own use, as well as be given to children . . . or be burnt in fire . . . for though the bread and wine remain, yet the consecration, the Sacrament of the Body and Blood of Christ, do not remain longer than the holy action itself remains for which the bread and wine were hallowed; and which being ended, return to their former use again?)[117]

Later, when discussing this same rubric in his *Particulars,* he urged that the consecrated elements that remained be consumed *in Church*:

And therefore for the better clearing of this particular, some words are needful here to be added, whereby the priest may be enjoined to consider the number of them which are to receive the Sacrament and to consecrate the bread and wine in such a near proportion as shall be sufficient for them; but if any of the consecrated elements are left, that he and some others with him shall decently eat and drink them in the church before all the people depart from it.[118]

To some extent, Cosin's position on the Real Presence was strikingly similar to that of Bucer.[119] He referred to the elements as "exhibiting" Christ's Body and Blood. "The receiving of which Sacrament, or participating of which sacrifice exhibited to us, we say is profitable only to them that receive it and participate of it." He interpreted the words about "creatures of bread and wine" as teaching that these elements exhibited Christ: "That together with the hallowed elements of bread and wine, we may receive the Body and Blood of Christ, which are truly exhibited in this Sacrament, the one as well as the other." [120] The elements remained, but when consecrated they communicated Christ's Body and Blood:

Hence it is most evident that the bread and wine (which, according to S. Paul, are the elements of the holy Eucharist) are neither changed as to their substance, nor vanished, nor reduced to nothing; but are solemnly consecrated by the words of Christ, that by them His blessed Body and Blood may be communciated to us.[121]

A union resulted between the bread and the exhibited Body of Christ; the names of sign and thing signified were interchanged:

The words of Christ make the form of this sacrament to consist in the union of the thing signified with the sign, that is, the exhibition of the Body of Christ with the consecrated bread, still remaining bread: by divine appointment these two are made one . . . by their being one with another, yet it is so straight and so true, that in eating the blessed bread, the true Body of Christ is given to us, and the names of sign and thing signified are reciprocally changed. . . .[122]

What was proper to Christ's Body was attributed to bread; and what was proper to bread was attributed to Christ's Body. Both were united in time, "though not in place; for the presence of Christ in this mystery is not opposed to distance, but to absence." [123]

Since Christ was exhibited and presented in the elements, adoration was due to Him, but not to bread and wine:

. . . whosoever so receiveth them, at that time when he receiveth them, rightly doth he adore and reverence his Saviour there together with the Sacramental Bread and Cup exhibiting His own Body and Blood unto them. . . . our kneeling, and the outward gesture of humility and reverence in our bodies, is ordained only to testify and express the inward reverence and devotion of our souls toward our blessed Saviour. . . .[124]

Cosin believed the English Service taught Real Presence more clearly than the Mass:

. . . we deny not the bread and wine to remain there still, as God's creatures. And I wonder the papists should so contend for the same *desitio panis et vini,* whereas in their own service or mass, they abstain not from these words, "thy creatures," after consecration, as we do.[125]

He returned to this same idea: "Before consecration, we called them God's creatures of bread and wine, now we do so no more after consecration; wherein we have the advantage against the Church of Rome, who call them still creatures . . . after consecration." The English Church abstained from these words after the Consecration that recipients could concentrate on the Body of Christ: "[We] think no more of bread and wine, but have our thoughts taken wholly up with the Body of Christ; and therefore we keep ourselves to these words only, abstaining from the other, (though the bread remains there still to the eye)." [126]

As a homilist, Cosin compared the Eucharistic elements to Baptismal water: "The water in Baptism, the bread and wine in the blessed Sacrament, naturally they are no more than other such elements are; but being consecrated and set apart once to these holy uses." [127]

In a sacramental union with Christ, the elements signified His Body and Blood.[128] The eating and drinking was not corporal, but spiritual and mysterious:

> We believe a presence and union of Christ with our soul and body, which we know not how to call better than sacramental, that is, effected by eating; that, while we eat and drink the consecrated bread and wine, we eat and drink therewithal the Body and Blood of Christ, not in a corporal manner, but some other way, incomprehensible, known only to God, which we call spiritual. . . .[129]

Cosin taught that the *fact* of the Real Presence was revealed; but the *manner* was a mystery. The English Church accepted the fact, and did not invent and impose an explanation of the manner. He thought Christians should assent to the doctrine, and leave the mystery to God's power and wisdom:

> As to the manner of the presence of the Body and Blood of our Lord in the blessed sacrament, we that are protestant and reformed according to the ancient Catholic Church, do not search into the manner of it with perplexing inquiries; but, after the example of the primitive and purest Church of Christ, we leave it to the power and wisdom of our Lord, yielding a full and unfeigned assent to His words.[130]

The very substance of Christ was received in Communion, and not just the benefits of His Passion. Unlike Rome, the English Church taught a true eating and union, not a corporal one:

> We do not say that in the Lord's Supper we receive only the benefits of Christ's death and passion: but we join the ground with its fruits, that is, Christ with those advantages we receive from Him, affirming with S. Paul, that "the bread which we break is . . . the communion of the Body of Christ, and the cup which we bless the communion of His Blood" of that very substance which He took of the blessed Virgin, and afterwards carried into heaven; differing from those of Rome only in this, that they will have our union with Christ to be corporal, and our eating of Him likewise, and we, on the contrary, maintain it to be indeed as true, but not carnal or natural.[131]

The man who "discerned" Christ's "Body as torn, and His Blood as shed, for the redemption of the world," truly received

Christ. But Christ was not "received with the mouth and ground with the teeth, so that not only the most wicked and infidels, but even rats and mice, should swallow Him down." [132]

In Cosin's doctrine, the Presence of Christ seemed to involve an almost ontological change in the elements. He did in fact admit explicitly that they were changed: "We confess the necessity of a supernatural and heavenly change, and that the signs cannot become sacraments but by the infinite power of God." He expressed the same idea in different words: "The bread and wine, by the power of God and a supernatural virtue, be set apart and fitted for a much nobler use, and raised to a higher dignity, than their nature bears." [133] In another context, Cosin identified the conversion with a change in the condition, use, and office of the elements: "There is a conversion of the bread into the Body (and consequently of the wine into the Blood) of Christ: for they know and acknowledge that in the sacrament, by virtue of the words and blessing of Christ, the condition, use, and office, of the bread is wholly changed." [134]

Cosin's Eucharistic doctrine went a long way toward rapprochement with Roman teaching jettisoned by the sixteenth-century reformers. He taught that Christ's Sacrifice was pleaded at Mass and that the Mass was propitiatory. He also professed change in the elements. It was natural, therefore, that he desired to restore a clear Offertory to the English liturgy and to inculcate therein the doctrine of a true and real Presence of Christ.

ROBERT SANDERSON

One of those Cosin had to reckon with in the proceedings for revision was Bishop Robert Sanderson of Lincoln. Sanderson was as conservative as he was influential. His conservatism in Eucharistic matters was reflected in his Eucharistic writings as well as in his alignment with those who wanted a settlement involving the 1604 Prayer Book. At the time of revision, power in Church and State rested with a group of Oxford men.[135] Sanderson aligned himself with this group and was able to thwart the advanced Laudians by his presence at Savoy and Convocation.

It is very significant that, during the time of persecution, Sanderson devised his own Eucharistic Office along *very conservative lines*.[136] He was only consistent when at the Savoy conference he pressed for the rejection of Presbyterian demands and maintenance of the *status quo*.[137] His prominence there contributed to the impossibility of revision along Laudian lines as well. If the liturgy was too hallowed for Presbyterian changes, it was also too hallowed for Laudian innovation.

When the Convocation revision committee was chosen, Sanderson was one of the eight members. He was joined by three others firmly in the Oxford camp. Of the four remaining, two Bishops, Skinner and Warner, were in disfavor with those in power and anxious to ingratiate themselves. This left only Cosin and Wren as advocates of substantial revision.

Sanderson's famous biographer, Izaak Walton, extolled Sanderson's influence at Convocation. According to Walton, "Convocation valued him so much, that he never undertook to speak to any point in question, but he was heard with great willingness and attention." [138] It is a fact that Sanderson was chosen to compose a Preface for the new Prayer Book, and that the Preface clearly expounded the dominant attitude of conservatism.[139]

In brief, Sanderson's alignment with the Establishment, his presence at Savoy, his committee membership at Convocation, and his selection to compose the new Preface, all indicate a position of influence in the revision proceedings. And the proceedings of 1661, as all past revision proceedings, were primarily concerned with the Communion Service.

Sanderson and the Eucharist

In the 1662 Preface, Sanderson expressed his conservative attitude toward the 1559 Prayer Book. He thought it "fairly defensible" against any opposition:

But such alterations as were tendered to us, (by what persons, under what pretences, or to what purpose soever tendered) as seemed to us in any degree requisite or expedient we have willingly, and of our own accord assented unto: not enforced so to do by any strength of argument, convincing us of the necessity of making the said alterations: for we are fully persuaded in our judgments (and we here profess it to the world) that the Book, as it stood before established by law, doth not contain in it any thing contrary to the Word of God, or to sound doctrine, or which a godly man may not with a good conscience use and submit unto, or which is not fairly defensible against any that shall oppose the same. . . .[140]

After describing the "several variations from the former Book, whether by alteration, addition, or otherwise," Sanderson hoped that the new revision would be "also well accepted and approved by all sober, peaceable, and truly conscientious sons of the Church of England." [141]

Sanderson's actions during the "times of trouble" give an indication of his conservative attitude toward the 1559 Prayer Book, especially the Communion Service. He followed the "ancient" rites of 1559: ". . . in the Administration of the Sacraments . . . I constantly used the ancient forms and rites to every of them respectively belonging, according to the appointment in the Book." [142]

In 1647 he was prepared to defend the English Prayer Book against "Papists and other oppugners or depravers thereof whatsoever":

> Which [the Prayer Book] we verily believe not to contain any thing which, with such favourable construction as of right ought to be allowed to all manner of Writings, is not justly defensible; which hath not been by learned and godly men sufficiently maintained against such exceptions as have been heretofore taken thereat; and which we are not confident, by the assistance of Almighty God, we shall be able to justify as occasion shall be offered, against all Papists, and other oppugners or depravers thereof whatsoever.[143]

Sanderson was soon delated by one of "the Presbyterian gang" for his well-known liturgical conservatism:

> About nigh two years ago, I was advertised (but in a very friendly manner) by a Parliament man of note in these parts, that at a public meeting in Grantham great complaint was made by Some Ministers (of the Presbyterian gang, as I afterwards found) of my refractoriness to obey the Parliament's Order in that belief.[144]

The "Parliament man" warned Sanderson that his actions had been known for some time. Public complaint had compelled officialdom to take action. Sanderson was provided with a dilemma; he could either forbear the traditional Service or suffer loss of his station.[145] His response to this dilemma indicated another conviction of his, namely, that discretion was the better part of valor:

> I having long ago considered of the case, and resolved what I might with a good Conscience do, and what were fittest for me in prudence to do, if I should ever be put to it, viz. to forbear the use of

the Common Prayer Book, so far as might satisfy the letter of the Ordinance, rather than forsake my station.[146]

Sanderson went so far as to provide a rite of his own that
would not bring danger to himself or "scandal to my brethren by
the disuse of the established liturgy":

My next business then was, to bethink myself of such a course to
be thenceforth held in the public worship in my own Parish, as might
be likeliest neither to bring danger to myself by the use, nor to bring
scandal to my brethren by the disuse of the established liturgy.[147]

Sanderson composed his own Communion Service, entitled
The Office of the Communion.[148] This short Service was the only
work of Sanderson devoted completely to the Eucharist. Outwardly,
the Service seemed to contradict his liturgical conservatism. But
a closer reading reveals a conservative tone that resembles Cranmer's theology more than that of the Laudian party.

Sanderson's rite began with an Exhortation, disguised by the
label "Instruction." In this exhortation-instruction, Sanderson
taught that men should approach the Eucharist with Faith in God's
mercy. It was by trust in God's mercy and the Death of Christ
that the benefits of the Passion were received. Sanderson referred
to the Sacrament as a representation of Christ's Passion and Death:

Thirdly, we ought to come to this holy Sacrament with a lively
and stedfast faith in God's mercy through Christ our Saviour, by the
breaking of whose Body, and the shedding of His most precious Blood
upon the Cross, (represented unto us in this Sacrament,) we and the
whole Church trust to obtain remission of our sins, and all other benefits of His passion, to our great and endless comfort.

The Eucharist was instituted for a manward remembrance of
Christ's efficacious Sacrifice for sins:

Lastly, forasmuch as this Sacrament was ordained by our Saviour
Jesus Christ Himself for this end especially, that the remembrance of
His death, wherein He offered up Himself a sacrifice for our sins (and
the innumerable benefits that we receive thereby) might be the better
remembered in the Christian Church to all succeeding generations.

We were to give thanks to the Trinity for the Redemption
by Christ:

We are therefore bound to give most humble and hearty thanks to God the Father, the Son, and the Holy Ghost, for the redemption of the world by the death and passion of our Saviour Christ, who, being the eternal Son of God, laid aside His glory and humbled Himself even to the death upon the cross, for us, miserable sinners, which lay in darkness and in the shadow of death, that he might make us the children of God, and exalt us to everlasting life.

An Invitation, Confession, Absolution (labeled "Benediction"), and several Prefaces followed.

After the Sanctus, there was a "Prayer" which was Sanderson's version of the traditional Prayer of Humble Access. In this prayer, he connected Communion with the Cranmerian idea of indwelling: "Grant us therefore, gracious Lord, so to eat the flesh of Thy dear Son Jesus Christ and to drink His blood that our sinful bodies and souls, being sanctified by His body, and washed through His most precious blood, we may evermore dwell in Him and He in us." [149]

Sanderson's Consecration prayer was very short.[150] It taught that Christ by His "own" oblation had made the traditional "full, perfect, and sufficient sacrifice." The Eucharist was commanded "to continue the memory of that His precious death." Communicants received "creatures of bread and wine" and became partakers of His most blessed Body and Blood:

Almighty God our Heavenly Father, whose only Son Jesus Christ by his own oblation of Himself, once offered upon the cross, hath made a full, perfect, and sufficient sacrifice, and satisfaction, for the sins of the whole world; and did in His Holy Gospel command us to continue the memory of that His precious death, until His coming again; grant, O merciful Father, we beseech Thee, that we, receiving these creatures of bread and wine, according to His holy institution, and in remembrance of His death and passion, may be made partakers of His most blessed body and blood; who, at His Last Supper, took bread; and, when He had given thanks, He brake it, and gave it to His disciples, saying,—Take, eat, this is my Body which is given for you; Do this in remembrance of me. Likewise, after supper, He took the cup and gave it to them, saying, Drink ye all of this; for this is my Blood of the New Testament, which is shed for you and for many, for the remission of sins. Do this, as oft as ye shall drink it, in remembrance of me.

As had been the English practice since 1552, Communion was distributed immediately after the Consecration. The formulas were the same as in the 1559 Service.

An "Act of Worship" provided a Post-Communion. This consisted of three prayers. The first was the Our Father. The second referred to Communion as a spiritual reception: ". . . Thou hast vouchsafed to feed us with the spiritual food of the most precious Body and Blood of Thy Son. . . ." The third contained the Cranmerian idea of Sacrifice as an offering of ourselves, our souls and bodies: "And here, O Lord, we offer and present ourselves, our souls and bodies, to be a reasonable, holy, and lively sacrifice unto Thee, which we beseech Thee mercifully to accept, as our bounden duty and service. . . ." [151]

Sanderson's Service concluded with a "Hymn" (almost identical with the *Gloria*), a Collect, and the traditional Anglican blessing, labeled "The Mission."

Sanderson's scanty Eucharistic writings suggest that he was more in the tradition of Cranmer than of the Catholic party as exemplified by Cosin. Furthermore, he aligned himself with those Royalists who wanted little change in the Prayer Book. It is because of Sanderson and his colleagues of the new Establishment that the Church of England rebuffed the scholarship undertaken by the Caroline Divines. In preventing a return to more ancient forms and the 1549 tradition, Sanderson and his allies had to thwart not only John Cosin but also Cosin's lone ally in the revision proceedings, Matthew Wren.

MATTHEW WREN

Matthew Wren, Bishop of Ely, may well have been "the most considerable influence" in the revision of 1662.[152]

Wren was associated with royalty. In 1621 he visited Spain as chaplain to Charles I. On that occasion he prided himself that "he could never be induced to go within the Jesuits' gates, though all the English else did not stick to visit them." [153]

As Bishop of Ely, he was confined to the Tower for his Eucharistic practices before the Puritan moment in the sun. During those days of enforced leisure, he composed a list of "Exceptions" for Prayer Book revision.[154] He was not interested mainly in structural alteration or in new doctrinal emphases. His primary concern was to amend verbal imperfections.

Although Wren was not at Savoy, he was one of the eight appointed as a revision committee by Convocation. He, Cosin, and Sancroft worked feverishly to prepare for the meetings. But it seems that Wren's Eucharistic position was more conservative than that of Cosin.[155]

Wren was respected for his knowledge of the Communion Service. He was known to have assisted Laud when the latter perused Wedderburn's recommendations for the 1637 Service. It was probably this fact, as well as his days of incarceration for defiance of the Puritans in Eucharistic matters, that induced Convocation to appoint him to the revision committee. Although he was more literalistic and less enthusiastic for change than Cosin, it seems that he and Cosin were the two members of the committee responsible for the few, albeit significant, changes made in the Communion Service.

Unlike Cosin and Sanderson, Wren was not a prolific writer. His doctrine may be derived from his *Defence* at his trial and the "Exceptions" elaborated in prison. The few passages dealing with the Eucharist in these documents indicate a sympathy with the doctrine of Laud, Wedderburn, and Cosin, mingled with a conservatism for traditional doctrine and forms.

Wren and Sacrifice

In his *Defence* before Puritan accusers, Wren was understandably reluctant to reveal his deepest Eucharistic convictions. The reasons he alleged for his past directives were administrative and utilitarian, not doctrinal. He defended his elevation of the Table that "the Minister might thereby more conveniently be heard by the Parishoners, in his Administration there." [156] He denied he had so much as used the word "Altar" in his directives: "And he saith . . . that he believeth that he never did by any Words of his own, so much as name the Word *Altar,* in any of his Articles or Directives; much less did he ever term the Table an Altar." [157] As for his directives for an eastward location, he defended these as expedient for uniformity and "convenience":

He also saith, that his directing to have the Communion Table placed at East end of the Chancel was done by him, as well for an Uniformity to all cathedral and collegiate Churches, which he conceived did receive the Usage which had been therein from the Beginning of the Reformation, and to all the King's Chapels, and to very many Parish Churches, wherein it had never been otherwise: as also for a double Convenience. . . .[158]

He denied that he had altered the pews so that all would face East as to a Table "set Altar-wise," nor had he prohibited seats about the Table:

. . . this Defendent answereth, and denieth, that he in the Year 1636, did order all Pews to be altered, that they might kneel with their Faces Eastwards towards the Table set altar-wise; much less, that he did so, the more to advance blind Superstition; or that he did order, that there should be no Seats about, or up even with the Communion Table.[159]

He submitted three reasons for such an arrangement. First, "that in God's House, by the observing of due Order and outward Comeliness, Men might be put in Mind of the Beauty of inward Holiness." Second, "that God's house being ordained for an House of Prayer the People might have the Opportunity . . . to put themselves into the Posture of Prayer, to kneel down and humble themselves in God's Service." Third, "that as much as might be with Convenience, they might look, or turn their faces all one Way." [160]

Throughout the *Defence,* Wren continued to justify his actions *without* betraying his deepest convictions on the Eucharist. As for use of the surplice, he defended it on three grounds. First, "for Decency and Convenience." Second, "For an Uniformity to all other Persons, Places, and Times." And finally, "For Conformity to the Law itself. . . . That the Minister at the Time of the Communion, and at all other time in his Ministration, shall use such Ornaments in the Church, as were in Use in the second Year of K. *Edward* the VIth." [161]

Years later, in safer days, Wren demanded a clear and specific vestments rubric:

But what is now fit to be ordered herein, and to preserve those that are still in use, it would be set down in express words, without these uncertainties which breed nothing but debate and scorn. The very words too of that Act. 2 Edw. VI, for the Minister's Ornaments, would be set down, or to pray to have a new one made. . . .[162]

In the years since his indictment, his views on the position of the Altar had become more evangelical. Communion Service was to be in the Chancel, "where it may well be done. But leave nothing ambiguous." The Priest was to stand "at the North of the Table, the people all kneeling. . . ." [163]

The offerings of the people were connected with Sacrifice to some extent when Wren remarked that the Offertory sentences should refer in part to freewill offerings to God:

These Sentences now are all the same here that were before, but . . . the seven that stand first will appear to be in general for all kind of charitable gifts; the seven next to tend particularly to that which they called *Prosphora* in the Primitive Church, that is a freewill Offering unto God; and the six last, to be especially for the *Eleemosyna*, that is, our Alms Deeds to the Poor.[164]

The "freewill Offering unto God" was to be delivered "in private to the Minister, with their other accustomed Offerings, such as are their due from them." [165]

The alms for the poor were also associated with Offering. These were to be placed on the table by the Minister. Significantly, they were to remain in that honored position until the conclusion of the Service:

As for the Devotion of the People to the Poor, the Church Wardens, or some appointed by them, shall presently after the Sentences go about and gather it, and then shall bring it unto the Minister, by him to be placed on the Holy Table, till the Divine Service be finished, and then to be put into the Poor Men's box, or to be presently given, as need shall be.[166]

The elements likewise were connected with offering when Wren urged that the "Priest" place bread and wine on the "Lord's Board." In this suggestion, Wren also revealed his belief in perduring Real Presence when he prescribed that only necessary elements be offered while others remained ready at hand:

The last Rubrick . . . would be thus: Here shall the Bread and Wine which is provided for that Communion, be in a decent manner presented by the Church Wardens, or some other for them, to the

Priest, who shall with due reverence set as much thereof, in both kinds, as he shall conceive there will be then use of upon the *Lord's* Board, and the rest to remain, ready at hand by him, if need should be of it.[167]

In view of this connection of elements with Sacrifice, it is surprising that Wren's suggestions are Cranmerian when he treats of Sacrifice itself. He seemed to consider the Sacrifice an act of *thanksgiving*; when he discussed remembrance and representation, these ideas seemed to involve a remembrance and representation before *men*.

He advocated verbal clarification to emphasize the thanksgiving aspect of the Eucharist. The Mass was a giving of thanks as well as being thankful:

Yet let it now be well weighed, whether it shall go so still, or be, *and give Him thanks*. For the Latin of which it was turned for us, was *et gratias age.* Also the verb in Greek . . . from which this Sacrament is rightly called the Eucharist, signifies not only *gratum esse,* to be thankful, but also *gratias agere,* to give thanks.[168]

In his suggested wording for the Consecration prayer, it seems he believed "shewing" or representation was made before men that thereby they could partake of Christ's Body and Blood: ". . . according to Thy Son our Saviour Jesus Christ's holy Institution, *for a* remembrance of *Him by shewing* His Death and Passion, may be partakers of His most blessed Body &c." [169] His suggestion for rewording the exhortation continued to stress the idea of a pledge or remembrance before men:

At the first line, put these words thus: He hath *to our great and endless comfort* instituted and ordained *these* holy mysteries *for* pledges of His love and for a continual remembrance of *Him who died for us.* . . .[170]

Wren's proposed Communion formulas reiterated his stress on the representative elements as a remembrance of Christ offered to men. The feeding was "in thy heart" with thanksgiving. "Take and eat this in remembrance of *Christ,* Who died for thee; and feed on Him in thy heart by faith with thanksgiving." And for the cup, "Drink this for a remembrance of *Christ,* whose Blood was shed for thee and be thankful." [171]

His suggestion for manual acts revealed the influence of Laud:

The first Rubrick to read thus:
Then the Priest standing before the Table shall so order and set the Bread and the Wine that, while he is pronouncing the following Collect, he may readily take the Bread and break it, and also take the Cup, to pour into it (if he pour it not before). . . .[172]

Nor did Wren oppose wafer bread. He wanted it allowed in the rubric, "because in some places (at Westminister, if I remember aright, and elsewhere) plain Wafers have ever been used." [173]

In a remark that indicated some historical confusion on his part, Wren urged restoration of the Saints to the Communion Service as part of the thanksgiving to God. He thought there was no longer danger that the "Vulgar" would interpret a commemoration as praying to or for the dead:

Of all right, it would now be added again. For in the Primitive Church, they ever had here a Commemoration, and Thanksgiving for the Saints. It was also here in this Prayer in Edward vi days. But in the beginning of Queen Elizabeth, that the Vulgar might not think they did either pray to the Dead or for the Dead, they chopped off the end of this Prayer, never thinking of the proposal made in the beginning of it. Thanks be to God, there can be no pretence at all now, why it should not be restored.[174]

Wren and Real Presence

At his arraignment, Wren defended bowing of the head as a "reverence" no different than other reverences. But he carefully avoided giving his real convictions on the Real Presence:

Also this Defendant considered, that lifting up of the Hands, or casting down of the Eyes, or smiting the Breast, or giving a Sigh, or any other like Gestures, as liable to just Offence as bowing is, are no way prohibited. And he could never apprehend why the using of this particular Reverence, should not be as free as is the using of no kind of Reverence at all.[175]

He defended bowing at the "Table" because the Table bears God's name, suggests the hypostatic union, and is a reminder "of the venerable Mystery of Christ's Death and Passion." He did not commit himself on a special Presence of Christ in the elements:

. . . because the Table bears God's Name, and particularly suggests the Memorial of the hypostatical *Union* of God and Man, and of the venerable Mystery of Christ's Death and Passion. . . . Therefore this Defendant limited himself to the forenamed Occasions only of performing of such Adoration unto the Lord Almighty.[176]

He denied any superstitious or idolatrous "Actions and Gestures in the Administration of the Lord's Supper." He defended his use of manual acts, Invocation, and Words of Institution as actions "which the Church of *England* has appointed." Once again, there is no clearcut indication of his convictions on the *effect* of these actions:

. . . this Defendant answereth and denieth, that in *Anno* 1636. he did in his own Person use any superstitious or idolatrous Actions and Gestures in the Administration of the Lord's Supper.

But he saith, that he doth ever use, and observe the Form of preparing or consecrating the Bread and Wine for the holy Sacrament which the Church of *England* hath appointed, and not other. . . .[177]

In his denial that he elevated the host and chalice, Wren *did* reveal his conviction on Transubstantiation and adoration of Christ's transubstantiated Body. He vigorously anathematized "any superstitious or idolatrous Usages, or Intentions by him in that kind ever had." But he did not give his *own* position; he merely professed allegiance to Article 28:

. . . he never lifted his Hand from the Table, whereon it rested: and no otherwise did he with the Cup also, whereas then in the Popish Church the use is, that the Priest after the Consecration, elevating the Bread and the Chalice, does it so, as not to be seen over his Shoulder only, but holds it up over his Head, meaning that then he does sacrifice *Christ's* Body, which there he hath transubstantiated, and therefore to that End elevates it, that the people beholding, may fall down and adore it: this Defendant is ready, according to the Decision in such Cases used in the ancient Councils, to pronounce *Anathema* to any superstitious or idolatrous Usages, or Intentions by him in that kind ever had, and to profess, that he doth faithfully and totally adhere to the Article of the Church of *England*. . . .[178]

Wren was no more tolerant of Transubstantiation in his "Exceptions" than he had been in his *Defence*. But he was at one with Laud in admitting Roman usages when these latter were susceptible of Anglican interpretation: "The Church of Rome to gain some colour to their fancy of transubstantiation, next after these words

. . . put in *Amen* there. Now, though we approve not of that, yet there is not reason why it should be quite omitted." [179]

In the safe atmosphere of Restoration England, Wren was willing to state his views on Real Presence. They were consistent with his position on Sacrifice as a remembrance before men; the Real Presence consisted in "holy mysteries" and "spiritual food": "[We] heartily thank Thee, for that Thou *hast vouchsafed to feed us who of thy Grace have received these holy mysteries from Thee,* with the spiritual food of the most precious body and blood of Thy Son &c." [180] Yet Wren was at one with Cosin in advocating reconsecration. Therefore, it seems he believed in efficacious consecration of the elements: "And if afterwards there prove to be use for any more Bread or Wine than that of which he brake and blessed at first, he shall use the very Form, and say over the words audibly, before he gives it." [181]

He also agreed with Cosin in his proposal for consumption of consecrated elements. Once again, this seems to indicate a belief in efficacious Consecration and perduring Real Presence:

. . . What remaineth of the Bread of any Loaf or Wafer that was broken for the use of the Communion, or of the Wine that was poured out, or had the Benediction, the Curate shall, after the Service is ended, take some of the Communicants to him, there to eat and drink the same. But all the rest in both kinds, the Curate shall have to his own use.[182]

Wren stood midway between Cosin and Sanderson. He was not the theologian Cosin was, nor did he go as far as Cosin in teaching propitiatory Sacrifice and change in the elements. But he was more favorable to revision along Catholic lines than was Sanderson. He would be ready to cooperate with Cosin in restoring emphasis on Offertory and perduring Real Presence.

THE COMMUNION SERVICE OF 1662

St. Bartholomew's Day is a fateful day in Church history. On the eve of that feast, August 23, 1645, the Long Parliament forbade the Book of Common Prayer. Seventeen years later, the Episcopal party got its revenge. Rubbing salt in Puritan wounds, the Cavalier Parliament required consent to that Book, as revised in 1662, on the feast of that gentle saint.[183]

Prayer Book settlement was part of political settlement, and the Communion Service was part of the Prayer Book. No party, even the government, could be thoroughly satisfied with the new Communion Service.[184] Obviously the Presbyterians were thoroughly rebuffed by the obduracy of Savoy. But by the same token, the Laudians were unable to claim victory. It had been their desire to return to the Sacrificial and Real Presence emphases of 1637 and 1549. That they succeeded in commanding any such changes at all was probably due to the careful homework of Cosin and Wren before the Convocation committee met.

The Communion Service

The Presbyterians found no mitigation of Sacrificial overtones in the 1662 ornaments rubric which still prescribed the vestments of the second year of Edward VI.[185]

There were only minimal changes in the introductory rubrics, all of them doctrinally insignificant. Communicants were directed to inform the Curate "at least some time the day before." The latter was to inform the Ordinary of any excluded communicant "within fourteen days after the farthest." In such cases the Ordinary was to take action "according to the Canon."

During the Lord's Prayer and Collect for purity, the people were directed to kneel. They remained "still kneeling" for the penitential litany, in which they implored mercy for past transgressions and grace "to keep the same for the time to come."

Since the 1662 revision was part of a political settlement, it is understandable that royalty was flattered by the transposition— as in 1637—of the Collects for the king to the more prestigious location preceding the Collect for the day.

The Puritan request for more specific indications of Epistle and Gospel selections was granted, and there was an option for saying or singing the Creed. The people were to stand.

In 1662, the announcements were to be read *before* the Sermon, not after as in 1559. At this time, "if occasion be," the Curate was to give notice of the Communion, Banns, Briefs, Citations, and Excommunications. There were to be no extempore announcements. This was indicated by the direction that "nothing shall be proclaimed or published in the Church, during the time of Divine Service, but by the Minister: nor by him any thing, but what is prescribed in the Rules of this Book, or enjoined by the King, or the Ordinary of the place."

A most significant change occurred in the rubric after the Sermon or Homily. This part of the Service was again called the "Offertory." This was an indication that the new Service embodied a more Sacrificial doctrine than its two predecessors. The emphasis was more Sacrificial than 1559, but less so than 1637. The three rubrics are compared below to indicate the divergent emphases:

1559	1662	1637
. . . and earnestly exhort them to remember the poor, saying one or mo of of these sentences following, as he thinketh most convenient by his discretion.	Then shall the Priest return to the Lord's Table, and begin the Offertory, saying one or more of these sentences following, as he thinketh most convenient by his discretion.	. . . and earnestly exhort them to remember the poor, saying (for the Offertory) one or more of these sentences following, as he thinketh most convenient by his discretion, according to the length or shortness of the time the people are offering.

The Offertory sentences of 1662 were the same as 1559. They were, therefore, less indicative of Sacrifice than the additions of Wedderburn in 1637.

But the two rubrics succeeding the sentences connected the elements and alms most intimately with the offering. Once again, the emphasis is more Sacrificial than in 1559, but less so than in 1637:

1559	1662	1637
Then shall the Churchwardens, or some other by them appointed, gather the devotion of the people, and put the same into the poor men's box: and upon the offering days ap-	Whilst these sentences are in reading, the Deacons, Churchwardens, or other fit person appointed for that purpose shall receive the Alms for the Poor, and other de-	While the Presbyter distinctly pronounceth some or all of these sentences for the Offertory, the Deacon or (if no such present) one of the Churchwardens shall receive the de-

1559	1662	1637
pointed, every man and woman shall pay to the Curate the due and accustomed offerings: after which done, the Priest shall say,	votions of the people in a decent bason to be provided by the Parish for that purpose; and reverently bring it to the Priest, who shall humbly present and place it upon the holy Table. And when there is a Communion, the Priest shall then place upon the Table so much Bread and Wine, as he shall think sufficient after which done the Priest shall say,	votions of the People there present for that purpose. And when all have offered, he shall reverently bring the said bason with the oblations therein, and deliver it to the Presbyter, who shall humbly present it before the Lord, and set it upon the holy Table. And the Presbyter shall then offer up and place the bread and wine prepared for the Sacrament upon the Lord's Table, that it may be ready for that service. And then he shall say,

Two significant changes in the Prayer for the Church Militant continued the Sacrificial emphasis of the Offertory.

The first change, a verbal one, added "and oblations" to the petition to "accept our alms." The correlative rubric for omitting mention of "alms" when none were offered also added "or oblations." Whether "oblations" referred to the elements or the alms themselves,[186] the emphasis was more Sacrificial by the very addition of the word. There may have been ambiguity in the use of "oblations"; but there was *studied* ambiguity since 1552 in such words as "alms," "devotion," "remember," and "pay."

A second addition to the prayer restored the commemoration of the departed. The new phrase read as follows:

And we also bless thy holy Name for all thy servants departed this life in thy faith and fear; beseeching thee to give us grace so to follow their good examples, that with them we may be partakers of thy heavenly kingdom:

The prayer for the Church was followed by an exhortation, the same that had appeared second in 1559. A preceding rubric adumbrated the waning of frequent Communion by its provision that this exhortation was to be read on Sundays as well as Holy Days preceding a Communion. There was one interesting addition in the transferral of specific sins from the third exhortation to this preparatory one. Apparently there had been danger of unworthy reception when these sins were read at the Service itself due to the embarrassment entailed in withdrawing in the presence of family and friends.

The exhortation composed in answer to Bucer's pleas for more penitential emphasis was to be read when people were negligent about communicating. Significantly, the word "sacrifice" appeared when the priest urged parishioners to attend to "remembrance of the sacrifice of his death." Previously, the words were "in remembrance of his death." There was another approach to traditional usage when the strictures against "gazing and looking on" were deleted. Apparently, these strong words had given the impression that non-attendance was preferable to passive attendance.

In the exhortation provided for the Service itself, as mentioned above, the references to heinous crimes were deleted, having been transferred to the preparatory exhortation when there was no danger of embarrassment or unworthy reception as a result of shame.

The Invitation and Confession were unchanged, except that the latter was to be said "by one of the Ministers."

There was perhaps a rapprochement to private Confession in the rubric for Absolution. In 1559, the Priest or Bishop was to "say thus." In 1662 he was to "pronounce this Absolution."

The Comfortable Words, Prefaces, and Prayer of Humble Access were unchanged, except that in the rubric for the latter, "Lord's Table" replaced "God's board."

The only changes in the Consecration Prayer involved manual acts. The rubric specified:

When the Priest, standing before the Table, hath so ordered the Bread and Wine, that he may with the more readiness and decency break the Bread before the people, and take the Cup into his hands, he shall say the Prayer of Consecration, as followeth.

After Communion, two important new rubrics indicated increased emphasis on the presence of Christ. The first provided for contingencies when the supply of consecrated elements was exhausted during distribution of Communion. In such cases the "Priest" was to consecrate more by reading the narration of the Institution and Words of Institution. The rubric was as follows:

> If the consecrated Bread and Wine be all spent before all have communicated, the Priest is to consecrate more according to the Form before prescribed; beginning at (Our Saviour Christ in the same night,) for the blessing of the Bread; and at (Likewise after Supper,) for the blessing of the Cup.

The second new Communion rubric directed the "Minister" to place remaining consecrated elements on the Table with reverence and to cover them with a linen cloth.

After these two rubrics, the Service concluded with the same prayers as that of 1559.

There were several further changes in the concluding rubrics. There was an indication that lay participation in the Communion Service had dwindled in the provision that a truncated Service could be said not only on Holy Days but even "Upon the Sundays." More important doctrinally was a rubric, following the lead of 1637, indicating reverence for remaining consecrated elements. No longer was the Curate to have these sacred elements for his own use. They were to be consumed reverently within the Church:

1559	1662	1637
And if any of the bread or wine remain, the Curate shall have it to his own use.	And if any of the Bread and Wine remain unconsecrated, the Curate shall have it to his own use; but if any remain of that which was consecrated, it shall not be carried out of the church, but the Priest and such other of the Communicants as he shall then call unto him, shall, immediately after	And if any of the bread and wine remain which is consecrated, it shall be reverently eaten and drunk by such of the communicants only, as the Presbyter which celebrates shall take unto him; but it shall not be carried out of the church.

1559	1662	1637
	the Blessing, reverently eat and drink the same.	

Although the stricture for ecclesiastical duties at Easter remained, there was no provision for weekly payment to the parish. As in 1637, money offered at the "Offertory" was disposed of by the Minister and Churchwardens, and if necessary, the Ordinary.

There was, moreover, a very important addition to the 1662 Service, doctrinally significant for its emphasis on true and real Presence. Paradoxically, the "Black Rubric" was restored, but *with a highly important verbal change*. Cosin, Wren, and the great Carolines had taught a "true and real" Presence while denying corporal or carnal presence. In 1552, Cranmer's "Black Rubric" even denied a "reall and essenciall presence there beeyng of Chrystes naturall fleshe and bloude." In 1662 the word "corporal" neatly replaced "reall and essenciall." The "Black Rubric" had come full circle. It now taught Real Presence. The two versions of this historic rubric are compared below with the significant verbal change italicized:

1552	1662
Wheras it is ordeyned in the booke of common prayer, in the administracion of the Lordes Supper, that the Communicantes kneelynge shoulde receiue the holye Communion: whiche thyng well mente, for a sygnificacyon of the humble and grateful acknowledgeynge of the benefites of Christe, geuen unto the woorthye receyuer, and to auoyde the prophanacion and dysordre which about the holye communion myghte elles ensue. Lest yet the same kneelynge myght be thought or taken otherwyse, we dooe declare that it is not mente thereby, that any adoracion is doone, or oughte to bee doone,	Whereas it is ordained in this Office for the Administration of the Lord's Supper, that the Communicants should receive the same Kneeling; (which order is well meant, for a signification of our humble and grateful acknowledgement of the benefits of Christ therein given to all worthy Receivers, and for the avoiding of such profanation and disorder in the holy Communion, as might otherwise ensue;) yet, lest the same kneeling should by any persons, either out of ignorance and infirmity, or out of malice and obstinacy, be misconstrued and depraved; It is hereby declared, That

1552	1662
eyther unto the Sacramentall bread or wyne there bodelye receyued, or unto anye reall and essenciall presence there beeyng of Chrystes naturall fleshe and bloude. For as concernynge the Sacramentall bread and wyne, they remayne styll in theyr verye naturall substaunces, and therfore may not bee adored, for that were Idolatrye to be abhorred of all faythful christians. And as concernynge the natural bodye and bloud of our sauior Christ, they are in heauen and not here: for it is agaynst the trueth of Christes true naturall bodye, to be in moe places then in one at one tyme.	thereby no adoration is intended, or ought to be done, either unto the Sacramental Bread or Wine there bodily received, or unto any *Corporal* Presence of Christ's natural Flesh and Blood. For the Sacramental Bread and Wine remain still in their very natural substances, and therefore may not be adored; (for that were Idolatry, to be abhorred of all faithful Christians;) and the natural Body and Blood of our Saviour Christ are in Heaven, and not here; it being against the truth of Christ's natural Body to be at one time in more places than one.

The Restoration Service of 1662 was substantially the Service molded by Thomas Cranmer in 1552. It had acquired the aura of martyrdom and was identified with all that was best in a united Church of England. Neither Presbyterians nor Laudians were pleased with the conservative 1662 revision. Concessions granted the Presbyterians were doctrinally insignificant. The Laudians, however, through the astute insistence of John Cosin, did win some concessions. This conservative revision was used by the Church of England in America. It was destined to provide the basis for the first native American Service a century hence. It has been to the present day the official Lord's Supper of the historic Church of England. But it was clear in the seventeenth century that if ever a group of Laudians or "Catholics" broke away from the Establishment, they would be free to evolve a Service more consonant with ancient liturgies and the Service of 1549, a Service that would clearly connect elements with Sacrifice and perduring Real Presence. This is precisely what happened in the interesting Nonjuror phenomenon.

CHAPTER V

The Communion Services of 1718 and 1764

The Restoration settlement really did not "settle" religious contro- versy in England. Charles II was succeeded by still another Stuart, James II, but James did not last long. In 1688 he was deposed and William of Orange was offered the English throne.

With the accession of William and Mary, a portentous phe- nomenon occurred. Archbishop Sancroft, eight Bishops, some four hundred priests, and many laymen refused to take the oath of allegiance to the new sovereigns.[1] Their refusal resulted in the Nonjuror phenomenon which was to influence future Communion Services to an extent far exceeding the number of Nonjurors.[2] Their schism flourished at least until the death of their last Bishop in 1805.[3]

At first the Nonjurors, with certain adjustments in the Collects for the King, adhered to the established Communion Service. Soon, however, a sizeable group of Nonjuror laymen and clergy, aware of their novel freedom from Erastianism, sought a return to ancient practices.[4]

Those advocating a return to ancient (and 1549) practices were known as Usagers. Those opposed to deviation from 1662 were Non-Usagers. With this division in sentiment the seeds for still another schism were sown. Controversy raged over return of four usages to the Communion Service: the mixed Chalice, remem- brance of the departed, an oblation, and an invocation.[5]

As further schism seemed imminent, leading Nonjurors con- vened in 1716 to discuss the controversy. At that tempestuous meeting Thomas Brett was adamant for the Usagers. But the Non- Usagers were equally obdurate and refused compromise. Finally, the latter group retired from the conference in anger resolved to follow the established Service. Another schism was finalized. Never again did Nonjurors meet as a single body.[6]

Usager Bishops again convened in December, 1717. At that meeting an important step was taken for the future of the Communion Services of Scotland and America. The Bishops agreed to publish a new Communion Office "agreeable to the primitive liturgies, taking in as much of the present established office as might be conveniently done." [7]

For the interim an injunction was issued to Nonjuror clergy authorizing certain usages "untill a fuller & better Form can be fram'd." Henceforth, a recitation of the two great commandments was to replace the Decalogue; water was to be mixed "openly" with wine; "militant here on earth" was to be omitted from the Prayer for the Church; a clear petition for the departed was to be added; and most significant, an Oblation and Invocation were to follow the Words of Institution.[8]

Except for Jeremy Collier, who sometime in that confused period was elected Primus, only Thomas Brett signed the injunction. But it should be noted that one Thomas Deacon signed also as one of three witnesses.[9]

The promised "better Form" Communion Service was issued on March 1, 1718. Until Thomas Deacon drew up a similar Office in 1748,[10] the Communion Service of 1718 served Nonjuror Usagers. This Service of 1718 was destined to exert profound influence on the Scottish Communion Office of 1764, and through that Service on the first American Service in 1789.

The immediate literary authorship of 1718 is shrouded in the mists of Nonjuror history.[11] Nevertheless, two men who were prominent in all the steps leading to revision and who wrote profusely were Thomas Brett and Thomas Deacon. Both of them clearly expressed Nonjuror Eucharistic doctrine. The doctrine expressed in their writings is the doctrine of the Communion Service of 1718.

JOHN JOHNSON

To understand the Eucharistic theology of the Nonjurors, it is necessary to know something of the theology of John Johnson, Rector of Cranbrook in Kent. Johnson was not one of the authors of the 1718 Service; in fact, he consistently adhered to the 1662 Service despite a preference for earlier forms. Yet he reflected mature High Anglicanism, and it was to his writings that the Usagers frequently referred as a defense and explanation of their Eucharistic position.[12]

Johnson and Sacrifice

Johnson argued that the Lord's Supper was a Sacrifice. It was necessary to attain forgiveness of sins not committed and not repented at the time of Calvary. Christ instituted the Eucharist as a Means to obtain Pardon for these sins:

> Sin cannot be forgiven, 'till they who are guilty of it, have sincerely repented, and used the proper Methods of obtaining Pardon; and that therefore, if Christ Jesus have instituted any Sacrifice, as necessary to be offer'd, in order to obtain this Pardon; we are never to presume, that we have gain'd the End, 'till we have us'd the Means.[13]

Unlike the sixteenth-century reformers, Johnson taught that Christ offered *Himself*, His Body and Blood, at the Last Supper. There was no evidence of any other offering of Himself: "Neither Christ nor his Apostles have declar'd that He did at any other Time or Place, as a Priest, offer his Body and Blood to the Father here on Earth." [14]

The reformers had denied that Christ offered Himself at the Last Supper. Since He was not offered then, He was not offered in the Mass.[15] Johnson met this traditional argument head-on. Christ *did* offer Himself at the Last Supper:

> It has been thought an Objection against the Sacrifice of the Eucharist, that St. *Paul* says, Christ was *but once offered:* And if, indeed, He had offer'd Bread and Wine only, when He had instituted the *Eucharist,* and had afterwards on the Cross made a distinct, Priestly Oblation of his natural Body and Blood; then there would have been some force in this Objection: but it appears by the account now given, that He did, as a Priest, offer his Body and Blood, in the *Eucharist,* under the Pledges of Bread and Wine; that He was afterwards slain as a Sacrifice on the Cross: but there is no Evidence, that He did again on the Cross make the Oblation of his Body and Blood, as a Priest. . . .[16]

In arguing that the Redemption was one act, Johnson countered the arguments of those who distinguished the oblations of the Last Supper, Cross, and heavenly priesthood:

Christ entered upon his Priestly Office in the Eucharist. . . . there he began the One Oblation; there he offered himself in a spiritual mystical Manner, as he afterwards did corporally upon the Cross. . . . In the institution of the Eucharist this Sacrifice was first made, in our Saviour's Will and Intention; then that he made the tender of his Body and Blood, after which the actual Payment presently followed. . . .[17]

Johnson professed a presence of Christ in the elements.[18] The bread and wine remained in their natural substances, but in mystery and power they were the Body and Blood of Christ. The offering in the Mass was an oblation of the "Sacramental Body and Blood":

. . . the Bread and Wine then offer'd are in Mystery and inward Power, tho' not in Substance, the Body and Blood of Christ: this raises the Dignity of the Christian Sacrifice above those of the Law of *Moses*, and all that were ever offer'd by mere Men: As it is Natural Bread and Wine, 'tis the Sacrifice of *Melchisedeck*, and of the most ancient Philosophers: As it is the Sacrifice of the Sacramental Body and Blood of Christ, it is the most sublime and divine Sacrifice that Men or Angels can offer.[19]

Johnson reflected mature high Anglicanism in his portrayal of the Eucharist as a Memorial and Representation. He agreed with his predecessors that it was not the "Substantial Body and Blood" that was offered. It was a spiritual offering that propitiated God:

When we say, we offer Bread and Wine, we don't only mean the products and first-fruits of the earth; but the Memorials of Christ's Passion, the Authoritative Representations of Christ's Body and Blood; or if you will speak with the primitive Church, the true Body and Blood of Christ; and on the other side, when you say we offer the Body and Blood, we don't mean, what is commonly call'd the Sacrifice of the Mass, not the Substantial Body and Blood of Christ, much less his Divinity; but the Bread and Wine, substituted by the Divine Lord for his own Body and Blood; and upon which God at the Prayers of the Priests and People, sends down his peculiar spiritual Benediction, by which it becomes a Sacrifice of a sweet-smelling Savour, as being therefore fully consecrated into the spiritual Body and Blood of Christ, and therefore fit therewith to propitiate the Divine Mercy.[20]

Johnson did not believe the Eucharist could be offered for the "sins" of the dead;[21] it was "only for the Sins of the Living." [22] Yet he argued that the Eucharist should be applied to the "Souls of particular Persons." It was the "main Channel" of Grace: "Christ instituted the Sacrifice of the Eucharist, as the main Channel, by which all divine Graces and Favours should be constantly communicated to his Church, and apply'd to the Souls of particular Persons. . . ." [23]

Johnson and Real Presence

In Johnson's doctrine, Christ was present in a true but not a substantial sense. He went beyond his Laudian predecessors in his development of this "true but not substantial" presence. By true, he meant that the force, dignity, and effect of Christ's Body was present even before reception. The elements offered remained bread and wine, but they were "in Mystery and inward Power, tho' not in Substance, the Body and Blood of Christ." [24]

He was a keen student of the primitive Church. It was his conviction that the early Christians believed the elements to remain bread and wine; that they called them Types of Christ's Body and Blood, but meant something more than the imperfect Types under the Law; that they believed these elements to be Christ's Body and Blood, not substantially, but in power and effect. He attempted to express this conviction by enumerating early beliefs:

I. That the primitive Church believ'd the Body and Blood in the Sacrament to be Bread and Wine.

II. That they believ'd them not to be the Body and Blood of Christ in Substance; and therefore often call'd them Types, Figures, Symbols of the Body and Blood.

III. That they did not esteem the such cold and imperfect Types, as those before and under the Law. Nay,

IV. They believ'd them to be the true spiritual Body and Blood of Christ, tho' not in Substance, yet in Power and Effect.[25]

The elements were Christ's Body and Blood because, after Consecration, they had "all the beneficial Effects, that his natural Body and Blood, influenc'd and anointed by the Holy Ghost, could have done, if it had been capable of Oral Manducation." [26] The elements were, therefore, "the very Body and Blood, tho' not in Substance, yet in Spirit, Power, and Effect." [27]

The ancient Church believed there was a great mystery in the Real Presence. "The Ancients believ'd this to be the Mystery

couch'd in the Sacramental Bread and Wine; viz. that they were in
Substance what they were before, but by the especial Presence of
the Spirit," they were also Christ's Body and Blood.[28]

Because the elements were more than a figurative Body and
Blood, yet less than substantial, Christ's presence in the Eucharist
was "the middle between these Extremes." The Holy Spirit "made"
these elements the Body and Blood, but in a mysterious sense that
could only be apprehended by faith:

> They are the mysterious Body and Blood. . . . I mean neither
> substantial nor yet merely figurative, but the middle between these
> Extremes, viz. the Bread and Wine made the Body and Blood of Christ,
> by the secret Power of the Spirit. . . .[29]

Despite the efficacy he attributed to the Holy Spirit, Johnson
denied a presence of Christ's soul and Divinity.[30] His Body and
Blood were truly present, but "not the Divinity and Human Soul of
Christ Jesus." [31]

Johnson had little patience with the teaching that Christ was
present only *in use*. His Body and Blood was made present by the
energy of the Holy Spirit, and that took place independently of any
faith on the part of the recipients. Johnson stated bluntly that faith
cannot make present what is absent:

> And indeed, if the Eucharist were not the Body and Blood before
> Distribution, it could not be made so by a Post-fact of the Communi-
> cants; for Faith can give Existence to nothing; cannot make That pres-
> ent which is absent.[32]

The Holy Spirit was all-important in Johnson's system. "We
may from hence learn, for what Reason the Ancients call'd the
Eucharistical Bread, the spiritual Body of Christ, *viz*. because it
was what it was by the peculiar Energy of the Holy Ghost." [33] The
Holy Spirit made Christ objectively present; the elements became
"Divine powerful Representations of the Original Body and
Blood." [34] Therefore, Christ was present even to an unworthy recipient, who did indeed *truly*, albeit not spiritually, partake of the
sacrament.[35]

The descent of the Spirit resulted in the "further consecration"
of the elements:

> . . . after the Oblation of the Bread and Wine as the Memorials
> of the Grand Sacrifice; there is a solemn Prayer, that God would sent

his Spirit or his Divine Benediction, for the further Consecration of them, after they had been first offered as a Sacrifice to God.[36]

Not only the Words of Institution, but the Oblation and Invocation "contribute toward the Consecration of the Elements into the Body and Blood":

> Now I have already proved, that the Holy Ghost was, by the Vote of Antiquity, the principal Cause of the Bread and Wine's becoming the Body and Blood. It now remains only that I show, that the Subordinate or Mediate Cause is, 1. The Reciting the Words of Institutions. 2. The Oblation of the Symbols. 3. The Prayer of Invocation. All these three did, in the Ancient Liturgies, immediately follow each other, in the order that I have mentioned them; and each of them was believed to contribute toward the Consecration of the Elements into the Body and Blood.[37]

The ancients believed that the Eucharist was the Body and Blood not by the faith of communicants, but by the Holy Spirit. It was "perfectly" a Consecration by means of the Invocation, Oblation, and Words of Institution:

> It is evident, that they believ'd the Eucharist to be made the Body and Blood, not by the Faith of the Communicant, but by the Power of the Holy Ghost, or divine Benediction, imparted to it by Means of the Invocation. (I mean perfectly, and finally imparted by this Means, not exclusively of the Words of Institution, and the Oblation.)[38]

According to Johnson, the necessary rites were: 1) the placing of elements on the table; 2) the Words of Institution; 3) the fraction of the bread and pouring of the wine; 4) the priest's Oblation after the Words of Institution in commemoration of Christ's Death, Resurrection, and Ascension; 5) the Invocation; 6) intercessions for all states of the Church.[39]

Nonjuror (and early American) theologians frequently referred to the writings of John Johnson of Kent as justification for their Eucharistic doctrine. Although loyal to the established Service, Johnson never reconciled this loyalty with his mature Laudian doctrine. His influence on the Nonjuror Services and the first American Service was freely acknowledged by the immediate framers of those rites.

THOMAS BRETT

Thomas Brett was consecrated a Nonjuror Bishop in 1716. Throughout the Usage controversy, he was a moderate and convinced Usager. As a Bishop, he played a prominent role in the meetings and discussions that eventually resulted in a new Communion Service.[40]

Brett was primarily a liturgist, and less a theologian than John Johnson. However, he fortified his liturgical arguments with doctrinal reasons. His Eucharistic position appears clearly in his book on Episcopacy and in his many liturgical writings.

Brett and Sacrifice

At the Last Supper, Christ offered and instituted as "proper a Sacrifice as any of the Jewish Sacrifices." [41] He offered bread and wine; but these elements were His Body and Blood in power and effect. We are to follow His example and offer bread and wine that have become His Body and Blood in power and effect:

> For though he offered *Bread and Wine* he made them his *Body* and *Blood* in Power and Effect. And by that Oblation consigned and offered his own Natural Body to be broken, and his most precious Blood to be shed on the Cross for our Sins. And if *Christ* offered *Bread and Wine* in the Holy Eucharist, we must also do the same, for we are commanded to do as he did, only with this Difference, he offered in Order to his Suffering upon the Cross, we offer in Remembrance of his Death there.[42]

Christ offered the elements before He consecrated them. "He plainly made a Sacrificial Oblation of the Bread and Wine to God, he first presented them to him as an Offering . . . and then Consecrated them to represent his own Body and Blood. . . ." [43] Brett, therefore, argued for a preliminary Oblation. This was done by placing the elements on the altar:

> Now by an Oblation or a Sacrifice, we understand a Reverend and Solemn Presentation of some visible material Gift, to the God we worship. . . . And the Place whereon we offer, present, or lay this material visible Gift or Element, is that which we therefore call the Altar; because the Element or Gift being there laid, from that Moment becomes God's peculiar Property. . . .[44]

The Eucharist was a Sacrifice "perfectly representing by Virtue of its Institution that great and truly meretorious Sacrifice of Christ Himself." It was a Godward Memorial in which "we plainly engage and induce Him to confer on us all the Mercies and Graces purchased for us by that All-sufficient Sacrifice: As Pardon of Sin, Reconciliation to God, Union with *Christ*, a Pledge or Earnest of Eternal Life. . . ." [45]

Because the Eucharist was a Godward Sacrifice or Memorial, it was offered by priests who were given authority "to offer the *Christian Sacrifice. The Representative Sacrifice of the Body and Blood of Christ in the holy Eucharist.*" [46]

The Nonjurors still interpreted the Roman position as teaching that Christ was somehow destroyed in the Eucharist. In Nonjuror theology the bread was Christ's Body in power and effect, the wine His Blood. But "as offered in the Church of *Rome*, as the individual Body and Blood of *Christ* broken on the Cross, we detest and abominate it, as a scandalous Corruption of his holy Institution." [47]

Nor did the elements represent Christ's soul and Divinity. The offering was a representation of the Passion, but "it is evident from the Scriptures that it is not the whole Christ, Body and Soul, and Divinity Hypostatically united, as the Papists also blasphemously teach." [48]

Brett departed from Rome in denying that the Eucharist was an offering of Christ. His doctrine was that the elements were a representation of Calvary whereby Christ's Sacrifice was pleaded. Since the offering was a representation, the Person represented could not be offered. Nevertheless, it was a "true and proper" Sacrifice:

> For the *Representative* cannot be the Person *Represented;* the Thing *signifying,* cannot be the Thing *signified:* For the very notion of a *Representative* implies something distinct from that which is *Represented* by it. Those therefore who charge the Doctrine of the *Eucharistical Sacrifice* as savouring of *Popery,* either know not what *Popery* is, or do not understand what a *Sacrifice* is, or have no right Notion of the *Eucharist* itself: For nothing can be more directly opposite to the doctrine of *Transubstantiation,* or to *the Sacrifices of Masses in the which it was commonly said that the Priests did offer* Christ *for the Quick and the Dead,* than this Doctrine of the *representative Sac-*

rifice of the Eucharist. For if the *Representation* of *Christ's* Body and Blood be there offered; then it is most certain *Christ* himself cannot be there offered. . . .[49]

Since the Eucharist was an unbloody Sacrifice, Christ's actual Blood was not offered. "For how can this be an unbloody Sacrifice, or a Sacrifice without Blood, if therein the very Blood of Christ was offered up to God." [50]

Brett urged a petition for the departed, as in the first liturgy of Edward VI. It should be placed after the Oblation: "And as to the Petition for the Saints departed, as in the first liturgy of King Edward VI, from whence it is taken into this, I trust I have . . . proved the necessity of it; This intercession is also removed to its proper Place after the Oblation. . . ." [51]

Christ commanded us to give Thanks at the Eucharist. He gave Thanks at the taking and breaking of the bread, "and therefore to take the Bread and break it without Thanksgiving, is not doing as he did, and commanded us to do." [52] The Thanksgiving should be restored before the Words of Institution as in the ancient liturgies: ". . . in all of them, except the *Roman*, there is an Eucharistical Prayer immediately preceding the Words of Institution, wherein Thanks are given for the Creation and Redemption of Mankind." [53]

Brett and Real Presence

In 1720, Brett explained the 1718 Communion Office. His defense was an excellent exposition of the Usager rite:

We had special Regard to the Communion Office of the Church of *England*. . . . In the Order wherein the Prayers have been placed, we have followed that Liturgy, and particularly have set the Confession, Absolution, comfortable Sentences of Scriptures, and Prayer of humble Access, immediately before the Distribution of the Elements: In which Order of Prayers, that Liturgy has followed the general Practice of the Ancient Church, and the present established Liturgy has deviated from it. But then where both these have deviated from the Practice of the Church, there we thought it necessary to follow the much elder Liturgies, rather than either of them. . . . As to the controverted Points, (for the sake of which only we thought it necessary to alter the Communion-Office) we have followed the first Liturgy of King *Edward* VI, excepting where we found it not so agreeable as we could with to the ancient Liturgies. Therefore we directed the Elements to be placed on the Table, and Wine to be put into the Cup, and a little pure and clean Water to be put into it immediately after the Offertory. And our Prayer for the Saints departed is in the very Words of that Liturgy. And our Oblation and Invocation had been the same as there, but that upon Examination we found the Order of those Prayers to be inverted . . . we chose rather to follow the much more ancient Practice of the Church, than the first Liturgy of King *Edward* VI.[54]

The Usages were necessary and primitive practices of Catholic worship. "For I am fully convinced that all of these are necessary, primitive and Catholic parts of Divine Worship, and therefore that no Human Authority can abolish or dispense with our Obligation to the Practice of them." [55]

Brett reiterated Johnson's arguments for the Oblation and Invocation. Both were necessary for a "perfect" Consecration. The stress on perfect Consecration led to insinuations that Brett advocated Transubstantiation. Anyone familiar with Brett's doctrine of Representation and Memorial would not so interpret him. His statement in the *Dissertation* denied such teaching unequivocally and polemically: "However, hoping what I have said may satisfy the unprejudiced at least, that we are as far from favouring Transubstantiation, or any other corrupt or erroneous Doctrine of the Church of *Rome,* as any of those that most zealously oppose us." [56]

Bread and wine were received; these were His *Sacramental* Body and Blood: "I do believe the Bread and Wine to be the only Body and Blood appointed to be received in the Holy Eucharist. And I believe them to be made his Sacramental Flesh and Blood." The Sacramental Flesh and Blood was "the full and perfect Representative of his Body and Blood; his very Body and Blood in Power and Effect." [57]

It was a quickening "Virtue" from the descent of the Holy Spirit that made the elements Christ's Body and Blood in power and effect:

The Holy Ghost descending upon, and operating in the Bread and the Cup, may give it a quickening, life-giving Virtue, and so make it Christ's Body in Power and Effect; and it may then as properly be called Christ's Body and actually be so. . . . His Sacramental or Spiritual Body, that is, Bread and Wine mixed with Water, made his Body and Blood in full Power and Effect by the Operation of the Holy

Ghost, is as effectual by Virtue of his Institution, as his natural Body and Blood could be.[58]

The elements represented Christ's Body and Blood; the latter were discerned by the eye of Faith:

For if it be still *Bread* and *Wine,* even at the very time it is to be eaten and drank, as St. *Paul* plainly declares it to be, and yet the *Body* and *Blood* of *Christ* is there also to be *discern'd* or seen, as the same Apostle also teaches, then must the Bread and Wine fully and perfectly represent the *Body* and *Blood* of Christ, and we must believe it to do so, and discern or see it by the Eye of Faith. . . .[59]

The elements, however, represented neither soul nor Divinity. Nor did the wine represent Blood "as in the Body," but as shed. The bread represented the Body as separate from the Blood. Therefore, the glorified Body of Christ was not present in the Eucharist:

That which is represented in the Eucharist is neither the Divinity nor the *Human Soul* of *Christ,* but only his *Body* and *Blood* separated from both, and from one another. The Blood is not represented by the Element of Wine, as in the Body, but as shed and separated from it; which is utterly irreconciliable with, and plainly contradictory to the Popish Doctrine of the Mass. . . . The *Bread* and *Wine* therefore representing *Christ's* Body as broken, and his Blood as shed and poured out from it, can by no means represent, much less really be, the very individual glorified Body of *Christ* now in Heaven, and Personally united, not only to the Human Soul, but also to the Divine Nature.[60]

The Oblation that followed the Words of Institution dedicated the elements to *God:* "For Consecration consists in the Oblation or Dedication of something to God, and therefore must be performed by some address made to him, and not by Words directed and applied to men." [61]

The Invocation called upon the Holy Spirit to complete and perfect the Consecration. Therefore it should follow the Words of Institution and Oblation, "which certainly is the most natural Order, the Holy Spirit by His descent completing and perfecting the Consecration." [62]

The Consecration Prayer of the English Church was inadequate. "How can the Form of Consecration in the Church of England be justified, where no Prayer is added after this Word of God is recited, but that Word concludes all, and the Priest, after he has pronounced it, proceeds immediately to receive and distribute. . . ." [63]

As a corollary to the above argument, Brett opposed the rubric for a second Consecration by mere recitation of Words of Institution:

> The Rubric directs that he shall only recite the Words of the Institution. Is not this a demonstrative Argument that this Church teaches that nothing more is necessary to the Consecration of the Elements, than the pronouncing over them the Words of Institution.[64]

England had departed from Tradition. Antiquity was on the side of the Nonjurors:

> We have an universal uninterrupted Tradition, that this Sacrament was consecrated by pronouncing the Words of Institution, by making an Oblation of the Elements as the Representative Body and Blood of Christ, with a thankful Remembrance of his Death, and by a Petition for the divine Benediction, or the holy Spirit to descend upon the Elements. . . .[65]

Reflecting Nonjuror scholarship, Brett embraced the 1549 Service where it accorded with his view of antiquity and departed from it where it did not. Most important for the Services he influenced was his insistence that "universal uninterrupted Tradition" taught that elements were consecrated by Words of Institution, Oblation, and Invocation. Although there were shades of difference between his writings and those of John Johnson, Brett was pervasively influenced by the scholar from Kent, especially in the importance of Oblation and Invocation to make the elements Christ in virtue, power, and effect. Brett was not alone in this teaching. He found a Nonjuror ally in Thomas Deacon, the Manchester Nonjuror.

THOMAS DEACON

As in the case of Brett, the precise extent of Deacon's role in 1718 will be forever a matter of conjecture. It is clear that he played a prominent part in the deliberations immediately preceding the famous Nonjuror revision. At one time Henry Broxap went so far as to state that "it appears extremely probable that Deacon had the chief share in translating and drawing up the new liturgy. . . ." [66]

Broxap's statement probably exaggerated Deacon's influence, but it is indicative of his prominence that in 1719 when a complete Nonjuror Prayer Book was issued, Deacon's name again appeared as a principal witness.[67]

Deacon and Sacrifice

Deacon's Eucharistic theology moved within the tradition of John Johnson and Deacon's fellow Nonjurors. Unlike Johnson and Brett, however, his doctrine appears exhaustively under the cover of *one* book.[68]

Deacon's doctrine on Sacrifice appears succinctly in a series of questions and answers in his *Shorter Catechism*. The Eucharist was an offering of Christ's Body and Blood to the Father. However, it was an offering through representative elements which were not that natural Body and Blood. At the Last Supper Christ offered His natural Body and Blood through representative elements. Once again, the elements were *not* that natural Body and Blood, but representations of the same. The bread represented His broken Body; the mixed wine his shed Blood. The Eucharist is a representative offering of that same great Sacrifice, an act of thanksgiving that procures all the blessings of Christ's Sacrifice:

Q. When did our Saviour begin to offer himself for the sins of all men?
A. When he instituted the Eucharist.

Q. What Sacrifice did he then offer?
A. His natural Body and Blood.

Q. In what manner?
A. As separate from each other.

Q. Why?
A. Because his Body was considered as broken, and his Blood as shed, for the sins of the world.

Q. But was it natural for him to break his own Body and shed his own Blood?
A. No; and therefore he did it in mystery, and offered his broken Body and shed Blood under the symbols of Bread and mixt Wine, which he therefore called his Body and Blood.

Q. How was the great sacrifice of CHRIST represented before it was performed?
A. By all the sacrifices of the old law.

Q. And how is it represented since?
A. By the Eucharist, which is a sacrifice of thanksgiving.
Q. What is the nature and design of the Eucharistic Sacrifice, when it is celebrated according to CHRIST's institution?
A. It is a solemn commemorative oblation of CHRIST's great sacrifice to God the Father, and procures us the virtue of it.[69]

The priest sets forth the elements and thereby represents the all-sufficient Sacrifice of Christ. "The priest acts as the visible Representative of Jesus Christ himself in his Priestly character, and does by visible signs represent and set forth before the Almighty Father, the all-sufficient and meritorious death and Sacrifice of his . . . beloved Son." [70]

Because the bread represented Christ's Body, and the wine His Blood, the elements assumed great importance in Deacon's system. He joined Brett in stressing the necessity of preliminary oblation. The people were to participate intimately in this important rite; they were to offer financial oblations for the purchase of the elements:

The Oblations are made in money, the common value of all things; however, that the ancient custom notwithstanding may be preserved, of the Eucharist's being taken out of the free-will-offerings of the people, the Bread and Wine prepared for the Eucharist be paid for out of those offerings.[71]

Deacon subscribed to the theory that destruction was involved in Sacrifice. Therefore he had to reconcile his doctrine of representative elements that were not Christ's natural Body and Blood with the necessity of destruction. He did this by distinguishing destruction from offering. "The offering of it, and making the atonement are never imputed to the act of killing, but to what was done before or after it." [72] The necessary rite in *every* Sacrifice (and therefore the Mass) was an Offertory prayer. "The only rite necessary to the offering of all Sacrifice, as never being omitted either by *Jew* or *Gentile* was that of Prayer, addressed to that god to whom the sacrifice was presented." [73]

Deacon argued from St. Paul's words about eating the Body of Christ. Because the Apostle spoke of eating, he must have meant a Sacramental and not natural Body. "And it is further to be observed that the prepared body of Christ mentioned . . . does

. . . imply a body fit to be eaten; and therefore the Apostle must mean, the Sacramental Body of Christ." [74]

Anglicans had always called the Eucharist an act of praise and thanksgiving. This traditional description could be maintained because the principal design of the offering of Christ's Sacrifice through representative elements was "to praise and glorify God for the great work of redemption in Christ Jesus." [75]

But Deacon displayed his Nonjuror theology when he stressed that Christ made His sacrificial oblation in will and intention at the Last Supper:

> Upon the cross the ransom was paid, the satisfaction made; his natural Body and Blood were the price, which he had agreed to deposit for the salvation of all men: but in the institution of the Eucharist this sacrifice was first made in our Saviour's will and intention; it was then, that he made the tender of his Body and Blood, and the actual payment followed soon after. . . .[76]

Because Christ offered the Sacrifice while yet alive, he offered the bread and wine as separated from each other. The bread represented His Body, the mixed wine His Blood. But there was no separation of Body from Blood in a substantial or natural sense:

> Our Saviour, as being both owner and priest, made the oblation while he was yet alive: and because it was impossible for him to make the priestly atonement, as was the common course, while the sacrifice was dead; therefore he did both in one: for he offered the Bread and mixed Wine, as his Body and Blood, apart from each other; and so did that by representation which could not be done by him in real substance.[77]

By the "do this" of Scripture, Christ commanded the Apostles to make a memorial of His Sacrifice. Therefore, in Deacon's terminology, memorial and Sacrifice are synonymous. The Apostles were commissioned to perpetuate this memorial: "Do or offer this for a memorial of me, he gave them a commission to continue the use of this sacrifice: and when he thus consecrated them, he further gave a perpetual duration to this commission. . . ." [78]

The representative offering is made to God for all blessings and mercies. It is the most efficacious of prayers:

> . . . when can we pray with more reasonable hope of success, than when we put up our petitions to God in virtue of that sacrifice

instituted by his Son, in virtue of Body and Blood represented to God by Symbols of his own appointment.[79]

Deacon was confronted with another difficulty that faces those who deny a substantial presence of Christ in the consecrated elements. He wanted to teach that the sacrifice of the Mass and Calvary were identical. But how could they be identical if the elements were not, when all is said and done, Christ's natural Body and Blood? He solved the difficulty by saying the Mass was one with Christ's Sacrifice in mystery, albeit not in substance. Its efficacy flowed "not by any separate power that is in it as a sacrifice distinct from that of Jesus Christ, but by its being the same with it, the same in mystery though not in substance." [80]

The Nonjurors included the deceased in the offering. But they did not teach purgatory. "Upon the whole here is nothing introduced without unexceptionable warrant: nothing of late beginning. Here is no . . . praying the dead out of Purgatory." [81]

Deacon and Real Presence

Deacon derived his doctrine and practice concerning the Real Presence from what he considered the "doctrines, practices, worship, and discipline" of the primitive Church. He exhorted all Christians to do the same:

. . . the best method for all Churches and Christians to follow, is to lay aside all modern hypotheses, customs, and private opinions, and submit to all the doctrines, practices, worship, and discipline, not of any particular, but of the Ancient and Universal Church of Christ. . . .[82]

He was uncompromising on the four salient usages. "Though we always wished for several other things to be restored to the Church, yet we never insisted on more than these four necessary points." [83] The Invocation, an indispensable usage, "made" the elements the Body and Blood in power, energy, and effect. Deacon believed that one thing was made another; but he denied this entailed change of substance:

. . . The Bread thus consecrated by the secret influence of the Holy Spirit, was the very Body of Christ in power and energy, and to all intents and purposes of religion, and so far as it was possible for one thing to be made another without change of substance. . . .[84]

In his *Shorter Catechism,* Deacon compared consecrated elements to baptismal water. The elements remained as the water remained; but they represented and signified more than appeared to the senses:

Q. Are Baptism and the Eucharist Mysteries?
A. Yes.

Q. Why?
A. Because they are one thing, but represent and signify another.

Q. What other things are Mysteries?
A. All the ceremonies of the Church, which have any spiritual significancy in them.

Q. Why?
A. Because they represent something more to the understanding than appears to the outward senses.[85]

Deacon considered Roman teaching on substantial change an added article of faith. Conversely, he believed the English position a denial of Real Presence. He seemed to think that Nonjuror theology preserved a balance and represented primitive teaching. A remark he made in a letter offers interesting reading: "If Rome makes the Eucharistic elements the natural body and blood of Christ, England will not allow them to be the body and blood in any sense. If the first adds articles of faith, the last virtually renounces one." [86]

It was primitive Christian dogma that bread and wine remained, but in mystery they were Christ's Body and Blood. The Real Presence meant a religious, not natural, Presence:

The Primitive Church indeed never supposed any Body and Blood in the Eucharist, but what was seen, and what they believed to be Bread and mixed Wine: but they considered them there, as the Body and Blood of Christ in mystery, and in a religious though not natural sense; and as such they offered them to God, and therefore as a real sacrifice.[87]

Another primitive practice was distribution of both species. In Nonjuror theology the bread represented only the broken Body, the wine only the shed Blood. Therefore both species were distributed:

It is pretended, that the people in receiving the Body, do at the same time receive the Blood also; but this is all mere human invention. It is evident, that our Saviour intended his Body and Blood to be offered and received in the Eucharist, separate and distinctly from each other.[88]

The Words of Institution made the bread and wine representations of this Body and Blood. But Words of Institution alone were inadequate. The Oblation offers these representative elements to the Father. Finally, the Invocation pleads with the Father to send the Spirit to make the representative elements Christ's Body and Blood in virtue and effect. The elements then become the sacramental Body and Blood, the same as the natural Body and Blood in effect, but not in substance:

These efficacious words are called the words of Institution, and by them the bread and cup are made the Representative Body and Blood of Christ, that is, authoritative representations or symbols of Christ's crucified body and effused blood; and are therefore qualified to be offered to God as the great Christian sacrifice. Accordingly the Priest makes the solemn oblation of them in commemoration of our Saviour's passion, death, resurrection, ascension, and second coming. . . . the Priest acts as the visible Representative of Jesus Christ himself in his Priestly character, and does by visible signs represent and set forth before the Almighty Father, the all-sufficient and meritorious death and sacrifice of his only-begotten and dearly-beloved Son . . . and in order to make the gifts efficacious instruments of conveying those great advantages, the Priest prays to God the Father to sanctify them, by sending his Holy Spirit upon the Bread and Cup offered to him, that he may enliven those Representations of Christ's dead Body and effused Blood, and make them his spiritual life-giving Body and Blood, by filling them with the divine virtue and power of his natural Body and Blood, and thereby making his Sacramental the same thing with his Natural Body and Blood in effect though not in substance. . . .[89]

Thomas Deacon was a young man in 1718; but, together with his Primus, Jeremy Collier, and Thomas Brett, he was instrumental in framing a Communion Service in the tradition of Cranmer's 1549 Service, the Nonjuror Communion Service of 1718. This Service was to have far-reaching influence on all future Services within the Catholic Anglican Eucharistic tradition.

THE COMMUNION SERVICE OF 1718

When it was possible within their theology, the Nonjurors of 1718 followed the 1662 Communion Service. To that extent their liturgy was conservative. But they also incorporated features of 1549 and 1637 and the ancient liturgies.

The Nonjurors were unwilling to restore "Mass" to their title. The title was, therefore, conservative: "The Order for the Administration of the Lord's Supper or Holy Communion." [90]

Although the Service was vividly sacrificial, there was only one minor addition to the rubrics for disposition of communicants. The first rubric provided that "Every priest shall take particular care not to admit any to the Holy Sacrament of the Eucharist, but those whom he knows to be in the Communion of the Church, or else is certified thereof by sufficient testimony."

The "Altar" location was even more sacrificial than in 1637. It was to stand at the "East end." There was another abrupt divergence from current English practice in the restoration of the Introit.

The Altar at the Communion time having a fair white linen cloth upon it, shall stand at the East end of the Church or Chapel. And the Priest and People standing with their faces towards the Altar, shall say or sing (in the same manner as the Psalms for the day are said or sung) for the Introit the Psalm appointed for that day according to that Translation which is in the *Book of Common-Prayer*.

An additional rubric for the Priest indicated that even the Nonjurors were still wedded to the "Northside" of the Altar:

Note, that whenever in this office the Priest is directed to turn to the Altar, or stand or kneel before it, or with his Face towards it, it is always meant that he shall stand or kneel on the Northside thereof.

Psalms were provided for Sundays and Holy Days throughout the year. In most cases, the Introit (as well as Collect, Epistle, and Gospel) was to "serve all the week after."

After "The Lord be with you" and response, a novel adaptation of the penitential litany followed:

Priest

Let us pray.

Then the People shall kneel with their faces toward the Altar; and the Priest turning to it, and standing humbly before it, shall say,

Lord, have mercy upon us.

People

Christ, have mercy upon us.

Priest

Lord, have mercy upon us.

At this point, the Our Father and Collect for Purity were inserted into the litany. The litany continued as follows:

Then shall the Priest turn him to the People, and say,

Jesus said, Thou shalt love the Lord thy God with all thy heart, and with all thy soul, and with all thy mind. This is the first and great Commandment. And the second is like unto it, Thou shalt love thy neighbor as thy self. On these two Commandments hang all the Law and the Prophets. Matth. xxii. 37, 38, 39, 40.

People

Lord, have mercy upon us, and write all thy laws in our hearts, we beseech thee.

The Nonjurors followed the practice of saying the Collects for the King before the Collect of the day.

The rubrics for Epistle and Gospel were similar to 1637 and 1662. The Creed was unchanged except for the oft reiterated direction of 1718 that Priest and People were to face the Altar.

As in 1662, the announcements followed the Creed. The Sermon or homily was followed by the three exhortations in the same order as 1662.

There were two changes in the first exhortation. Instead of an unworthy reception increasing "damnation," it increased "Condemnation." The second change eliminated some of the ambiguity about private Confession and the power of priestly absolution. The change is interesting and significant enough that the two versions (1662 and 1718) are compared below:

1662	1718
. . . let him come to me, or to some other discreet and learned Minister of God's Word, and open his grief; that by the ministry of God's holy Word he may receive the benefit of absolution, together with ghostly counsel and advice, to the quieting of his conscience, and avoiding of all scruple and doubtfulness.	. . . let him come to me or to some other discreet and learned Priest, and confess and open his sin and grief, that of us (as of the Ministers of God) he may receive the benefit of Absolution, together with ghostly counsel and advice, to the quieting of his conscience, and avoiding of all scruple and doubtfulness.

The Nonjuror Offertory was patently sacrificial. An explicit rubric introduced this important part of the Service:

Then shall the Priest begin the Offertory, saying one or more of these Sentences following, as he thinketh most convenient in his discretion, the People kneeling with their faces towards the Altar.

The only change in the Offertory sentences was an elimination of the two longest verses, and the substitution of two short verses teaching generosity to the poor. Four of Wedderburn's sentences were retained; all the sentences Laud had retained from the 1559 rite were used except the longest one.

Another Offertory rubric connected elements with offering even more intimately than 1637 and 1662; it taught in effect that all, even the most indigent, were to offer *something*. This interesting rubric is compared with its immediate predecessors to illustrate Nonjuror emphasis on congregational offering:

1637	1718	1662
While the Presbyter distinctly pronounceth some or all of these sentences for the Offertory, the Deacon or (if no such be present) one of the Churchwardens shall receive the devotions of the People there present in a	Whilst these Sentences are in reading, the Deacons, Churchwardens, or other fit person appointed for that purpose shall receive the devotions of the People there present, in a decent Basin provided for that	Whilst these Sentences are in reading, the Deacons, Churchwardens, or other fit person appointed for that purpose, shall receive the Alms for the Poor, and other devotions of the people, in a decent ba-

1637	1718	1662
bason provided for that purpose. And when all have offered, he shall reverently bring the said bason with the oblations therein, and deliver it to the Presbyter, who shall humbly present it before the Lord, and set it upon the holy Table.	purpose. And that no one may neglect to come to the Holy Communion, by reason of having but little to give, the person who collects the Offerings shall cover the Basin with a fair white linen cloth, so that neither he himself nor any other may see or know what any particular person offers. And when all have offered, he shall reverently bring the said Basin with the Oblations therein to the Priest, who shall humbly present and place it upon the Altar.	son to be provided by the Parish for that purpose; and reverently bring it to the priest, who shall humbly present and place it upon the holy Table.

A third rubric, providing for the mixture and the placing of elements on the Altar, was derived from the Service of 1549:

Then shall the Priest take so much Bread and Wine, as shall suffice for the Persons appointed to receive the Holy Communion; laying the Bread in the Paten, or in some other decent thing prepared for that purpose; and putting the Wine into the Chalice, or else into some fair and convenient Cup prepared for that use, putting thereto in the view of the People a little pure and clean Water; And then setting both the Bread and the Cup upon the Altar, he shall turn to the People, and say,

The Priest then pronounced an Offertory prayer that identified the elements ("Offerings") with the unbloody Sacrifice.

Let us pray.

Then the Priest shall turn to the Altar, and standing humbly before it, he shall say the Collect following.

O Almighty God, who has created us, and placed us in this ministry by the power of thy holy Spirit; may it please thee, O Lord, as we are ministers of the New Testament, and dispensers of thy holy mysteries, to receive us who are approaching thy Holy Altar, according to the multitude of thy mercies, that we may be worthy to offer unto thee this reasonable and unbloody Sacrifice for our Sins and the Sins of the People. Receive it, O God, as a sweet smelling savour, and send down the grace of thy Holy Spirit upon us. And as thou didst accept this worship and service from thy Holy Apostles: so of thy goodness, O Lord, vouchsafe to receive these Offerings from the hands of us sinners, that being made worthy to minister at thy Holy Altar without blame, we may have the reward of good and faithful servants at that great and terrible day of account and just retribution; through our Lord Jesus Christ thy Son, who, with Thee and the Holy Ghost, liveth and reigneth ever one God, world without end. Amen.

After the Preface and Sanctus, the long, magnificent Nonjuror consecration prayer was inaugurated with a doxology for the whole of salvation history, from Creation to Redemption. The signs of the cross were restored to the narration of the Institution, and the people participated intimately by pronouncing "Amen" after both *logia* of Institution.

Johnson and the Nonjurors had insisted on the importance of Oblation and Invocation. Their doctrine bore fruit in this consecration prayer with its Oblation of "this bread and this cup" and an Invocation to the Holy Spirit to descend on these gifts, this bread and cup, to "make" them Christ's Body and Blood. The prayer concluded with a reference to Holy Communion and the Priest's "Amen." The entire prayer, containing Nonjuror doctrine that the elements become "in mystery" the representative Sacrifice through Words of Institution, Oblation, and Invocation is reproduced below:

Immediately after, the Priest shall say,

Holiness is thy nature and thy gift, O Eternal King; Holy is thine only begotten Son our Lord Jesus Christ, by whom thou hast made the worlds; Holy is thine Ever-blessed Spirit, who searcheth all things, even the depths of thine infinite perfection. Holy art thou, almighty and merciful God; thou createdst Man in thine own image, broughtest him into Paradise, and didst place him in a state of dignity and pleasure: And when he had lost his happiness by transgressing thy command, thou of thy goodness didst not abandon and despise him. Thy

Providence was still continued, thy Law was given to revive the sense
of his duty, thy Prophets were commissioned to reclaim and instruct
him. And when the fulness of time was come, thou didst send thine
only begotten Son to satisfy thy Justice, to strengthen our Nature, and
renew thine Image within us: For these glorious ends thine Eternal
Word came down from heaven, was incarnate by the Holy Ghost, born
of the Blessed Virgin, conversed with mankind, and directed his life
and miracles to our salvation: And when his hour was come to offer
the Propitiatory Sacrifice upon the Cross; when he, who had no sin
himself, mercifully undertook to suffer death for our sins, in the same
night that he was betrayed* (a) took bread; and when he had given
thanks, (b) he brake it, and gave it to his disciples, saying, Take, eat,
(c) THIS IS MY BO✠DY, which is given for you, Do this in remembrance of me.

Here the People shall answer,

Amen.

Then shall the Priest say,

Likewise after Supper, (d) he took the Cup; and when he had given
thanks, he gave it to them, saying Drink ye all of this, for (e) THIS
IS MY BLO✠OD of the New Testament, which is shed for you and
for many for the remission of sins; Do this, as oft as ye shall drink it,
in remembrance of me.

Here the People shall answer,

Amen.

Wherefore, having in remembrance his Passion, Death, and Resurrection from the dead; his Ascension into heaven, and second coming with
glory and great power to judge the quick and the dead, and to render
to every man according to his works; we Offer to Thee, our King and
our God, according to his holy Institution, this Bread and this Cup;

---

* Marginal rubrics: "(a) Here the Priest is to take the Paten into
his hands; (b) And here to break the bread; (c) And here to lay his
hand upon all the Bread. (d) Here he is to take the Cup into his hands;
(e) And here to lay his hand upon every vessel (be it Chalice or
Flagon) in which there is any Wine and Water to be consecrated.
(f) Here the Priest shall lay his hand upon the Bread. (g) And here
upon every vessel (be it Chalice or Flagon) in which there is any
Wine and Water."

giving thanks to thee through him, that thou hast vouchsafed us the honour to stand before thee, and to Sacrifice unto thee. And we beseech thee to look favourably on these thy Gifts, which are here set before thee, O thou self-sufficient God: And do thou Accept them to the honour of thy Christ; and send down thine Holy Spirit, the witness of the passion of our Lord Jesus, upon this Sacrifice, that he may make this (f) Bread the Body of thy Christ, and this (g) Cup the Blood of thy Christ; that they who are partakers thereof, may be confirmed in godliness, may obtain remission of their sins, may be delivered from the Devil and his snares, may be replenished with the Holy Ghost, may be made worthy of thy Christ, and may obtain everlasting life, Thou, O Lord Almighty, being reconciled unto them through the merits and mediation of thy Son our Saviour Jesus Christ; who, with Thee and the Holy Ghost, liveth and reigneth ever one God, world without end. Amen.

The prayer of intercession, with "militant here on earth" eliminated,[91] *followed* the Consecration. Petition for Bishops and Curates *preceded* the petition for rulers. The congregation was gathered "to celebrate the commemoration of the most glorious death of thy Son." There was provision for special prayers requested by members of the congregation. The 1549 reference to the Blessed Virgin and particular classes of Saints was restored. God's *mercy* was asked for the departed, and there was again a reference to the Mystical Body and general resurrection.

The Communion resembled that of 1549. The Lord's Prayer, *Pax,* Paschal Lamb prayer, Invitation, Confession, Absolution, Comfortable Words, and Prayer of Humble Access all immediately preceded reception as had been the case in Cranmer's first Service. There was no directive to distribute Communion "in their hands." But the recipient was to respond "Amen" and the Priest was to say "me" and "my" when receiving himself.

The directive for reverent covering of consecrated elements adumbrated perduring Real Presence. Very significantly, considering Nonjuror insistence on Oblation and Invocation, there was no rubric for reconsecration by Words of Institution.

The Service concluded with the 1549 Collect of Thanksgiving, the *Gloria,* and traditional Anglican blessing.

The truncated Service, when had, was to end well before the Offertory, at the conclusion of the Creed or sermon.

Two concluding rubrics reflected the emphasis on Sacrifice. If "two persons" were present, celebration was allowed. And *every* Priest was to "administer or receive" the Holy Communion every Sunday or Holy-day, unless hindered by sickness, some other urgent cause, or inability to get "two persons to communicate with him."

Another rubric provided for those unable to offer substantial sums of money. They were still to give *something;* as in the Service itself, the Nonjurors insisted on at least this pittance of offering in further recognition of the connection between elements and "oblations."

Although wheat bread was still allowed, there was an interesting addition to the 1637 and 1662 rubric for consumption of superfluous consecrated elements. It was now provided that elements could be reserved and transported out of Church to the sick or disabled:

> If there be any persons who through sickness or any other urgent cause are under a Necessity of communicating at their houses, then the Priest shall reserve at the open Communion so much of the Sacrament of the Body and Blood, as shall serve those who are to receive at home. And if after that, or if, when none are to communicate at their houses, any of the consecrated Elements remain, then it shall not be carried out of the Church; but the Priest, and such other of the Communicants as he shall then call unto him, shall immediately after the Blessing reverently eat and drink the same.

Finally, the 1637 and 1662 rubric for distribution of the "oblations" was changed significantly in further recognition of the connection of these financial offerings and the elements.

> The Money given at the Offertory being solemnly devoted to God, the Priest shall take so much of it as will defray the charge of the bread and Wine: and the remainder he shall keep or part of it, or dispose of it or part of it to pious or charitable uses, according to the discretion of the Bishop.

The Nonjuror Service of 1718 reflected the influence of ancient liturgies, the Scottish Service of 1637, and the English Services of 1549 and 1662. It embodied the doctrine of John Johnson and his Nonjuror disciples. The clear Offertory, Oblation, and Invocation emphasized Sacrifice and perduring Real Presence to an extent unprecedented in previous Anglican rites. Among the many Catholic Anglican Services it influenced was the Scottish Communion Service of 1764.

The Communion Service of 1764

Even after the 1660 Restoration, the Communion Service returned to Scotland very slowly. At first the Eucharist was celebrated as infrequently as once a year, and sometimes not even that often.[92] Furthermore, in the liturgical chaos of the highlands, the form followed sometimes differed little from that of the Presbyterians.[93]

Gradually the Book of Common Prayer began to spread throughout the north. By 1707 the English Service was celebrated with some frequency. But many Scottish Churchmen preferred— and used—the Communion Service of 1637. Many of those who used the established English rite admired the scholarship and doctrine of the Nonjurors. As a result the "Usages" were frequently interpolated into the 1662 Service. There was little scruple about innovation such as inverting the order of prayers so that the English Post-Communion prayer frequently followed the Consecration.

Dowden writes that "an event of deep moment in the history of the Scottish Office was the posthumous publication in 1744 of Bishop Rattray's work, *The Ancient Liturgy of the Church of Jerusalem.*" [94] Rattray's liturgical studies corroborated those of the Nonjurors and gave momentum to a movement for a Scottish Communion Office resembling that of 1718.

In 1755 Bishop William Falconar published an Office reflecting the influence of the Canterburian party of 1637, the Nonjurors of 1718, and the corroborative testimony of Rattray. Only about a thousand copies were printed, but it approached the form finally assumed in 1764.

In 1762 or 1763 Falconar, the Primus, proposed the composition of a new Communion Office. Those responsible for the ensuing Service were Falconar and Bishop Robert Forbes.[95]

Except for the liturgy mentioned above, there are no available works of William Falconar. The doctrine of the Service of 1764 must be derived from a published work of Robert Forbes.

ROBERT FORBES

No less an authority than John Dowden considered Bishop Robert Forbes "the chief hand in giving us the Scottish Communion Office in the form in which we now possess it." [96]

The areas of Ross and Caithness where Forbes served had suffered grievously in the religious upheavals.[97] But he still found time for liturgical study. Another Scottish Bishop, John Skinner of Aberdeen, later remarked that the 1764 Communion Service was undertaken by "two of our Bishops who were well versed in these matters." [98] Apparently all the Bishops approved the choice of Forbes as principal author of the new Communion Service.[99]

As a priest Forbes had used the Communion Service of 1637. He arranged for his congregation to make financial "Offerings" after the sermon, which offerings were then placed on the Altar as "Oblations to God." This usage of 1637 with emphasis on offering to God reveals that Forbes was influenced by Johnson and the Nonjurors. There is a notice in his handwriting at the Edinburgh College Library. It was to be read in his Church at Ayr:

Air, March 24 Easter Eve, 1744. I desire that such as are to communicate may stay after Prayers in order to receive copies of the Scots Communion-Office, by which we consecrate the Holy Sacrament of the Lord's Supper. It is that Office which stands authorized by King Charles 1st of Blessed Memory; and for which, it may indeed be said that truly great and good Monarch suffer'd Martyrdom; and therefore it is the more worthy of all esteem and regard from us. Please know, that tomorrow the Communicants do not give in their Offerings till Sermon is ended, when one will come about and receive them at their hands in a decent manner; and then they will be placed upon the Altar-Table, as their Oblations to God promoting that good work now "by the Blessing of Heaven" so happily commend'd in this place.[100]

Forbes reflected mature Laudian doctrine of the eighteenth century. It was his Eucharistic doctrine that was instilled in the Communion Service of 1764, a Service that became *ab omnibus receptus* and introduced a good measure of uniformity into the Scottish Church.

Forbes and the Eucharist

Forbes's views on the Eucharist are expressed with admirable clarity in his Catechism.[101] In this catechetical exposition he stressed Nonjuror doctrine on Real Presence. Apparently he wrote the Catechism to stimulate frequent Communion.

His views on Sacrifice were well known from his practice at Ayr. He favored the 1637 Communion Service with its connection of "oblations" and elements. It was the people, as well as the priest, who offered. In his Catechism he remarked that "several other particulars" might be derived from Patristic writings, among them "that the Holy Eucharist is a sacrifice." [102]

The Eucharist was a remembrance or memorial of Christ's Sacrifice. Frequent Communion was necessary for a lively remembrance:

Q. What is the end and design of its Institution?
A. To keep a constant lively remembrance in our minds of the Sacrifice of the Death of Christ, and of the benefits which we receive thereby; which only can be done by frequent communicating.[103]

The fraction represented the broken Body of Christ; the pouring of the wine represented the shedding of His precious Blood:

Q. What doth the breaking of the bread represent?
A. The breaking or piercing of the Body of Christ.

Q. What doth the pouring out of the Wine represent?
A. The shedding of the most precious Blood of Christ.[104]

Forbes interpreted the "Do this" of Christ as referring to frequent Communion. The more frequently men communicate, the better Christians they are:

Q. How do you prove this?
A. From the very words of our Saviour himself, in St. Luke, Chap. 22nd, ver. 19th, "This do in remembrance of me;" which are a positive and express command, as sacred and binding as any of the ten Commandments of the Moral Law.

Q. How long is the obligation of this Commandment of our blessed Saviour to last?

A. Even to the end of the world.

Q. What proof can you give for this?

A. These words of St. Paul, in the First Epistle to the Corinthians, Chap. 11th, ver. 26th, "as often as ye eat this Bread, and drink this Cup, ye do shew forth the Lord's death till He comes." Hence we may plainly see, that there lies an obligation upon all Christians to eat the Sacramental Bread, and to drink the Sacramental Wine, in remembrance of Christ's death, even unto the end of the world, because our Saviour is not to come till then. And the more frequently we perform this solemn and necessary duty, still the better Christians we are.[105]

But the Sacrament was more than a bare remembrance. It was the renewal of our Baptismal Vow. It sealed our pardon and infused grace. It was an assistance in future duties:

Q. Is the Sacrament only a bare Remembrance or Memorial of Christ's Death and sufferings?

A. No, it is more than that: For by receiving of it we solemnly renew our Baptismal Vow; and if we partake worthily, we therein have the pardon of our former sins sealed unto us, and we receive new supplies of the grace of God to repair those breaches the enemies of our salvation have made, and to assist us to perform our duty for the time to come.[106]

For a worthy reception, preparation was necessary. Forbes distinguished between mediate and immediate preparation. Habitual or mediate preparation surpassed actual or immediate preparation:

Q. Can any person then be said to receive worthily?

A. Yes.

Q. How comes that to pass?

A. Because God's goodness is such, that he accepts of our serious tho' imperfect endeavors, in place of a sinless perfection; of our sincere repentance, instead of innocence.

. . . .

Q. How many kinds of preparation for the Communion are there?

A. Two.

Q. What are they?

A. An habitual and an actual preparation.

Q. What is meant by an habitual preparation?

A. A virtuous and good life.

Q. What is meant by an actual preparation?

A. When a person, knowing beforehand of the approach of the Holy Communion, sets apart some portions of his time for acts of devotion, meditation, and examination of his life; and such is the season of Lent before Easter, and of Advent before Christmas.

Q. Which of these is the best?

A. Certainly the habitual preparation is the only available one; for without a good life the actual preparation is nothing else but a mocking of God, and an imposing upon ourselves.[107]

The influence of John Johnson and the Nonjurors was obvious in Forbes's exposition of the "sense" of Real Presence. He denied the presence of Christ's "natural and substantial" Body. Christ was present in a spiritual manner, that is, the consecrated elements became His Body and Blood in power, virtue, and effect:

Q. Are not Christians to believe the Consecrated Bread in the Holy Eucharist to be the Body of Christ, and the Consecrated Wine to be the Blood of Christ?

A. Yes, certainly they are; because our Saviour himself, in his Institution of this most holy Sacrament, has expressly declared the Bread to be his Body and the Wine to be his Blood. . . .

Q. In what sense are we to believe this mysterious doctrine?

A. Though we cannot believe that the Bread and Wine are the very *natural* and *substantial Body and Blood of Christ,* that were upon the Cross; yet we are to believe them to be so in a spiritual manner; that is to say, That the Consecrated Bread and Wine are the Body and Blood of Christ in *Power, Virtue* and *Effect.*[108]

At the Last Supper Christ Himself consecrated the elements. In the daily Eucharist it is the Holy Spirit, His Divine Substitute on earth, who sanctifies and works in the bread and wine. Forbes praised the 1637 Communion Service for its Invocation of the Holy Spirit:

Q. By what power is this wonderful change made upon these weak Elements of Bread and Wine?

A. 'Tis certain (as I have already said) from the Words of Institution, that Christ did make the Elements to be his Body and Blood, for he expressly tells us they are so: But no power inferiour to his own could make them so. As therefore the Holy Ghost is his Divine

Substitute upon earth, by which he is present with his Church unto
the end of the world, so whatever operations he now performs in
his Church are wrought by that Divine Spirit. Therefore, that the
Bread and Wine may become his Body and Blood, though not in
Substance, yet in *Power, Virtue,* and *Effect,* it is necessary that this
Holy Spirit should bless and sanctify them, and work in them and
with them; because, as St. John says (Chap. 6th. ver. 63rd) He is
the Spirit that quickneth. Hence it is, that in the excellent Communion Office, authorized by King Charles the First, which we use,
we have . . . petition for the operation of the Holy Ghost, to
make the Elements the Body and Blood of Christ.[109]

Nonjuror doctrine, as expressed by Forbes, was a middle
ground between the position of Rome and the mere representation
of many Protestant persuasions. The elements were not the Body
and Blood; nor were they mere representations or resemblances of
the Same. In the Consecration, through the power and operation of
the Holy Spirit, they "are made" as effectual as Christ's natural
Body and Blood would be *if* they were present:

Q. As the whole of this doctrine is plain, and easy to understand; so I
earnestly desire, you would endeavour to give me a short account
of it in as few words as possible, that so we may have it in one view,
and thereby comprehend the meaning of it the more easily.
A. I think, it may all be summed up in this: That the Bread and Wine
are the Body and Blood, not in themselves considered, nor merely
by their resembling, or representing the sacred Body and Blood of
the adorable Jesus; but by the invisible *Power* and *Operation* of the
Holy Ghost, by which the sacramental Bread and Wine, in the Act
of Consecration, are made as *powerful* and as *effectual* for the ends
of religion, as the natural Body and Blood themselves could be, if
they were present before our eyes.[110]

In Nonjuror doctrine Christ was present in virtue, power, and
effect. Forbes applied an interesting scriptural analogy, comparing
the "spirit and power" of the absent Elias in John the Baptist to
the "power, virtue and effect" of the absent Christ in the Eucharist:

Q. Are there any similitudes in Scripture, from the consideration of
which this interpretation of our Saviour's Words [*This is my Body,
This is my Blood*] can receive any light?
A. There are several similitudes to be found there, which might be
condescended upon to clear up this point; but there is one in par-

ticular so much to the purpose, that I shall pitch upon it without mentioning any of the rest; and it is that St. John the Baptist is by our Saviour (St. Matth. Chap. 17th, ver. 12th and 13th; St. Mark Chap. 9th, ver. 13th compared with Mal. Chap. 4th, ver. 5th) called the prophet Elias, who had flourished so many hundred years before his time, for this could not readily be believed, seeing the time and place of St. John the Baptist's birth were so well known. But the reason assign'd why he is called Elias, is this, namely, Because he came in the *spirit* and *power* of Elias; as we have it in St. Luke Chap. 1st, ver. 17th. Even so, in the Holy Eucharist the Consecrated Bread and Wine are called by Christians, and believed to be, the Body and Blood of Christ, according to his own positive declaration, because attended with the same *power, virtue,* and *effect* for the ends of religion, that his natural *Body* and *Blood* could be were they existing with us.[111]

Forbes composed his own prayer for the mixture, in which he mentioned the mystical union with Christ the Head:

. . . grant, that those thy Servants, who are to partake of this mixed Cup, may no more be separated from Christ their Head than this Water can now be separated from this Wine, but they may continue their unmerited Union with him by a firm and steady perseverance in that Faith once delivered to the Saints, and by the serious Practice of all virtuous and godly Living, till at last they arrive at that unspeakable Bliss in the glorious Mansions above, which thou hast prepared for those who are thy faithful Servants, through the same Jesus Christ, who liveth and reigneth with Thee, O Father, and the Holy Ghost, ever one God, World without End. Amen.[112]

Robert Forbes was in the tradition of John Johnson and the English Nonjurors. His 1764 Communion Service was another Service in the Catholic Anglican tradition. He composed it for a small Episcopal Church in the misty Scottish Highlands. But it was a Service that was to have immense influence in the New World.

THE COMMUNION SERVICE OF 1764

Forbes's Communion Service of 1764 apparently began at the Communion exhortation. The earlier part of the Service was printed only in 1844. Therefore, references to this earlier part are derived from the reconstruction of John Dowden.[113]

One notable feature of this Service was the severe curtailment of rubrics. Another was the thoroughgoing emphasis on Sacrifice and Real Presence.

Dowden's reconstruction begins with the Our Father and Collect for Purity. The penitential litany followed, but it was more traditional than its 1718 predecessor. It consisted of Decalogue and *Kyrie;* however, a "Summary" of the Law was provided as an alternative at the Minister's discretion.

There was another alternative in a new Collect provided as a substitute for the Collects for the King. Paradoxically, however, the two Collects for the King still preceded the Collect for the day. The rubric and alternative Collect were as follows:

Then shall follow one of these Collects and the Collect for the day, the Presbyter standing up and saying,

Let us pray.

O Almighty Lord, and everlasting God, vouchsafe, we beseech thee, to direct, sanctify, and govern, both our hearts and bodies, in the ways of thy laws, and in the words of thy commandments; that through thy most mighty protection, both here and ever, we may be preserved in body and soul; through our Lord and Saviour Jesus Christ. Amen.

Epistle, Gospel, Creed, and Sermon followed the Collects, but there was no rubric prescribing announcements after the Creed.

One very notable and felicitous simplification was the omission of the first two exhortations. Forbes's Service began with the Communion Exhortation immediately following the Sermon.

After the exhortation there was a vividly Sacrificial Offertory. The introduction set the tone of offering; a rubric indicated that the people offered *to God*.

Then the Presbyter, or Deacon, shall say,

Let us present our offerings to the Lord with reverence and godly fear.

Then the Presbyter shall begin the offertory, saying one or more of these sentences following, as he thinketh convenient by his discretion, according to the length or shortness of the time that the people are offering.

The Godward direction of the Offertory was clear from the Offertory sentences. These were the Sacrificial sentences favored by Laudian Divines of the seventeenth and eighteenth centuries and suggested for the 1637 Service by Wedderburn. Even the long sentence about the widow's mite was restored. While the Sentences were recited, a Deacon collected devotions in a basin, brought the same "with the oblations therein" to the Presbyter who presented it to God and placed it on the "holy table." There was no rubric for covering the oblations as a protection to small offerers.

After the vivid Sacrificial actions of the Presbyter, he said the following Offertory doxology. This prayer too taught Sacrifice in the sense that the offerers "give" to God of His own riches:

> Blessed be thou, O Lord God, for ever and ever. Thine, O Lord, is the greatness, and the glory, and the victory, and the majesty: for all that is in the heaven and in the earth is thine: thine is the kingdom, O Lord, and thou art exalted as head above all: both riches and honour come of thee, and of thine own do we give unto thee. Amen.

After the Preface and *Sanctus,* the Laudian rubric of 1637 introduced the Consecratory prayer: "Then the Presbyter standing at such a part of the holy table as he may with the most ease and decency use both his hands, shall say the prayer of consecration as followeth."

This prayer varied somewhat from 1718, notably in its shortened commemoration of Salvation history. The important thing to be observed, however, is that it contained Oblation and Invocation as the Nonjurors (and Johnson) had directed. The Invocation prayed that elements "become" Christ's Body and Blood. Because of this prayer's influence on Samuel Seabury, and because of its intrinsic merit, it is reproduced in full:

All glory be to thee, Almighty God, our heavenly Father, for that thou of thy tender mercy didst give thy only Son Jesus Christ to suffer death upon the cross for our redemption; who (by his own oblation of himself once offered) made a full, perfect, and sufficient sacrifice, oblation, and satisfaction, for the sins of the whole world, and did institute, and in his holy gospel command us to continue a perpetual memorial of that his precious death and sacrifice until his coming again. For in the night that he was betrayed,* (a) he took bread; and when he had given

---

* Marginal rubrics: "(a) Here the Presbyter is to take the paten in his hands; (b) And here to break the Bread; (c) And here to lay his hands upon all the Bread. (d) Here he is to take the Cup into his

thanks, (b) he brake it, and gave it to his disciples, saying, Take, eat, (c) THIS IS MY BODY, which is given for you: DO this in remembrance of me. Likewise after supper (d) he took the cup; and when he had given thanks, he gave it to them, saying, Drink ye all of this, for (e) THIS IS MY BLOOD, of the new testament, which is shed for you and for many, for the remission of sins: DO this as oft as ye shall drink it in remembrance of me.

The Oblation.

Wherefore, O Lord, and heavenly Father, according to the institution of thy dearly beloved Son our Saviour Jesus Christ, we thy humble servants do celebrate and make here before thy divine majesty, with these thy holy gifts, WHICH WE NOW OFFER UNTO THEE, the memorial thy Son hath commanded us to make; having in remembrance his blessed passion, and precious death, his mighty resurrection, and glorious ascension; rendering unto thee most hearty thanks for the innumerable benefits procured unto us by the same.

The Invocation.

And we most humbly beseech thee, O merciful Father, to hear us, and of thy almighty goodness vouchsafe to bless and sanctify, with thy word and holy Spirit, these thy gifts and creatures of bread and wine, that they may become the body and blood of thy most dearly beloved Son. And we earnestly desire thy fatherly goodness, mercifully to accept this our sacrifice of praise and thanksgiving, most humbly beseeching thee to grant, that by the merits and death of thy Son Jesus Christ, and through faith in his blood, we (and all thy whole church) may obtain remission of our sins, and all other benefits of his passion. And here we humbly offer and present unto thee, O Lord, ourselves, our souls and bodies, to be a reasonable, holy and lively sacrifice unto thee, beseeching thee, that whosoever shall be partakers of this holy Communion, may worthily receive the most precious body and blood of thy Son Jesus Christ, and be filled with thy grace and heavenly benediction, and made one body with him, that he may dwell in them, and they in him. And although we are unworthy, through our manifold sins, to offer unto thee any sacrifice; yet we beseech thee to accept this our bounden duty and service, not weighing our merits, but pardoning our offences, through Jesus [Christ] our Lord: by whom, and with whom, in the unity of the Holy Ghost, all honour and glory be unto thee, O Father Almighty, world without end. Amen.

---

hand; (e) And here to lay his hand upon every vessel (be it chalice or flagon) in which there is any wine to be consecrated."

The Nonjurors believed in a perduring Real Presence. They also believed in Sacrifice. Therefore it was fitting that the prayer of intercession follow the *Consecration*. As in 1718, Forbes placed this prayer immediately after the Consecration. He referred to the offering of alms "and oblations"; the Service commemorated Christ's death "and Sacrifice"; however, there was no intercession for the departed, nor was there explicit mention of Mary and certain classes of Saints. And Forbes reverted to the strange procedure of mentioning Kings and Rulers *before* the clergy as had been done in 1549.

The emphasis on Real Presence continued with the Invitation, Confession, Absolution, Comfortable Words, and Prayer of Humble Access. These prayers, as in 1718, *immediately* preceded the Communion. In 1552 Cranmer had transferred them to a safe distance from the Communion and placed them *before* the Consecration. The Nonjurors restored them to their 1549 location.

As in 1718 there was no rubric for distribution in the hands. In the simplified 1764 Service, the Presbyter apparently received with the same formula as did the people.

An extremely important rubric followed the Communion. It provided that, in cases of reconsecration, the Presbyter was to begin at the beginning of the Consecration prayer and end only with the words "become the body and blood of thy most dearly beloved Son." This rubric was important because it stressed Nonjuror doctrine on the necessity of Oblation and Invocation for a complete Consecration.

Another rubric directed the Presbyter to cover remaining consecrated elements. A prayer of thanksgiving stressed the reception of the "precious body and blood of Christ." The two rubrics and the concluding thanksgiving prayer were as follows:

If the consecrated bread or wine be all spent before all have communicated, the Presbyter is to consecrate more, according to the form before prescribed, beginning at the words, All glory be to thee, &c. and ending with words, that they may become the body and blood of thy most dearly beloved Son.

When all have communicated, he that celebrates shall go to the Lord's table, and cover with a fair linen cloth that which remaineth of the consecrated elements, and then say,

Having now received the precious body and blood of Christ, let us give thanks to our Lord God, who hath graciously vouchsafed to admit us to the participation of his holy mysteries; and let us beg of him grace to perform our vows, and to persevere in our good resolutions; and that being made holy, we may obtain everlasting life, through the merits of the all-sufficient sacrifice of our Lord and Saviour Jesus Christ.

The Service closed with the traditional *Gloria* and Anglican blessing. At this point the 1764 curtailment of rubrics was most obvious. Gone were all concluding rubrics, including prescriptions for a truncated Service, a specified number of communicants, directions for a minimal offering, the type of bread, reservation and consumption of the sacred species, and the disposition of superfluous money. As in 1718, there was no "Black Rubric."

The 1764 Communion Service was the immediate predecessor of the first American Service. It rapidly became the *textus receptus* in the highlands and was the Service used by the consecrators of Samuel Seabury. The road that led to the American Communion Service was a long road with many diverse paths. It began with Thomas Cranmer and the *Order of the Communion* in 1548. It ended in 1764, far north of Canterbury, when a Bishop named Robert Forbes put his final period after the Anglican blessing.

CHAPTER VI

The American Service of 1789

The early colonists in America styled themselves members of "The Church of England in America." [1] In the frontier thirst for unshackled freedom, there was an inherent suspicion of prelacy. There were no native American bishops, only the distant Bishop of London, to whom the colonists owed a shadowy allegiance.[2]

From 1607 until 1662 the Elizabethan Communion Service prevailed in the rugged frontier chapels, and after the Restoration the Communion Service of 1662. But when "the shot heard round the world" was fired at Concord bridge, "patriot" Anglicans found themselves at war with Mother England. Within hours of the Declaration of Independence in 1776, some of these patriots met to alter prayers for the King in the Communion Service.[3] The American Church was torn asunder by divided loyalties, and wounds began to heal only with the welcome restoration of peace in 1783.

Obviously, subservience to the Bishop of London was now less popular than proposals for a native hierarchy. Connecticut was the first state to designate a Bishop. Samuel Seabury was duly elected and sent to England for consecration. But the English Bishops temporized about ordaining one who could not take the oath of allegiance, until Seabury in impatience applied to the Nonjuring Bishops of Scotland for a Scottish consecration.[4] At Aberdeen, Scotland, in 1784, the Connecticut churchman received the imposition of hands from three Scottish prelates. He signed an interesting Concordat with his Scottish consecrators. Article V was to have immense significance for the history of the American Communion Service, and for Anglican Eucharistic theology in general. For American Episcopalians, no less than other Anglicans, subscribe to the principle that *lex orandi est lex credendi.*

Art. V. As the Celebration of the Holy Eucharist, or the Administration of the Sacrament of the Body and Blood of Christ, is the princi-

pal Bond of Union among Christians, as well as the most solemn Act of
Worship in the Christian Church, the Bishops aforesaid agree in
desiring that there may be as little Variance here as possible; and tho'
the Scottish are very far from prescribing to their Brethren in this
matter, they cannot help ardently wishing that Bishop Seabury would
endeavour all he can, consistently with peace and prudence, to make
the Celebration of this venerable Mystery conformable to the most
primitive Doctrine and Practice in that respect: Which is the pattern
the Church of Scotland had copied after in her Communion Office, and
which it has been the Wish of some of the most eminent Divines of
the Church of England, that she also had more closely followed than
she seems to have done since she gave up her first reformed Liturgy,
used in the reign of King Edward VI, between which, and the form
used in the Church of Scotland, there is no Difference in any point,
which the primitive Church reckoned essential to the right Ministration of the holy Eucharist. In this capital Article therefore of the
Eucharistic Service, in which the Scottish Bishops so earnestly wish for
as much Unity as possible, Bishop Seabury also agrees to take a
serious View of the Communion Office recommended by them, and
if found agreeable to the genuine Standards of Antiquity to give his
Sanction to it, and by gentle Methods of Argument and Persuasion, to
endeavour, as they have done, to introduce it by degrees into practice,
without the Compulsion of Authority on the one side, or the prejudice
of former Custom on the other.[5]

By attaching his signature to that fateful document, Seabury
had agreed by "argument and persuasion" to urge adoption of the
Scottish Communion Office in the United States.

In 1785 a "convention" of only seven states, Seabury and
Connecticut being excluded, produced a "Proposed Book" of rites
which never met approval. The Standing Liturgical Commission
dismissed this early effort to adjust the Communion Service as
follows:

The treatment of the Communion Service in the "Proposed Book"
of 1785 had only one point in mind, namely the elimination of matter
which was duplicated when Morning Prayer, Litany, and Holy Communion (or more usually "Ante-Communion") were said as one
continuous service, as had been the English custom ever since the
Puritan Archbishop Grindal had ordered that "accumulation" in
1571.[6]

This truncated convention did accomplish one momentous feat. It christened the American Church "The Protestant Episcopal Church of the United States." [7]

Meanwhile, liturgical revision gathered momentum in dissident Connecticut. In August, 1785, prayers for the King preceding the Nicene Creed were abolished.[8] The next year, Bishop Seabury boldly "recommended" to Connecticut congregations a Communion Service substantially the same as the Scottish Service of 1764.[9] It is noteworthy that this Office was well received by Connecticut clergy who almost universally abandoned the Service of their youth and early priesthood in favor of Seabury's rite.

The year 1789 will always have a pleasant ring to Episcopalians. For it was in 1789 that the former colonies, now the United States, were united in one convention, consisting of an upper house of Bishops, and a lower house of clergy and laity. The two Bishops present, Seabury and William White, worked diligently on Prayer Book revision. The lower house established several committees for the same project.[10] On October 14, both houses ratified the new Communion Office. Seabury was enthusiastic that the Service adopted included Oblation and Invocation. Bishop White "without conceiving with some that the service as it stood was essentially defective . . . always thought there was a beauty in those ancient forms, and can discover no superstition in them." [11] The towering figure in the lower house was one Dr. William Smith who was instrumental in carrying the motion for the new Office despite potential opposition.[12]

As of October 14, 1789, the American branch of the Anglican Communion had its own Communion Service. The men primarily responsible for its creation, adoption, and doctrine were Samuel Seabury, William White, and William Smith.

SAMUEL SEABURY

Before the turbulent days of the War of Independence, Seabury worked quietly as Minister at Jamaica and Westchester. During the hostilities he favored the loyalist, or Tory, cause. Nevertheless, once that historic conflict was resolved, his fellow Connecticut churchmen honored him as Bishop designate, the first so honored in the States. Despite a well-documented Scottish consecration,[13] not all Episcopalians were impressed by Seabury's credentials. A loyalist war record and now a Nonjuror consecration rendered him suspect to many of his countrymen.[14] Nor did his willingness to ordain native priests win him popularity in more conservative and cautious circles.[15]

Seabury never dissembled his Nonjuror sympathies as far as the Communion Service was concerned. He was quoted as saying of the 1662 Canon: "To confess the truth, I hardly consider the form to be used as strictly amounting to a consecration." [16]

Seabury was convinced of the validity of his Orders as well as of the truth of his Eucharistic doctrine. Although he was eager to see the Nonjuror Canon prevail in all the states, as it already did in Connecticut, he stood fast in adamant refusal to accept a chair in the House of Bishops until the 1789 Convention unanimously recognized the validity of his Scottish consecration.[17] Through the conciliatory efforts of White and Smith, the Convention did recognize his episcopacy. Once he had achieved that goal, Seabury plunged eagerly into Communion Service revision as a member of the committee of two in the upper house.

Seabury's writings reveal a thorough acquaintance with Nonjuror doctrine. This was the Eucharistic doctrine that Seabury made his own. In other words, Article V of the Concordat with his Scottish consecrators was no act of expediency; it reflected his own deepest Eucharistic convictions.

Addressing Presbyterians and Independents, he espoused Nonjuror teaching that liturgies should concur with the practice of the primitive Church. "Any liturgy in which a due regard was paid to the analogy of the christian faith, and the approved practices and usages of the primitive church, would be much better than extempore prayer." [18] In 1786 he outlined general principles for liturgical revision; it should return to those halcyon years "uncorrupted by popery." He cautioned, however, that government, doctrine, and sacraments are settled by Divine authority:

> The Christians who lived in the next age after the apostles must have conversed with the Apostles, and were acquainted with their opinions and practice, in the conduct of the public worship, and administration of the sacraments, and discipline of the Church. Nor is it likely they would safely or quickly depart from that mode which they knew had been approved by them; especially at a time, when perpetual persecution and distress kept men close to God and their duty: And

the world and its concerns could have but little power over those, who daily expected to yield up that life in martyrdom, which they had passed in continual devotion to God, and in the service and edification of his Church. It would therefore be a good rule, in altering anything in our sacred Liturgy that might be thought to need it, to go back to early Christianity, before it was corrupted by Popery, and see what was then the practice of the Church—what its rites and ceremonies—and to conform our own as nearly to it as the state of the Church will permit. . . .[19]

But his principal concern was with the Communion Office. In 1789 he complained to White that "the most exceptionable part of the English Book is the Communion Office." He lamented the absence of Oblation and Invocation; mere Words of Institution were "not consecratory at all."

That the most exceptional part of the English Book is the Communion Office may be proved by a number of very respectable names among her clergy. The grand fault in that Office is the deficiency of a more formal Oblation of the Elements, and of the Invocation of the Holy Ghost to sanctify and bless them. The Consecration is made to consist merely in the Priests laying his hand on the elements and in pronouncing This is my body &c: Which words are not consecratory at all—nor were they addressed by Christ to the Father—but were declarative to the Apostles.[20]

Seabury and Sacrifice

Seabury's doctrine on Sacrifice resembled that of John Johnson. It seems that for him the Mass was more than an offering of representative elements together with a pleading of Christ's Sacrifice. In several passages he stated that the Eucharist was an offering of Christ's Sacrifice, an offering of His Body and Blood. However, the elements themselves were sacramental representations; they were not in themselves Christ's natural Body and Blood.

The faithful who approached the Table feasted "with their brethren on the sacrifice of the Holy Eucharist." [21] The Mass, therefore, was more than an empty remembrance; more than obedience to an arbitrary command; more than renewal of the Christian covenant. It was a commemorative sacrifice of Christ's Sacrifice:

The primitive Christians had very different sentiments from these, concerning the Holy Communion, and so I suppose our Church has also. They considered it not as the renewal of the Christian Covenant, but a privilege to which the Christian Covenant, into which we had been admitted by Baptism and which had been ratified by Confirmation entitled us. Nor as an arbitrary command of God to show his sovereign authority over us. Nor as a bare remembrance of Christ's death. But as the appointed means of keeping up that spiritual life which we received in our New-birth: and of continuing that interest in the benefits and blessings of Christ's passion and death which was made over to us when we became members of his mystical body. They called and esteemed it to be the Christian Sacrifice, commemorative of the great sacrifice of atonement which Christ had made for the sins of the whole world wherein, under the symbols of bread and the cup, the body and blood of Christ which he offered up, and which were broken and shed upon the cross, are figured forth and being presented to God our heavenly Father by his Priest here on earth, the merits of Christ for the remission of sins, are pleaded by him, and we trust by the great High Priest Himself in heaven.[22]

Christ offered His natural Body and Blood at the Last Supper: "When did He offer himself? I answer, in the institution of the holy eucharist. And though I do not say this is declared in express words, . . . a careful attention to what he did and said, will put the matter out of doubt." [23]

The words "Do this" connoted Sacrifice. The Eucharist, therefore, was more than mere eating and drinking:

The first thing that presents itself to our inquiry is the meaning of the command, *Do this.* Some understand the expression merely of eating and drinking the sacramental elements. This could be admitted with regard to the *bread,* it cannot be admitted with regard to the *cup:* And as the command must, in all reason, be understood in the same sense with regard to them both, it cannot be admitted with regard to either of them.[24]

Seabury distinguished memorial from remembrance. Memorial meant sacrifice; remembrance was only respectful recollection. The words "Do this" meant memorial or Sacrifice: "Less than this will not come up to the meaning of the expression 'This do in remembrance of me.' " [25] This memorial or representation of Christ's Sacrifice was "made before the Almighty Father." The Eucharist "is not only a commemoration of Christ's death, but a memorial or representation of His sufferings made before the Almighty Father, to put Him in mind of the meritorious sacrifice of His blessed Son on our behalf." [26]

Christ's natural Body and Blood could not be present on the Altar. Therefore it was Christ's mystical Body, a representation of His natural Body that the priest held in his hands. By mystical body or representation, Seabury meant the Body of Christ in virtue and effect, but not the substantial or natural Body:

For the command, "This do in remembrance of Me," relates not barely to eating bread and drinking wine in remembrance of Christ, as the Socinians teach, and some ill-informed Christians suppose, but to the whole transaction. By it the Apostles were enjoined, when they administered the Holy Communion, to do as Christ then did, take bread and break it, and offer it up to God, by thanksgiving and prayer, consecrating it to be His mystical body—the memorial or representative of that Body which Christ in the institution willingly offered up and devoted to God, a sacrifice and propitiation for the sins of the world; and which in consequence of His offering, was soon after slain upon the cross for our redemption—the Body of Christ in virtue and efficacy.[27]

The Eucharist was a Memorial of Christ's Sacrifice that procures for mankind the benefits of Christ's death:

We are to make a commemoration or memorial of His precious death and sacrifice before the Almighty Father, and plead before *Him* the merits of His dearly beloved Son dying for the sins of the world: Not that God will forget, unless we refresh His memory; but because in so doing we use the means that Christ has appointed to convey to us the benefits of that sacrifice which He offered for sin.[28]

Despite this clear teaching of application, Seabury was reluctant to call the Mass an offering for sin. This reluctance probably stemmed from a connection of propitiatory Sacrifice and death then current in American thought.[29] When he termed Calvary the only true and proper Sacrifice for sins, Seabury probably meant that only Calvary involved "the Death of Christ":

He was graciously pleased by his One Oblation of himself once offered for our redemption, to make a full perfect and sufficient Sacrifice, Oblation and Satisfaction for the sins of the whole world, which is here called the Sacrifice of the Death of Christ. Now this Sacrifice which our Blessed Lord made was the only true and proper Sacrifice for Sin, that ever was or ever can be offered for it.[30]

Yet the Eucharist was as truly and properly a Sacrifice as the Old Law Sacrifices which were figures to "typify and represent the

Sacrifice of the Death of Christ then to come." [31] In one passage Seabury called the Lord's Supper an oblation of Calvary which procures the blessings of the Atonement:

The H. Eucharist i.e. a Sacrifice of Thanksgiving or the Lord's Supper, as it is generally called, was ordained by him as a solemn commemorative oblation of the same great Sacrifice to God the Father, and procures us the virtue of it. This commemorative oblation therefore of the Sacrifice of the Death of Christ, as now already offered up, is as truly and properly a Sacrifice as any under the Mosaic institution, that is to say, only in Virtue of that Great Sacrifice which they prefigured and it commemorates. And indeed It alone is Instituted by Our Blessed Lord to supply the place of all those . . . Sacrifices of the Old Law.[32]

God had ordained the sacrifices of the Old Covenant to fore-shadow Christ's Sacrifice. The Mass was necessary in the New Dispensation to set forth, and represent, the death of Christ:

. . . it is as necessary for the continual remembrance of the sacrifice of the death of Christ and of the benefits which we receive thereby even to the end of the world, to set forth, represent or shew the Lord's death till he comes again, as those typical Sacrifices were from the be-ginning of the world to foreshow it.[33]

The broken bread represented "Christ's crucified Body" which was offered in the Mass; the mixed chalice represented "the Blood and Water that flowed from the dead Body of Christ." The Words of Institution made these elements "authoritative represen-tations or symbols of Christ's crucified Body and effused Blood." The Oblation to the Father of these elements was "the highest and most proper act of Christian worship." [34]

Clearly, the bread and wine assumed the same importance in Seabury's doctrine as they did in the teaching of his High Church predecessors. He connected the offering of the people with these elements. Urging frequent Communion, he recommended "that the collection shall be made only the first Sunday in the month; and I presume it will be sufficient for furnishing the elements for the intervening Sundays." [35]

Seabury taught that the Eucharist was joined to Christ's pre-vailing intercession in heaven. The High Priest was "our advocate in heaven, where he ever lives to make intercession for us." [36]

He assured his faithful of Christ's "prevailing intercession for us with the Almighty God in heaven, the true Holy Place." [37] Christians should remember that the Lord was "now in heaven making intercession for them." [38]

Seabury and Real Presence

Seabury dismissed Transubstantiation as the offshoot of literalistic exegesis contravening both reason and common sense. "We justly discard transubstantiation, and depart from the literal meaning of those texts which the papists alledge in support of it, because it contradicts the principles of reason and common sense." [39]

There was no evidence at the Last Supper of the elements changing into the natural Body and Blood of Christ. If the Words of Institution, when uttered by Christ Himself, did not effect change into His natural Body, much less would they do so when pronounced by a priest:

There is . . . no ground, from Christ's words, to infer any transubstantiation, or conversion of the bread and wine into his natural body and blood, by his pronouncing the words, "This is my body; this is my blood," over them. His natural body and blood were then present—his body unbroken—his blood unshed—and absolutely distinct from the bread and wine; for in his natural hands he held the bread and cup, even when he declared them to be his body and blood, *then* given for the remission of sins. And if those words, when pronounced by Christ, did not change the bread and cup into the natural body and blood of Christ, no such effect is to be expected from them, when pronounced by a priest.[40]

Yet all who communicated received Christ really and truly, though "mystically and spiritually." In Nonjuror fashion, Seabury added that this was to partake in the Atonement:

And they [the primitive Christians] did believe, that all who worthily partook of the consecrated Elements, did really and truly, though mystically and spiritually, partake of the Body and Blood of Christ. Our Church evidently teaches the same thing in her Catechism defining "the inward part, or thing signified," by the bread and wine in the Holy Communion, to be "the body and blood of Christ, which are verily and indeed, taken and received by the faithful in the Lord's Supper." . . . We have therefore a right to believe and say, That in the Holy Communion the faithful receiver does, in a mystical and spiritual manner, eat and drink the Body and Blood of Christ represented by the consecrated bread and wine; and does thereby partake in the atonement made by the passion and death of Christ, having remission through Him, of all past sins, and eternal life assured to him.[41]

In Seabury's system, the outward elements remained bread and wine. But he consistently professed some type of change in the bread and wine. They remained bread and wine by nature, but Christ's words made them to be what by nature they were not:

Naturally they were only bread and wine, and not the body and blood of Christ. When he had blessed them, he determined them to be his body and blood. They were, therefore, by his blessing and word, made to be what by nature they were not.[42]

Along with the bread and wine, Christ was sacramentally present. The consecration made the elements the sacramental Body and Blood:

Before he was so much as apprehended by his enemies, he offered to his Father his natural Body and Blood voluntarily and really, tho mystically, under the Symbols of Bread and Wine mixed with Water: for which Reason he called the Bread at the Eucharist his Body, which was then broken, given or offered for the Sins of many: and the Cup his blood which was then shed or offered for the Sins of many: and commanded us, i.e. All Christians to receive the same as his Sacramental Body and Blood.[43]

Such a change of bread and wine into the sacramental Body and Blood is effected only by a priest or Bishop. By the words of the priest the elements—remaining what they are—"become" the Body and Blood:

The Bread and Cup become the Body and Blood of Christ by consecration which is performed validly only by a Bishop or a Priest, who first gives God Thanks for all his Benefits and mercies: and then recites how J.C. instituted this Sacrament the night before his passion and performs his Command by doing what He did.[44]

Seabury's doctrine on Real Presence and change in the elements is expressed succinctly in the unpublished discourse on the Catechism. He denied substantial change, but affirmed a change in qualities. By nature bread and wine remained what they were before, but in mystery, power, signification, and effect they are "changed" into the Body and Blood:

Thus I say we see that by the Consecration of the Eucharist, the Bread and Cup are not destroyed but sanctified: they are changed not in their Substance, but in their qualities: they are made, not the natural, but the Sacramental Body of Christ: so that they are both Bread and Wine and the Body and Blood of Christ, at the same time, but not in the same manner. They are Bread and Wine by nature, the Body and Blood of Christ in Mystery and signification. They are Bread and Wine to our senses, the Body and Blood of Christ to our Understanding and they are Bread and Wine in themselves, the Body and Blood of Christ in *power* and *effect*.[45]

Such a change in qualities differentiated consecrated from ordinary bread. To approach consecrated elements unworthily was to become guilty of Christ's Body and Blood:

. . . a person who approaches the Holy Table without due reverence and devotion, without considering the dignity of the Holy Mystery, and the difference between receiving the Body and Blood of the Lord, and eating and drinking common bread and wine, does not receive the Lord's Body, is guilty of the Body and Blood of Christ, and is in danger of bringing God's judgments upon him by his unworthy receiving.[46]

Seabury's attempt to explain change in the elements while denying the Roman doctrine of substantial mutation was his development of Nonjuror doctrine. He repeated Nonjuror tenets that the worthy recipient "in a spiritual and mysterious manner" receives the Body and Blood, "i.e. all the benefits of His passion, death, and resurrection." [47] Worthy communicants are "made partakers of all the benefits of His death." [48] Through the all-important Invocation, ordinary elements "become through the operation of the Holy Ghost, the Body and Blood of Christ in power and effect." [49] Seabury also reiterated the Anglican doctrine that a worthy recipient "dwells in Christ, and Christ in him. He is one with Christ and Christ with him." [50]

In his unpublished sermon on frequent Communion, the Connecticut prelate bemoaned lay negligence—"especially the men"—in availing themselves of the benefits of Holy Communion.

He also encouraged frequent Administration of the Lord's Supper, and to him frequent meant more than once a month:

> The consideration of the Great backwardness of people, especially the men, to attend on the H.C. hath been the subject of much complaint and grief among several of the Clergy, who think with me that the most likely method to bring men back to a due reverence of the . . . Institution, is its more frequent administration. For if the H.C. be only necessary once in a month or two months, why is it necessary then? This practice ought to begin here: and I hope your good example will provoke very many.[51]

Seabury looked askance at the English Communion Service with its lack of Oblation and Invocation. His own doctrine moved in the Nonjuror tradition, and he considered Oblation and Invocation necessary for a true consecration. In some passages he seemed to say that the Sacrifice was an offering of Christ's Sacrifice and more than an offering of representative elements together with a pleading of Calvary. He also attempted to develop a theory of change in the elements. His doctrine was close to Roman Catholic teaching. He was committed to the Scottish Canon, and, if he was to succeed in having this adopted in America, he would need the cooperation of the other Bishop at the 1789 convention, his more Evangelical colleague William White.

WILLIAM WHITE

Bishop William White was one of the great influences—perhaps *the* great influence—in the foundation of the Protestant Episcopal Church. Through him, Samuel Provoost, and James Madison, the *English* episcopacy was transmitted to the United States.

In October, 1786, White presented to General Convention the necessary testimonials that he had been chosen Bishop-designate by Pennsylvania. Soon after, he embarked with Samuel Provoost of New York for an English consecration.[52] On February 4, 1787, at Lambeth Palace,

"Dr. White and Dr. Provoost were ordained and consecrated bishops, by the Most Rev. John Moore, archbishop of Canterbury. The Most Rev. William Markham, archbishop of York, presented. And the bishops who joined . . . in the imposition of hands, were the Right Rev. Charles Moss, bishop of Bath in Wells, and the Right Rev. John Hinchliff, bishop of Peterborough.[53]

White strove to unite Connecticut and the North with the new Church. "In regard to the Church in Connecticut, it had been all along an object with the author, which he never endeavored to conceal, to bring its Episcopacy within the Union." [54] In August, 1789, he assured Seabury that the Convention would tolerate no question "which implied even a doubt of the Validity of your Consecration; and the Proceedings of the present Convention on that Subject, we are persuaded, will be more than sufficient to remove every Objection to our future Union, which might have been apprehended on that score." [55]

The principal act of the second session of 1789 "was the preparing of the Book of Common Prayer, as now the established liturgy of the Church." [56] White and Seabury worked on revision in the upper house, Provoost being absent due to alleged illness. The two Bishops worked well together. "To this day, there are recollected with satisfaction, the hours which were spent with Bishop Seabury, on the important subjects which came before them; and especially the Christian temper which he manifested all along." [57]

White's words about the restoration of Oblation and Invocation are worthy of note. He concurred readily with that very significant change, but his reasons for the restoration were less doctrinal than those of Seabury. White's remarks also reveal that he considered the Eucharist a Sacrifice in a *figurative* sense:

In the service for the administration of the communion it may perhaps be expected that the great change made, in restoring to the consecration prayer the oblatory words and the invocation of the Holy Spirit, left out in King Edward's reign, must at least have produced an opposition. But no such thing happened to any considerable extent; or at least, the author did not hear of any in the other house, further than a disposition to the effect in a few gentlemen, which was counteracted by some pertinent remarks of the president. In that of the bishops, it was very near to the heart of Bishop Seabury. As for the other bishop, without conceiving with some, that the service as it stood was essentially defective, he always thought there was a beauty in those ancient forms and can discover no superstition in them. If indeed they could have been reasonably thought to imply, that a Christian minister is a priest, in the sense of an offerer of sacrifice, and that the table is an altar and the elements a sacrifice, in any other than figurative senses, he would have zealously opposed the admission of such unevangelical sentiments—as he conceives them to be.[58]

White and Sacrifice

White's terminology differed considerably from Seabury's. But a careful reading of his discourses reveals some similarity in doctrine. White lamented the misunderstanding of Sacrifice that continually erupted even within Protestantism. Therefore, he thought the word "Sacrifice" should be used only when all safeguards were taken against superstitious misunderstanding. He feared the word induced belief in propitiatory Sacrifice, destruction of Christ's "animal" Body, and a material Sacrifice in the Eucharist. He disagreed with Seabury who called the Eucharist a Sacrifice as true and proper as Old Law Sacrifices. White explicitly denied this. In his explanation the Old Law Sacrifices were material, the Eucharist spiritual. His favorite expressions for the Eucharist were Memorial, spiritual or figurative Sacrifice, a Sacrifice of ourselves, our souls and bodies.

Another interesting tendency in White's writings is his recurring criticism of Laud, Johnson, and the Nonjurors. Yet, despite his misgivings about their Eucharistic doctrine, his writings reveal that he was influenced by their insights.

White thought revision of the liturgy a serious enterprise. He believed "the united wisdom of the Church should be employed in the establishing of the Articles and Liturgy." [59] Although "the providing of them is left to that prudence which may have regard to various circumstances of time, of place, of character, and of custom," [60] great respect should be had for the "early ages of the Church; it being especially understood of the first three centuries." [61] In this he was at one with the Nonjurors.

Throughout his writings, White denied that the Eucharist was a "material" Sacrifice. It was spiritual. "It had for its most distinguishing property, its being a spiritual sacrifice." [62] The very wording of the Communion service referred to a *spiritual* Sacrifice:

And as to the term "sacrifice" the only places in which it appears . . . with a reference to the Eucharist, is in the prayer of consecration; where it is said—"We offer and present unto thee, O Lord, ourselves, our souls and bodies, to be a reasonable, holy and living sacrifice unto thee"; and again—"Although we are unworthy, through our manifold sins, to offer unto thee any sacrifice, yet we beseech thee to accept this, our bounden duty and service." [63]

White's ideas on the Oblation and Invocation differed from Seabury's. He opposed their use if superstition threatened. The reason Cranmer incorporated them into the 1549 Service was that such superstition was demolished by the English reformers:

The English reformers carefully exploded every thing of this sort, at the time of their issuing of the first book of Common Prayer, which contained the oblation and invocation. Although they were left out on a subsequent review; yet it was done at the instance of two learned foreigners; and in order to avoid what was thought the appearance of encouragement of the superstition, which had been done away with.[64]

The key to White's hesitation in the use of "Sacrifice" may be found in the conviction that the true meaning of Sacrifice "is to be sought in the Old Testament, in which, it will always be found to comprehend the circumstance of animal oblation." [65] Furthermore, he seemed to misunderstand Roman doctrine, believing that Rome taught a daily destruction of Christ's animal Body in the Mass:

It is thought that Protestants should be aware, how they adopt a term, which, possessing the said property, may land them by fair consequence, on the sacrifice of the mass; in which the animal nature of the Redeemer of the world is supposed to be as truly offered, as it was at first on the cross.[66]

Although White's doctrine was actually close to that of Laud, he often spoke in Evangelical terms as if the Eucharist were commemoration before *men*. Although the commemoration was more than "a man's celebrating of the memory of a deceased friend," [67] the elements were memorials to men of Christ's Sacrifice:

As our Lord's command was simply, "Do this in remembrance of me;" it seems as if no more were necessary on the part of the receiver, than the act of commemoration, provided there be adequate apprehensions of the commemorated subject; that is, of the death of Christ, not merely as for human benefit, for so were the deaths of St. Peter and St. Paul, but as a propitiatory sacrifice, the antitype of that paschal sacrifice, at the close of which the eucharist was instituted. In this point of view, the bread and wine are memorials of the body and the blood of Christ as a sacrifice for sin.[68]

Caution was urged in the use of priest and Altar.[69] But once again, White was not denying that the Mass was a Memorial or representative Sacrifice. What he denied was that there was destruction of Christ:

> . . . the definitions of sacrifice have been so numerous, that it might perhaps be resolved into a strife of words, although in the scriptural sense of sacrifice, except when used metaphorically, slaying was an essential circumstance. But to the idea of a sacrifice in the eucharist, there is attached that of an altar, and that of priest, in the Jewish sense of the terms, which is unauthorized either by Scripture or by our Church, or rather in violation of the authority of both.[70]

White remarked that sacrifice, priest, and altar were not found in the Latin Prayer Book. To avoid the overtones of animal sacrifice associated with "priest," he preferred the use of "presbyter." "That neither sacrifice nor altar is found in her liturgy is evident. . . . In the Latin Prayer Book, which is of equal authority with the English, 'Priest' is not 'Sacerdos', but Presbyter; this even in the sacramental service." [71]

On one hand, White denied there was "sacrifice in the elements." By this he meant there was no animal sacrifice there, no carnal separation of Christ's Body and Blood. The Eucharist, on the contrary, was a spiritual Sacrifice:

> If the communion service be examined, it is easy to perceive places in which the eucharist itself might have been called a sacrifice, had any such thing been thought desirable; but in no such manner is the term applied. In the prayer of consecration, our prayers and thanksgiving are called a sacrifice; and we offer ourselves as "a living sacrifice." But these are evidently in the same latitude of sense in which our alms are so called in Scripture. As to there being a sacrifice in the elements, or a sacrificing in them, nothing like it is to be found.[72]

However, it should be stressed that White considered the elements a "typical" or representative Sacrifice. That is, once it was understood that there was no material sacrifice or destruction, the elements should be understood as types of Christ's Body and Blood. Christ presented such elements to *the Father* at the Last Supper; Christians do the same today.

> And therefore, I never could perceive any reason in the objection which some have made to that part of our consecration of the elements in which we offer them to the Father, as typical of His blessed Son's body and blood . . . and it seems involved in the act of our Saviour,

when, in the original institution, he invoked a blessing on the elements, in which act there must have been a religious presentation of them.[73]

White hesitated to say Christ was "verily and indeed" present in the elements. Once again, he feared the horrendous misunderstanding of a carnal or animal presence. Therefore, he said Christ was "spiritually" present.[74] He described the elements as representations of Christ's Body and Blood; "We consider as in themselves bread and wine, although made by consecration representative of that body and that blood." [75] In his understanding of the representative sacrifice, White, unwittingly, was at one with William Laud. When Laud said Christ was "truly and really" present, he had meant the same spiritual presence as White.

In the second letter to John Hobart, White manifested his deep suspicion of definitions of Sacrifice:

The points which I propose to handle are these: Is there in the Eucharist a Sacrifice? If not, is there a feast or sacrifice? And if neither, what is the import of its being the commemoration of a sacrifice:

The introducing of the third question shows that I answer the first and the second in the negative; and in regard to the first, I consider it as no small objection to the doctrine of the eucharistic sacrifice, in the strict and proper sense, that they who affirm it find so great difficult in agreeing in a definition of the word.[76]

The American prelate was well aware that most definitions of sacrifice involved destruction. He curtly contemned the definitions of learned men, cited by John Johnson, as arbitrary and "so is his own." [77] This latter swipe at Johnson shows that White was familiar with Nonjuror doctrine, but that he did not realize how close that doctrine was to his own. White feared that the myriad definitions prevalent in his day eventually ended in propitiation and animal destruction, the worst of "Roman Catholic superstition":

. . . there was a time when I was disposed to look on the present question as merely one of words. But when I came to consider maturely the opinions which go along with the affirmative side of the question, in the writings of those who hold it; and when I perceived, as I thought, a train of sentiment, which by a consistent progression ended in the worst of all the bad tenets of Roman Catholic superstition, I became uneasy at the appearance in our Church of any of that leaven which has shown itself capable of leavening the whole lump.[78]

Once again White did not realize how close, almost identical, his own doctrine was with Laud's. Laud preferred to call the Eucharist a Sacrifice; White a Memorial. Although their words differed, their doctrine came to the same thing. White displayed his suspicion of Laud by blaming him for much of the rampant superstition. "We are charged to 'take heed lest of the memory it be made a sacrifice.' To the best of my recollection this continued a universal sentiment to the time of Archbishop Laud." [79]

None of the early or later Fathers preached material sacrifice. Even Chrysostom, despite rhetorical flourishes, clearly differentiated Christian from Jewish oblations. Christians offered a Memorial of Christ's one Sacrifice.[80] Material sacrifice set the stage for Roman absurdity: "No sooner throw in among their indistinct conceptions the notion of material sacrifice, than it looks so much like that of a propitiatory sacrifice for the dead and living, as must be a preparation of the mind for the error in all its absurdity and mischievous tendency." [81] The Eucharist resembled the peace offerings. It was not expiatory, but a commemoration of an Atonement made once for all:

. . . this holy ordinance answers not to sacrifice of expiation, but to that of the peace offerings, which are never said to make atonement, but, on the contrary, suppose the worshipper in a state of reconciliation. I forbear to dilate on the consequences of our leading of the people to believe that at every celebration of the Lord's Supper we are making atonement for sin. No; let it be a commemoration of an atonement made once for all.[82]

White clearly taught application. "This is a matter which cannot be commemorated without a recognizing and an applying of whatever is its effects." [83] Invisible grace "is involved in the subject commemorated, and therefore must be imparted by the means of the celebration." [84]

Christians themselves were identified with the offering. As a commemoration of Christ's Atonement, the Eucharist demanded unbounded love in return:

Suppose I were told that you had introduced into your family the stated celebration of the memory of a friend, cherished by you with affection, which you took this way of expressing and perpetuating. But suppose me further informed that the favor consisted in dying that you and your whole family might live, and this without your having merited any favor at his hands, and even under the weight of great demerit; and then I perceive that it is a case which, beyond any other that concerns your temporary being, challenges the unbounded love of you and yours. Now, apply this to the subject, and you will perceive that the doctrine of a mere memorial gives no such degrading representation as is supposed in the language which has been bestowed on it.[85]

But the Eucharist was more than a mere commemoration and offering of ourselves. Once adequate safeguards were taken, it should be admitted the Eucharist was an oblation that began with the offering of alms which were presented by the Minister in the name of all:

What the primitive Church meant by Eucharistic oblation, may be seen in the Rubricks of the Episcopal Church, where she makes the "Offertory to *begin* with the collecting of the alms and other devotions of the people." The sentiment is supposed to have come down to us from the earliest times, in which the oblation began with popular contribution; although it was not perfected, until what had been thus gathered were presented at the Lord's table, in a solemn act of adoration. And this was done by the minister, in the name of all.[86]

White realized his strictures against use of "Sacrifice" could lead many to believe he opposed even typical or representative or figurative sacrifice. He countered this danger by admitting "there would be a mistake in supposing, that in what has been said concerning sacrifice and altar, a censure is designated on the figurative use of the words, which may occasionally be made to the advantage of discourse and without danger of misleading any." [87]

White and Real Presence

White considered Transubstantiation inimical to reason. Along with images and purgatory it was one of those "matters which afterwards crept gradually into the Church." [88]

It represents him as telling his disciples, while his sacred body was before their eyes that he was even then bearing it in his hands. Since his ascension, we learn from many places in Scripture, that it is in heaven; while the doctrine in question describes it as extended to every place, wherein a Christian minister may be commemorating his passion. Even the nature of a sacrament is hereby overthrown, as is remarked in the Twenty-eighth Article of this Church. For a sacrament is an outward sign of an inward grace: but according to the hypothesis, the substance of the sign vanishes under the act of consecration. And, that the properties of the substance should remain, after this itself has vanished, is a contradiction in terms; and therefore, unlike to anything proposed to our belief in scripture.[89]

Cranmer and his associates did not consider Oblation and Invocation necessary for Consecration. However, they did not consider them superstitious in themselves, but as abused by the superstition of men:

Considering further the great learning and the independent spirits of Archbishop Cranmer and his associates; the latter must have entertained the opinion, that the parts of the service in question were not essential to the ordinance; and that having been much abused by superstition, they were best dispensed with. That the English reformers thought them superstitious in themselves ought not to be believed. . . .[90]

The Scottish clergy, however, considered Oblation and Invocation essential. Considering Seabury's affection for his Scottish consecrators and for Nonjuror theology, White spoke tactfully and irenically when describing Scottish convictions:

. . . when a liturgy was provided, in the reign of Charles I. for the established Church of Scotland, at that time Episcopal; they who had the direction of the business, of whom the principal was Archbishop Laud, took care to insert what they thought to have been unnecessarily omitted among themselves. The parts so restored were handed down in the Episcopal Church of Scotland, after it ceased to be an establishment. And there is no part of the service to which the clergy of that Church are more attached. For there is here reason to think, that the matters in question are not uncommonly considered among them, as essential to the sacramental act.[91]

Throughout his writings, White consistently cautioned against belief in a corporal Presence of Christ. The elements signified and represented Christ's Body and Blood. It was these significative and representative elements that were presented by the priest.[92] It is not surprising that White leaned to the Zwinglian translation of the "est" of the Words of Institution. But once again displaying his affinity to Laud's position, White equated "represents" with "signifies": "Therefore the sense of the place is—'This bread signifies' (or represents) 'my body': and—'This cup signifies' (or represents) 'my blood.' " [93] The oblation effected no change. The elements remained creatures of bread and wine:

Be it remembered that the matter is not here contended for so far, as to affirm the oblatory words to be essential to the commemorative eating of bread and wine. They are, however, advocated, not only as defensible, but as impressive and edifying. It would be another thing, were the elements spoken of as comprehending more than what is discernible by our senses.—"These thy gifts and creatures of bread and wine:" and the words are after the oblation; which therefore could never have been conceived of, as effecting any change.[94]

Nor did the Invocation effect change. The elements were sanctified through the Invocation, as was Baptismal water. But White did not teach a change in qualities as did his colleague, Bishop Seabury:

As to the other branch of the subject, the invocation of the Holy Spirit, not on ourselves only, for that is in the English service, but as sanctifying the bread and the wine to their religious application; it is no more than similar to what is done in our baptismal offices, when we implore God to "sanctify the element of water to the mystical washing away of sin." [95]

White insisted that the elements remained bread and wine, although representative of Christ's Body and Blood:

The extravagance of those errors, independently of any other cause, makes an irreconcilable division between us and the Church of Rome. The decisions of that Church, naturally and by fair consequence, lead to the adoration of what they call the body and the blood of the Redeemer; but what we consider as in themselves mere bread and wine, although made by that consecration representative of that body and that blood.[96]

White yearned for peace and unity in the fledgling Church.[97] Therefore he surmounted his fear of superstition and backed Seabury's efforts to instill a "complete" Consecration in the nascent Service. But subtly and indirectly, and without a hint of polemics, White dissociated himself from Seabury's view of Consecration:

Bishop Seabury's attachment to these changes may be learned from the following incident. On the morning of the Sunday which occurred during the session of the convention, the author wished him to consecrate the elements. This he declined. On the offer being again made at the time when the service was to begin, he still declined; and smiling, added—To confess the truth, I hardly consider the form to be used, as strictly amounting to a consecration. The form was of course that used heretofore; the changes not having taken effect. These sentiments he had adopted, in his visit to the bishops from whom he received his Episcopacy.[98]

In discussing Real Presence, White used receptionist terminology. The elements, although sanctified by Consecration, recalled Christ's benefits to *the mind*. They were *pledges* of these benefits. White did not restrict the attainment of these benefits to Holy Communion: ". . . it should be remarked, that the benefits thus assured, are not restricted to the times of receiving the pledges of them; although such times are peculiarly proper for the realizing of them to our minds." [99] White departed from the Nonjurors in denying the elements contained the effects of Calvary. They were pledges that strengthened and refreshed the soul:

> "What are the benefits whereof we are partakers thereby?" Answer—"The strengthening and refreshing of our souls by the bread and wine." This carries us from the results of the benefits of the sacrifice of Christ, as they are in themselves, to their beneficial influence on those who duly receive the pledges of them.[100]

Adoration of the species arose only in the thirteenth century, an historical innovation that proved the lateness of the doctrine that elements comprehended the Divinity. "It was not until the thirteenth century, that the idea was conceived of the adoration of the host: Which was so natural, on the supposition of its comprehending of the divinity; that the lateness of the ceremony is unanswerable evidence of the lateness of the doctrine." [101]

Extravagant parlance of fourth century writers who spoke of change in the elements eventually resulted in the error of Transubstantiation. White noted that these writers, while speaking of a heavenly virtue in consecrated elements, testified to the fact that bread and wine remained:

> . . . they spoke commonly of a change made in the elements by the act of consecration; conceiving of this change as superinducing a heavenly virtue on the elements, but not destroying their substantial properties. That they expressed the former sentiment in language which led to transubstantiation shall not be here denied; but is considered as

fruitful of caution, as to whatever may lead to the same result. Among the arguments which should clear them from the charge of that extremity of error, is the fact of their occasionally speaking of the bread and the wine, as remaining after the consecration.[102]

White strove as did Seabury for frequent Communion, which to him also meant more than once a month. He believed the primitive Christians received every Lord's Day:

Its being attended to in our Churches only monthly and on the three principal festivals is one of the many proofs existing, that the piety of Christians is not so ardent as in the beginning. There are few facts more satisfactorily proved, than that of the eucharist having been administered in the primitive Church every Lord's day.[103]

William Temple once remarked that the *via media* was not the middle ground but the comprehension of both extremes. To some extent this was the case when the Catholic Seabury and the Evangelical White agreed on the Scottish Canon. But White did admit a figurative Sacrifice of the elements and a true and real Presence. That he and Seabury succeeded in incorporating the 1764 Canon was made possible by the cooperation of the president of the lower house, William Smith.

WILLIAM SMITH

William Smith was a prominent educator and divine, who, along with Seabury and White, was a key figure in organizing the Episcopal Church and framing a new Prayer Book.

As chairman of the committee for the "Proposed Book" in 1785, Smith advocated considerable, albeit cautious, revision. In the words of his biographer, "Dr. Smith . . . was the person chiefly desirous of a further considerable review, and the person chiefly active in bringing on a discussion concerning the change, and in suggesting and introducing the particulars of it." [104]

Smith influenced the future Communion Service indirectly by his zeal to vindicate Seabury's consecration and to induce the Connecticut prelate to attend the 1789 convention. In early 1789 he wrote Seabury, begging him to attend the convention, and even proffering the hospitality of the Smith household.[105] Later he arranged reconciliation between Seabury and Bishop Provoost, a feat he "considered among the good acts of his life." [106]

It was a propitious omen for supporters of a new Communion

Service when Smith was chosen president of the lower house. From that lofty post, he succeeded by "pertinent remarks" in stemming any incipient recalcitrance.[107] Furthermore, it was his resonant and obviously sincere reading of the new Service that convinced the delegates of its value.[108]

Smith did not write extensively on the Eucharist. But his scanty writings on the subject reveal why he was a forceful advocate of the new Service on the House floor.

It should be remembered that, except for the Canon, the 1789 Service was basically a conservative revision of 1662. And Smith's attitude toward the latter Prayer Book was one of abiding reverence. He extolled the English liturgy as "our excellent liturgy." [109] In 1786 the Communion Service was "our excellent Church-Service." [110] In 1783 he pleaded for a conservative revision "which it is humbly conceived, may and will be done, without any other or farther departure from the venerable Order and beautiful Forms of Worship of the Church from whence we sprung, than may be found expedient in the change of our situation." [111] In 1785 he waxed rhetorical in his praise of the English liturgy: "We stood arrested, as it were, at an awful distance—It appeared almost sacrilege to approach the porch, or lift a hand to touch a single part, to polish a single corner, or to clear it from its rust of years." [112]

Smith and Sacrifice

Despite this reverence for the English Service, Smith was in sympathy with John Johnson in his views on Sacrifice. On one occasion he described his position as similar to "the author of the unbloody sacrifice." [113] He too sought Eucharistic doctrine from the "first Christians who were the Admiration of the World." [114]

The Eucharist was a real, representative Sacrifice. Unlike White, Smith did not hesitate to call the Eucharist a Sacrifice. The Lord's Supper was "a real Sacrifice representing Christ's death and passion:—and the Evangelical priests the proper offerers of that sacrifice." This doctrine was "indisputable if scripture and the primitive Fathers are allowed to adduce their testimony." [115]

In Nonjuror parlance, Smith believed "it was the judgment of the primitive church that Christ sacrificed himself ineffably and invisibly when he instituted the Eucharist, or communion of His body and blood." [116]

In one passage, Smith hinted that the Eucharist applied Christ's Sacrifice, but he did not develop the idea. "Whatever degree of excellency the primitive church ascribed to the representative sacrifice of the Eucharist, they never considered the atonement of Christ thereby diminished, but rather magnified and rendered so much the more efficacious." [117]

There was evidence "to prove the Eucharist is a sacrifice,—a representative Sacrifice, *shewing* forth or exhibiting Christ's death." [118] The laity would always consider "the holy communion as 'a sacrifice of praise and thanksgiving, shewing forth' their Redeemer's 'death until his second coming.' " [119] The Apostle Paul "taught the Galatians that the holy Eucharist was a sacrifice representing Christ's body broken and blood shed." [120] The Lord's Supper was a source of consolation to Christians because of its memorial aspect:

. . . let us dwell on the heights and the depths and the breadths of the love manifested to us, and seek every occasion to commemorate this love in the way he hath appointed, by drawing near to him at his holy table, on the great occasions appointed by his church for that heavenly service.[121]

The Supper of the Lord was "to be for ever observed in remembrance of the spiritual redemption procured by him." [122] The elements were witnesses of the covenant which kept up the remembrance of Christ's death until His second coming.

The great captain of our salvation . . . in that night before the bloody tragedy of his cross (knowing that his disciples and followers were soon to be dispersed over the whole earth) instituted the elements of consecrated bread and wine, to remain eternal witnesses of the new covenant between God and us, and to keep up the remembrance of his meritorious death, until he shall come again. . . .[123]

But the sacrifice was more than a mere manward remembrance. It was a Godward representation of Christ's death. Smith's defense of altar and priesthood reflected his belief in this Godward sacrifice:

Having shown a disposition to blot out the priesthood, to break down every altar sacred to Jesus, and to reduce the representative sacrifice of the holy Eucharist to a bare act of faith or memory in the recipient; you sum up all your benevolent intentions toward christianity, by saying—"we may be well content to resign the sacerdotal character to others, neither any longer calling our ministers priests, nor our communion tables altars." [124]

When Smith called the Eucharist a proper Sacrifice, he meant it was offered to God. He interpreted St. Paul's words about the Lord's table as referring to a proper altar. A Godward Sacrifice was intrinsically connected to the concepts of priesthood and altar:

Sacrifice is inseparable from the idea of priesthood, and both are closely connected with the idea of an altar; not that an altar is absolutely necessary for the offering of a proper sacrifice, for in the days of persecution, the christian priests might, in want of a proper altar, offer the Eucharist on the stump of a tree, or a common table, as acceptably as upon an altar of most exquisite workmanship. If you object to my calling the communion table an altar—and quote St. Paul calling it a table;—observe he does not call it a *table* simply but the *Lord's table*. The table of the Lord was the most honorable title, that the prophets and apostles could give to a proper altar.[125]

Smith concurred with Seabury and White that the Mass was not propitiatory. He considered purgatory a fabrication devised for lucre. He believed that neither Masses, prayers of the Church militant, or intercessions of Saints and Angels profited the deceased:

The Abuse of this Doctrine, the gainful trade instituted, or engrafted upon it, by *Deceivers,* and those willing to be *deceived* as I never thought it much worthy of an earlier attention in Life, I shall not think it worthy of a present discussion.[126]

Smith and Real Presence

Smith did not elaborate his doctrine of Real Presence. When he did discuss the subject, he made it clear that he considered the elements bread and wine that represented Christ's death. He was "equally opposed to the doctrine of transubstantiation as to that of consubstantiation, both of them being to me equally unintelligible." [127]

The elements were bread and wine. As a representative Sacrifice, they were witnesses "shewing forth Christ's death, 'till his second coming.'" [128] The elements were "forms of bread and wine." By this Smith meant that they remained in their natural substance and showed forth Christ's death. They were "a representative crucifixion, the *shewing forth Christ's death* in the holy communion, under the forms of bread and wine." [129]

The elements were compared to the unchanged elements of Melchisedech.[130] They were "eternal witnesses of the new covenant between God and us." [131] In the Old Law the Lamb had prefigured and represented Christ's death. Now the Eucharistic elements represented the same event. When Christ instituted the Sacrament he used the same bread and wine with which he had celebrated the Pasch. Smith does not imply any change in the elements:

> In the same chamber, and with a portion of the same bread and wine, with which Jesus had celebrated the paschal solemnities, he instituted the evangelical passover, the sacrament of his own body and blood to be a representative memorial of his "death and passion" until his second coming; the paschal Lamb had prefigured and represented his "death and passion" until his first. The manner of representation is different, but the object represented is the same.[132]

On one occasion Smith referred to reception of the benefits of Christ's death. But within the context of his writings, he probably meant the benefits through faith in a devout reception of the Eucharist. "Let us come to partake of it with a due sense of the benefits of Christ's death, with secret longings to make conformable to him, and to enjoy him, with stedfast resolutions to resist and amend all vice." [133]

Smith advocated a weekly celebration of the Lord's Supper as was done by the early Christians:

> The most superficial reading of Scripture will show us that the manner in which the inspired apostles and first Christians kept the Sabbath, was by praying and preaching, exhorting one another, joining together in psalms and hymns and spiritual songs, in celebrating the Lord's Supper, and in giving alms to the distressed.[134]

When history is being made, small events often seem insignificant. Only in retrospect do what once appeared to be accidents take on their true perspective. Such an apparently small event was Samuel Seabury's trip to Aberdeen for a Scottish consecration. Yet in retrospect it was the concordat he signed there that eventually put America squarely in the Catholic Eucharistic tradition of 1549. At the 1789 convention, Seabury was assisted in the lower house by William Smith. The Service that resulted from their zeal for Nonjuror theology is still substantially the Communion Service of the Protestant Episcopal Church.

THE COMMUNION SERVICE OF 1789

The American Communion Service was essentially a conservative revision of the 1662 English Service and, for the Consecration, the 1764 Scottish Service.

As in 1662, the title was "The Order For The Administration of the Lord's Supper or, Holy Communion." [135]

Perhaps in emulation of 1764, there was a tendency to simplify and even eliminate rubrics. At the outset, the rubric for transmission of names the day before Communion was deleted.

Only minor verbal changes occurred in the two rubrics for penitential preparation. The Minister was to report cases of exclusion from Communion "as soon as conveniently may be."

There was a noteworthy change in the rubric for the altar, although it did not have doctrinal significance. The Minister was to stand at the north side of the table, *or* where Morning and Evening Prayer were said. This strange provision was dictated by the design of St. Peter's in Philadelphia. The Standing Liturgical Commission described the Church and explained the changed wording of the rubric:

To this day this church has a "three-decker" reading-desk and pulpit at one end of the building, and the altar at the other. The congregation must reverse the way they are sitting in the square box pews when the service passes from Morning Prayer to the Holy Communion. Bishop White, who was then in charge of the parish, asked to be spared the needless effort and disturbance of walking from one end of the church to the other merely to read the "Ante-Communion," as was the invariable custom in those days, and then back again for the Sermon.[136]

The Lord's Prayer could be omitted if Morning Prayer had preceded immediately before. This change reflected the new Church's desire to avoid repetition. The entire rubric read as follows:

The Table, at the Communion-time, having a fair white linen cloth upon it, shall stand in the body of the Church, or in the Chancel; and the Minister, standing at the north side of the table, or where Morning and Evening Prayer are appointed to be said, shall say the

Lord's Prayer and the Collect following, the People kneeling, but the Lord's Prayer may be omitted, if Morning Prayer hath been said immediately before.

After the Our Father (when said) and the Collect for Purity, the Service continued with the decalogue litany. However, Nonjuror influence appeared in the permission to recite the Summary of the Law and the second prayer from the English Ante-Communion Collects.

There was, of course, no rubric prescribing a Collect for the King. Perhaps to compensate for this omission, there was a provision at the end of the Service that the optional Collects could be used at Communion according to the Minister's discretion.

Within the Service itself, the Collect for the day was followed by directions for the Epistle and Gospel. Another sign of Nonjuror influence was the restoration of "Glory be to thee, O Lord," after the Gospel.

The next rubric allowed a choice of Apostles' or Nicene Creed, *unless* one of them had been read in Morning Service.[137] The Creeds were printed within the texts for Morning and Evening Prayer.

The announcements and sermon followed the Creed (when said). But there was no mention of prescribed homilies.

After the sermon, the Minister "when there is a Communion" was to return to the Lord's Table, "and begin the Offertory, saying one or more of these sentences following, as he thinketh most convenient." The Sentences and rubrics followed 1662. The vividly sacrificial rubrics are reprinted below:

Whilst these Sentences are in reading, the Deacons, Churchwardens, or other fit persons appointed for that purpose, shall receive the Alms for the Poor, and other Devotions of the People, in a decent Basin to be provided by the Parish for the purpose; and reverently bring it to the Priest, who shall humbly present and place it upon the Holy Table. And the Priest shall then place upon the Table so much Bread and Wine, as he shall think sufficient. After which is done, he shall say. . . .

Another sign of Nonjuror influence was the omission of "here in earth" from the introduction to the prayer for the Church.

Instead of a petition for the King, the prayer read, "We beseech thee also, so to direct and dispose the hearts of all Christian rulers, that they may truly and impartially administer justice, to the punishment of wickedness and vice, and to the maintenance of thy true religion and virtue." The petition for the Clergy now read: "Give grace, O heavenly Father, to all Bishops and other Ministers."

The exhortations, Invitation, Confession, Absolution, and Comfortable Words followed the prayer for the Church.

There was one new preface. The Standing Liturgical Commission conjectured that "the impact of the outbreak of Unitarianism in New England by the secession of King's Chapel, Boston, may have influenced the adoption of a new alternative Proper Preface for Trinity Sunday." [138] The new preface was as follows:

> For the precious death and merits of thy Son Jesus Christ our Lord, and for the sending to us of the Holy Ghost the Comforter; who are one with thee in eternal Godhead: Therefore with Angels &c.

The Prayer of Humble Access was between Sanctus and Consecration.

In the one big change of the American Service, that of the Consecration prayer, the American text is so amazingly close—even in wording—to the 1764 Service that only one passage demands comparison. There was a notable change in the Invocation, probably because of a Declaration of the 1786 Maryland Convention. When William White proposed Seabury's rite to that Convention, they rejected "that they may become the body and blood of thy most dearly beloved Son" for the more familiar English wording.[139] This may have been due, in part, to White himself who was reticent to call the elements Christ's Body and Blood. The two texts are compared below:

1764	1789
And we most humbly beseech thee, O merciful Father, to hear us, and of thy almighty goodness vouchsafe to bless and sanctify, with thy word and holy Spirit, these thy gifts and creatures of bread and wine, that they may become the body and blood	And we most humbly beseech thee, O merciful Father, to hear us; and, of thy Almighty goodness, vouchsafe to bless and sanctify, with thy Word and Holy Spirit, these thy gifts and creatures of bread and wine; that we, receiving them according to thy Son

1764	1789
of thy most dearly beloved Son.	our Saviour Jesus Christ's holy institution, in remembrance of his Death and Passion, may be partakers of his most blessed Body and Blood.

Immediately after the Consecration prayer, there was provision for a Communion hymn: "Here shall be sung a Hymn, or Part of a Hymn, from the Selection for the Feasts and Fasts, &c."

The rubric and formulas for distribution followed the English Service, but Nonjuror influences appeared in the rubric for reconsecration. The *entire* Consecration prayer to the end of the Invocation was to be used:

If the consecrated Bread and Wine be spent before all have communicated, the Priest is to consecrate more, according to the Form before prescribed; beginning at—*All glory be to thee, Almighty God*—and ending with these words—*Partakers of his most blessed Body and Blood.*

Remaining elements were to be covered reverently.

There was a rubric for the Lord's Prayer with the people repeating the petitions after the Minister. Only the second "Post Communion" prayer of 1662 was to be said.

With the promulgation of the 1789 Communion Service, a long and complicated evolution reached a consummation. Cranmer's innovation in 1548 had inaugurated a long process of several centuries, involving theologians of three nations, that finally burst forth in the New World in 1789. This was the same year in which the American experiment in representative government really began. George Washington was an Episcopalian. When he first worshipped according to the new Communion Office, two traditions, one political and one spiritual, met at the Altar of God.

Conclusion

The scandal of a divided Christendom is most evident when Christians are unable to eat the Bread of Life at the same table. Early in the seventeenth century, the Anglican James Ussher remarked: "It is a lamentable thing to behold how this Holy Sacrament, which was ordained by Christ to be a bond whereby we should be knit together in unity . . . is made the principal occasion of that woeful distraction which we see amongst Christians at this day." [1]

In the study we have just concluded, we examined the historical development of Anglican Eucharistic doctrine during three centuries and on two continents. We have found that from the Reformation to recent times, Anglican doctrine has tended to converge with that of the Roman Catholic Church. The conclusion we have reached from a historical point of view concurs with that of a recent commission of Anglicans and Roman Catholics who have been studying contemporary doctrinal formulations of both churches. In a statement issued after a conference on formulations on Eucharistic Sacrifice, theologians and bishops of both churches said: "Since the time of the Reformation, the doctrine of Eucharistic sacrifice has been considered a major obstacle to the reconciliation of the Anglican Communion and the Roman Catholic Church. It is the conviction of our commission that this is no longer true." [2]

In our historical study we have also found that since the Elizabethan settlement, comprehensiveness has been a component of Anglican Services. The rite of the Episcopal Church is as susceptible as the Roman Mass to interpretation in terms of propitiatory Sacrifice and perduring Real Presence. In fact, there is one component of the Episcopal Canon—the Invocation insisted on by Seabury—that possibly teaches Real Presence more explicitly than the Roman Mass.

One Anglican scholar, Massey H. Shepherd, Jr., is well aware that the Mass of the Episcopal Church (and even the Methodist rites) are susceptible to Roman Catholic interpretation, including the disputed doctrine of Transubstantiation.

The divergencies of doctrine are not so much implicit in the formularies themselves as they are in the interpretations imposed upon them by theological confessions that are external to the rite. Doctrinal definitions of the Real Presence, for example, are not precisely stated in the liturgies. It is we who impose our niceties of distinction upon them. The dogma of Transubstantiation is read into, not read out of, the Roman Canon of the Mass. And the same dogma could be read into any liturgy that employs our Lord's Words of Institution. The Methodist liturgy as such is no more lacking in a proper doctrine of the Real Presence than is the liturgy of the English Prayer Book, which is its immediate parent. If the experience of Anglicans counts for anything, it is fair to say that a liturgy faithful to the language of Scripture and tradition can comprehend a certain variety of doctrinal emphasis without danger to a real unity in the fundamentals of the Christian faith.[3]

Shepherd's caution about "niceties of distinction" can serve as a reminder to Roman Catholics that the Eucharistic Sacrifice and Real Presence are profound mysteries. The Roman Catholic theologian Francis Clark has also noted: "Not only the Eucharistic Presence of Christ but likewise the Eucharistic sacrifice remains a profound mystery. A scholastic theory which would attempt to empty out the mystery and to explain the question, as if it lay wholly within the grasp of human understanding, would stand self-condemned." [4]

In 1897, when replying to Pope Leo XIII, the Anglican Archbishops of Canterbury and York had likewise called attention to the mystery in the Eucharist—a statement worthy of serious consideration by Anglicans and Roman Catholics today:

The matter is indeed one full of mystery and fitted to draw onwards the minds of men by strong feelings of love and piety to high and deep thoughts. But inasmuch as it ought to be treated with the highest reverence and to be considered a bond of Christian charity rather than an occasion for subtle disputations, too precise definitions of the manner of sacrifice, or of the relation which unites the sacrifice of the eternal Priest and the sacrifice of the Church, which in some way certainly are one, ought in our opinion to be avoided rather than pressed into prominence.[5]

Anglicans take justifiable pride in their historic adherence to the mystery of the supernatural. Roman Catholic theologians who speculate on the Eucharist within the framework of modern philosophy are to be commended, but they can learn caution not only from Pope Paul VI but from the Anglican Paul Elmer More, who wrote that "the rationalization of the supernatural is always in danger of pushing on to a formula which magnifies one half of the truth to an Absolute by excluding the other half." [6] Certainly theologians of both communions should seek *"aliqualem intelligentiam"* of the Faith, but in the last analysis there is much wisdom in the words of two Episcopal Divines, Walden Pell and P. M. Dawley: "No one has ever explained the Consecration satisfactorily. Men have tried again and again, and always failed." [7]

Over twenty-five years ago, the Anglican Dean William Palmer Ladd ventured that the American Prayer Book might provide an effective instrument for unity. Ladd went on to raise an intriguing question:

Ours is the responsibility and the duty to make the most of our Prayer Book Eucharist as a living, spiritual tradition. Thus it would attract far-flung and unsuspected loyalties, and the next one hundred and fifty years might witness its development into an increasingly effective instrument for the promotion of unity among all the churches of our sadly divided Christendom. May it not be the special vocation of our Church to make that contribution to the fulfillment of our Lord's great eucharistic petition "that they all may be one"? [8]

A final word remains to be said about the practical implications of the findings of this study and the similar findings of the recent colloquium between theologians of both churches.

In studying Anglican Eucharistic thought historically, we have found substantial identity developing between Canterbury and Rome. The theologians who met in May, 1967, studied statements of the contemporary position of both churches on Eucharistic Sacrifice. They reached the same conclusion from these contemporary sources as we have from a historical study. We also agree with the Commission's recommendation:

We believe that it is of utmost importance for the clergy and laity of our two churches to acknowledge their substantial identity in this area of Eucharistic doctrine and to build upon it as they go forward in dialogue. Whatever doctrinal disagreements may remain between our churches, the understanding of the sacrificial nature of the Eucharist is not among them.[9]

As one way for clergy and laity to "acknowledge their substantial identity" in the doctrine of Eucharistic Sacrifice, we would propose that Roman Catholic priests make use of the Communion Rite of the Episcopal Church. This should be done with proper authorization and on suitable occasions. This would serve as a vivid reminder to the faithful of both churches of their substantial agreement on the Eucharist.

We also propose concelebration by Anglican and Roman Catholic priests when this is authorized by both churches. Admittedly, there is still disagreement on Anglican orders, but the participation of Roman Catholic priests should satisfy everyone that there is a "valid" Mass. If the Mass takes place in a Roman Catholic Church, we would recommend the use of the Anglican Communion Service. If it takes place in an Anglican Church, we recommend the use of the Roman Catholic Service. As a further sign of unity, we recommend that the faithful present at such Services receive Communion from a priest *not* of their own church.

The Eucharist should be sign and cause of unity. We think and hope and pray that the polemical epithets of yesterday will never again wound and separate Anglicans and Roman Catholics, who share substantial agreement in Eucharistic doctrine. The rites of both churches reflect and admit this doctrine. It remains only for clergy and laity of both churches to gather around the same table and break the same bread. Common celebration of the Eucharist will be a sign of the new unity that exists and a cause of the deeper unity to come. Perhaps it was no coincidence that Roman Catholic Archbishop McGucken of San Francisco was in the sanctuary during consecration of Episcopal Bishop C. Kilmer Myers and that, a few months later, Bishop Myers summoned Christians to reconsider their thinking about Rome.

Appendix

Revisions of 1892 and 1928
in the Episcopal Church

Although the Communion Service revisions of 1892 and 1928 are not treated in this book, for the sake of completeness the few alterations are summarized here.

In 1892, largely through the efforts of William Reed Huntington, General Convention finally agreed to alter the Communion Service in a few details. The Decalogue could be omitted, provided it was said once on a Sunday. But when it was omitted, the Lord's Summary of the Law was to be read in its place, followed by the Lesser Litany. The Nicene Creed was printed after the rubric for the Gospel. It was required to be read on the five great festivals of the year. Acts xx. 35 (the last part) was prefixed to the Offertory Sentences. To the latter were added Exodus xxv. 2, Deuteronomy xvi. 16, 17, and I. Chronicles xxix, 11 and 14 (the last part). The Communion exhortation could be omitted if it were already said on one Lord's Day in the same month. The Sanctus was printed in a separate paragraph with a rubric that people and priest recite it conjointly. The Oblation and Invocation were divided into separate paragraphs. Finally, in a very felicitous change, the two penitential exhortations were transferred to the end of the Service.

In 1928, a commission, of which Bishops Whitehead and Slattery were Chairmen, succeeded in having another revision accepted. There were three new Proper Prefaces and an *intercession* for the departed. A more traditional prologue was prefixed to the Lord's Prayer. Several new Epistles, Gospels, and Collects were added. The Lord's Prayer and Prayer of Humble Access followed the Consecration Prayer.

Author's Notes

Introduction

1. Joseph M. Powers, "Mysterium Fidei and the Theology of the Eucharist," in *Worship*, Vol. 40, No. 1, January, 1966, p. 35. See also Cecil McGarry, "The Eucharistic Celebration as the True Manifestation of the Church," in *Church and Eucharist*, Michael Hurley, ed. (Dublin, 1966), pp. 33–35, 41–42.

Chapter I: The Communion Service of 1549

1. *The booke of the common prayer and administration of the Sacramentes, and other rites and ceremonies of the Churche: after the use of the Churche of England*, in *The Two Liturgies, A.D. 1549 and A.D. 1552: with other Documents Set Forth By Authority in the Reign of King Edward VI.* Joseph Ketley, ed. (Cambridge, Parker Society, 1844), p. 19. On this diversity of uses previous to 1549, T. M. Parker remarks, "There were indeed local rites; but they were not, as an unwary reader of the Act of Uniformity might suppose, different liturgies. All were varieties of the broadly uniform Roman rite, by the Middle Ages prevalent in all Western Christendom except a few isolated spots," in "The Problem of Uniformity 1559–1604," The Archbishop of Canterbury, *et al.*, *The English Prayer Book 1549–1662* (London, 1963), pp. 31–32.

2. Francis Procter and Walter Frere, *A New History of the Book of Common Prayer: With A Rationale of Its Offices* (London, 1951), p. 14.

3. F. E. Brightman, *The English Rite*, 2 Vols. (London, 1921), Vol. 1, pp. xcviii–ciii. See also Aidan Gasquet and Edmund Bishop, *Edward VI and the Book of Common Prayer* (London, 1928), pp. 164–176.

4. *Manuale ad Usum Percelebris Ecclesiae Sarisburiensis*, A. Jeffries Collins, ed., "Henry Bradshaw Society," Vol. 91 (Chichester, 1958), pp. 84–90. All references to the Sarum Canon are taken from this edition of the *Manuale*. For the preparation and the Mass preceding the Canon, see *The Order of the Communion 1548*, H. A. Wilson, ed., "Henry Bradshaw Society," Vol. 34 (London, 1908), pp. 30–36; for the parts subsequent to the Canon, see pp. 39–41, 44–45 (Appendix III).

5. The Standing Liturgical Commission of the Protestant Episcopal Church of the United States of America, *Prayer Book Studies IV, The Eucharistic Liturgy* (New York, 1953), pp. 25–26.

6. Christopher Wordsworth, *Notes on Medieval Services in England* (London, 1898), p. 93.

7. Wilson, ed., *Order of Communion*, p. xvi (Introduction by editor).

8. T. M. Parker, *The English Reformation to 1558* (London, 1950), p. 131.

9. *Ibid.* See also John Cheke, *Pio Lectori*, in Thomas Cranmer, *Defensio Verae et Catholicae Doctrinae de Sacramento Corporis et Sanguinis Christi*, in *Writings and Disputations of Thomas Cranmer Relative to the Sacrament of the Lord's Supper*, John Edmund Cox, ed. (Cambridge, Parker Society, 1844), p. 6 (Foreword). Hereafter cited as *Writings Relative to the Lord's Supper*.

10. Thomas Cranmer, *A Short Instruction into the Christian Religion, Being a Catechism Set Forth by Archbishop Cranmer in 1548, Together with the Same in Latin Translated from the German by Justus Jonas in 1539*, Edward Burton, ed. (Oxford, 1829), pp. 176–177, 207–208. The Latin had said: "Deinde de pane dicit, Hoc est corpus meum, et de calice, Hic est sanguis meus. Ideo credere debemus, quod vere corpus et sanguis ejus sit." Cranmer's translation was as follows: "Secondarily Christ saieth of the breade, this is my bodye, and of the cuppe he sayeth, this is my bloud. Wherefore we ought to beleue, that in the sacrament we receyve trewly the bodye and bloud of Christ."

11. In a parliamentary debate Cranmer said: "Eating with his mouth gyveth nothing to man, nor the bodye being in the bread. . . ." and "They be twoo things to eate the Sacrament and to eate the bodie of Christ," in J. T. Tomlinson, *The Great Parliamentary Debate in 1548 on the Lord's Supper* (London, [n.d.]), p. 39 (Appendix).

12. Bartholomew Traheron to Henry Bullinger, London, December 31, 1548, in *Original Letters Relative to the English Reformation Written During the Reigns of King Henry VIII, King Edward VI, and Queen Mary: Chiefly from the Archives of Zurich*, 2 Vols., Hastings

Robinson, ed. and trans. (Cambridge, Parker Society, 1846–1847), Vol. 1, p. 323.

13. *An Answer by the Reverend Father in God Thomas Archbishop of Canterbury, Primate of all England and Metropolitane, Unto a craftie and Sophisticall cauillation, deuised by Stephen Gardiner Doctour of Law, late Bishop of Winchester agaynst the true and godly doctrine of the most holy Sacrament, of the body and bloud of our Sauiour Jesu Christ,* in *Writings Relative to Lord's Supper,* pp. 53, 64, 79. That the *Answer to Gardiner* itself contained Cranmer's last word on the Eucharist seems clear from John Foxe's sympathetic account of the Archbishop's last words in St. Mary's Church, Oxford, a few minutes before his last walk to the stake at what is now Broad Street just opposite Balliol College, in *Acts and Monuments,* Josiah Pratt, ed., 8 Vols. (London, 1877), Vol. 8, p. 88.

14. *The Answer of Thomas, Archbishop of Canterbury, &c., Against The False Calumniations of Doctor Richard Smith, Who Hath Taken Upon Him to Confute the Defence of the True and Catholic Doctrine of the Body and Blood of Our Saviour Christ,* in *Writings Relative to Lord's Supper,* p. 369.

15. *Answer to Gardiner, ibid.,* p. 352.

16. *Ibid.,* p. 361.

17. *Ibid.,* p. 47.

18. "Disputations at Oxford," *ibid.,* p. 395.

19. *Answer to Gardiner, ibid.,* p. 352.

20. *Ibid.*

21. *Ibid.,* p. 86.

22. *Ibid.,* p. 349.

23. "Disputations at Oxford," *ibid.,* p. 399.

24. *Answer to Gardiner, ibid.,* p. 347.

25. "Disputations at Oxford," *ibid.,* pp. 396–397.

26. *Answer to Gardiner, ibid.,* p. 86.

27. *The Answer of Thomas, Archbishop of Canterbury &c Against the False Calumniations of Doctor Richard Smith, ibid.,* p. 369.

28. Thomas Cranmer, *A Defence of the True and Catholic Doctrine of the Body and Blood of Christ Our Saviour,* in *Archbishop Cranmer on the True and Catholic Doctrine of the Lord's Supper,* Charles H. H. Wright, ed. (London, 1907), pp. 45–47.

29. *Answer to Gardiner,* in *Writings Relative to Lord's Supper,* p. 348.

30. *Ibid.*

31. *Ibid.,* pp. 348–349.

32. *Ibid.*, p. 349.
33. *Ibid.*, p. 364.
34. *Ibid.*, p. 350.
35. *Ibid.*, p. 352.
36. *Defence,* in *Archbishop Cranmer on the True and Catholic Doctrine,* pp. 235, 240, 243.
37. *Answer to Gardiner,* in *Writings Relative to Lord's Supper,* p. 351.
38. *Ibid.*
39. *Ibid.*, p. 352.
40. *Ibid.*
41. Edward B. Pusey, *Eirenicon* (London, 1865), p. 25.
42. *Answer to Gardiner,* in *Writings Relative to Lord's Supper,* p. 34.
43. *Ibid.*
44. *Ibid.*, p. 46.
45. *Defence,* in *Archbishop Cranmer on the True and Catholic Doctrine,* p. 156.
46. *Ibid.*, p. 121.
47. *Answer to Gardiner,* in *Writings Relative to Lord's Supper,* p. 56.
48. *Ibid.*, p. 225. R. T. Beckwith, librarian of the evangelical Latimer House at Oxford University, wrote, "One can safely assert, and without qualification, that before the Oxford Movement the real presence of Christ's Body and Blood in the bread and wine was universally rejected by Anglican Divines," in *Priesthood and Sacraments, A Study in the Anglican-Methodist Report* (Plymouth, 1964), p. 62. In the case of Cranmer at least, Beckwith's strong statement is correct.
49. *A Preface to the Reader,* in *Answer to Gardiner,* in *Writings Relative to Lord's Supper,* p. 3.
50. *Defence,* in *Archbishop Cranmer on the True and Catholic Doctrine,* p. 156.
51. *Answer to Gardiner,* in *Writings Relative to Lord's Supper,* p. 247.
52. *Ibid.*
53. *Ibid.*, p. 52.
54. *Ibid.*, p. 89.
55. "Disputations at Oxford," *ibid.*, p. 395.
56. *Answer to Gardiner, ibid.*, p. 185.
57. *Ibid.*, p. 36.
58. *Ibid.*, p. 366.

59. *Ibid.,* pp. 60–61.
60. *Ibid.,* pp. 61–62.
61. *Ibid.,* p. 11.
62. *Ibid.*
63. *Ibid.,* p. 30.
64. *Ibid.,* p. 42.
65. *Ibid.,* p. 43. See also *Defense,* in *Archbishop Cranmer on the True and Catholic Doctrine,* p. 244.
66. Stephen Neill, *Anglicanism* (London, 1960), p. 72.
67. C. C. Richardson, *Zwingli and Cranmer on the Eucharist* (Evanston, 1949), p. 48; see also Dom Gregory Dix, *The Shape of the Liturgy* (London, 1945), pp. 646, 656; see also Dix, "Dixit Cranmer et Non Timuit I," in *The Church Quarterly Review,* Vol. 145, No. 290, January–March, 1948, pp. 145–176.
68. C. H. Smyth, *Cranmer and the Reformation Under Edward VI* (Cambridge, 1925), pp. 59–74. Theodore Maynard popularized this over-simplification in *The Life of Thomas Cranmer* (London, 1956), p. 221. The best refutation of Smyth's terminology is in Constantin Hopf, *Martin Bucer and the English Reformation* (Oxford, 1956), pp. 35–40. Nevertheless, Bucer's influence on Cranmer should not be underestimated.

There was also a time when it was fashionable to write that Cranmer had been considerably influenced by Luther, and that Lutheran influences were in the 1549 Communion Service. See, for example, John Strype, *Memorials of Thomas Cranmer,* 3 Vols. (Oxford, 1848–1854), Vol. I, p. 147. In 1898 A. J. Mason formulated the viewpoint which has since prevailed among scholars that there "was no period at which he taught a definite doctrine like Luther's, opposed to the Roman on the one hand, and to the Swiss on the other," in *Thomas Cranmer* (London, 1898), p. 125.
69. See, for example, Archbishop Cranmer to Joachim Vadian, [n.p.], 1537, in Robinson (ed.), *Original Letters,* Vol. 1, p. 13, where Cranmer states, "I have come to the conclusion that the writings of every man must be read with discrimination."
70. *Ibid.*
71. *Concilia Magnae Britanniae et Hiberniae Synodo Verolomiensi A.D. 446 Ad Londoniensem A.D. 1717. Accedunt constitutiones et alia ad historiam Ecclesiae Anglicanae spectantia,* David Wilkins, ed., 4 Vols. (Bruxelles, 1964), Vol. 4, p. 11.
72. Wilson (ed.), *Order of Communion,* no pagination.
73. *Ibid.*

74. See *infra,* p. 39.

75. Wilkins (ed.), *Concilia Magnae Britanniae et Hiberniae,* Vol. 4, p. 32.

76. Gasquet and Bishop, *Edward VI and the Book of Common Prayer,* p. 66.

77. Verney Johnstone and Ernest Evans, *The Story of the Prayer Book* (London, 1949), p. 22. See also Brightman, *The English Rite,* Vol. 1, p. lxxii.

78. Wilson (ed.), *Order of Communion,* pp. 49–51 (Appendix IV).

79. F. E. Brightman and K. D. Mackenzie, "The History of the Book of Common Prayer Down to 1662," in *Liturgy and Worship: A Companion to the Prayer Books of the Anglican Communion,* W. K. Lowther Clarke and Charles Harris, eds. (London, 1959), p. 144.

80. Footnote five, in Procter and Frere, *A New History,* p. 28.

81. *Philippi Melanchthonis Opera Quae Supersunt Omnia,* Carolus Gottlieb Bretschneider, ed., *Corpus Reformatorum* (Halis Saxonum, 1835), Vol. 5, p. 114.

82. Wilson (ed.), *Order of Communion,* pp. 49–51 (Appendix IV).

83. C. W. Dugmore writes that "Cranmer was not merely *one* of those who compiled the book. He was the prime mover. . . . His is the only name which the first Act of Uniformity definitely connects with the English Prayer Book of 1549," in "The First Ten Years 1549–1559," in The Archbishop of Canterbury, *et al., The English Prayer Book 1549–1662,* p. 10.

84. Parker, *The English Reformation,* p. 118. For Edwardian changes in worship prior to 1549 see Phillip Hughes, *The Reformation in England,* 3 Vols. (London, 1952–1954), Vol. 2, pp. 94–137.

85. "The Supper of the Lorde, and the holy Communion, commonly called the Masse," in *Liturgies of the Western Church,* Bard Thompson, ed. (Cleveland, 1962), pp. 245–268, is a verbatim transcription from the microfilm in the Huntington Library of the Whitchurch edition printed at London, March, 1549. All references to the 1549 and 1552 Communion Services are taken from *Liturgies of the Western Church.*

86. "Reformation, Preaching, and Ex Opere Operato," in *Christianity Divided,* Daniel Callahan, Heiko Oberman, and Daniel J. O'Hanlon, eds. (New York, 1961), p. 227. See also N. Dimock, *The History of the Book of Common Prayer* (London, 1910), pp. 4–5.

87. Brightman and Mackenzie say that vestment means "chasuble, stole, and maniple," but at the same time they concede that some

authorities believe the chasuble alone was meant, in "The History of the Book of Common Prayer Down to 1662," in Clarke and Harris. (eds.), *Liturgy and Worship,* p. 157.

88. Martin Bucer and Paul Fagius to the Ministers at Strasbourg, Lambeth, April 26, 1549, in Robinson (ed.), *Original Letters,* Vol. 2, pp. 535–536.

89. Wilson (ed.), *Order of Communion,* pp. 30–31 (Appendix III).

90. Footnote two in Gasquet and Bishop, *Edward VI and the Book of Common Prayer,* p. 188.

91. Wilson (ed.), *Order of Communion,* p. 31 (Appendix III).

92. Boniface Lautz, O.S.B., "The Doctrine of the Communion of Saints in Anglican Theology 1833–1963" (unpublished S.T.D. dissertation, Faculty of Theology, University of Ottawa), Ottawa, 1964, p. 10. Lautz states that "most of the collects for the saints days were newly composed in 1549. That saints should be in any way mediators between God and man was a concept rejected in the new liturgy."

93. C. W. Dugmore overlooks Cranmer's change of the Offertory in his brief treatment of the 1549 Communion Service in *The Mass and the English Reformers* (London, 1958), pp. 132–133. Dugmore is attempting to prove that in the late Middle Ages "the Mass came to be thought of as a distinct sacrifice in itself which does not derive its sacrificial character from its relation to the sacrifice of the Cross." He admits that Aquinas taught no such doctrine, but adds "it is evident from the attacks of many of the Reformers that this doctrine had gained currency in the period just before the Reformation. . . . ," but the only names he adduces are Canus, Suarez, DeLugo, and Bellarmine, all of whom wrote in a later period, and none of whom taught a "fresh immolation of Christ at each mass" (*ibid.,* p. 62).

94. See comparison in Procter and Frere, *A New History,* pp. 450–451.

95. It is the opinion of Gasquet and Bishop that Cranmer was able to find the forms for the invocation in the liturgies of Clement, James, Basil, and Chrysostom in a well-known tract of that time by Bessarion: *de Sacramento Eucharistiae.* For this, see footnote one in *Edward VI and the Book of Common Prayer,* p. 169. Brightman comments: "The Mozarabic and the Eastern Orthodox rites played some small part," in *The English Rite,* Vol. 1, p. lxxix.

96. Standing Liturgical Commission, *Prayer Book Studies IV,* p. 27. The English translation of the Latin Sarum is from pp. 28–34, *ibid.*

97. The 1549 Service is taken from Thompson, ed., *Liturgies of the Western Church.*

98. It is interesting to note that Gasquet and Bishop translate *hostiam* as "Victim" whereas the Liturgical Commission renders it as "oblation." See Gasquet and Bishop, *Edward VI and the Book of Common Prayer*, p. 172. The Liturgical Commission explains their rendering as follows: "It is true that in classical Latin the word always refers to a living animal to be killed in the pagan sacrifices; but in the liturgical language of the Christian Church this meaning had to be completely laid aside as irrelevant to a Sacrifice which did not employ animal food." (*Prayer Book Studies IV*, p. 36.)

99. Lautz, "The Communion of Saints," pp. 25–28.

100. Possibly because Cranmer used a continental reforming Catholic document for this passage. See Brightman, *The English Rite*, Vol. 1, p. lxxix.

101. Cranmer probably derived the Trinitarian invocation from the liturgy of St. Basil. See Standing Liturgical Commission, *Prayer Book Studies IV*, pp. 46–48.

Chapter II. Reactions to the 1549 Service

1. Quoted in *Troubles connected with the Prayer Book of 1549, documents now mostly for the first time printed from the originals in the Records Office, the Petyt Collection in the Library of the Inner Temple, the Council Book, and the British Museum*, N. Pocock, ed. (Westminster, 1884), p. x.

2. Francisco Dryander to Henry Bullinger, Cambridge, June 5, 1549, in Robinson, ed., *Original Letters*, Vol. 1, p. 350.

3. *Defence* in *Archbishop Cranmer on the True and Catholic Doctrine*, p. 257.

4. *Writings Relative to Lord's Supper*, pp. 53, 56, 79, 185, 271, 327.

5. Procter and Frere, *A New History*, pp. 55–57.

6. E. C. Ratcliff, "The Liturgical Work of Thomas Cranmer," in *Thomas Cranmer, 1489–1556, Three Commemorative Lectures Delivered in Lambeth Palace* (London, 1956), p. 40.

7. Brightman, *The English Rite*, Vol. 1, pp. cxlii–cxlvi.

8. Brightman limits Hooper's influence to the "Black Rubric," (*ibid.*, p. cl). Procter and Frere credit him with being "conspicuous as a leader in the attack on the Prayer Book," in *A New History*, p. 70. John Henry Blunt thinks his sermons influenced King Edward VI toward a new revision, in *The Annotated Book of Common Prayer, Being an Historical Ritual, and Theological Commentary on the Devotional System of the Church of England* (London, 1868), p. 20. G. J.

Van De Poll credits him as being, along with Gardiner, a prime "critic" of the Prayer Book, in *Martin Bucer's Liturgical Ideas* (Assen, 1944), p. 145.

9. John Hooper, "The Third Sermon Upon Jonas," in *Early Writings of John Hooper, D.D.*, Samuel Carr, ed. (Cambridge, Parker Society, 1848), p. 479. Hereafter cited as *Early Writings of John Hooper.*

10. "Biographical Notice of Bishop Hooper," in *Early Writings of John Hooper*, p. iii (Introduction by editor).

11. "The Third Sermon Upon Jonas," *ibid.*, pp. 478–479.

12. Martin Micronius to Henry Bullinger, London, October 13, 1550, in Robinson, ed., *Original Letters*, Vol. 2, p. 571. See also M. M. Knappen, *Tudor Puritanism* (Chicago, 1963), pp. 483–486 (Appendix I).

13. Micronius to Bullinger, postscript, in Robinson, ed., *Original Letters*, Vol. 2, p. 573.

14. Foxe, *Acts and Monuments*, Vol. 6, pp. 640–641.

15. Hooper to Bullinger, London, December 27, 1549, in Robinson, ed., *Original Letters*, Vol. 1, p. 72.

16. "The Third Sermon Upon Jonas," in *Early Writings of John Hooper*, p. 479.

17. Micronius to Bullinger, in Robinson, ed., *Original Letters,* Vol. 2, p. 571.

18. "The Third Sermon Upon Jonas," in *Early Writings of John Hooper*, p. 488.

19. *Ibid.*, p. 492.

20. "The Sixth Sermon Upon Jonas," in *Early Writings of John Hooper*, p. 534.

21. Hooper to Bullinger, December 27, 1549, in Robinson, ed., *Original Letters*, Vol. 1, p. 72.

22. In *Early Writings of John Hooper*, p. 341.

23. Hooper to Bullinger, Dated from prison, September 3, 1553, in Robinson, ed., *Original Letters*, Vol. 1, p. 100.

24. "The Sixth Sermon Upon Jonas," in *Early Writings of John Hooper*, p. 534.

25. *Ibid.*, pp. 536–537.

26. *A Declaration of the Ten Holy Commandments, ibid.*, p. 346. See also *Hyperaspismus De Vera Doctrina et Usu Coenae Domini*, in *Later Writings of Bishop Hooper*, Charles Nevinson, ed. (Cambridge, Parker Society, 1852), pp. 402–404.

27. *Answer to the Bishop of Winchester's Book*, in *Early Writings of John Hooper*, p. 112.

28. "The Fifth Sermon Upon Jonas," *ibid.*, p. 534.

29. Hooper, *A Declaration of the Ten Commandments, ibid.*, p. 346.

30. Hooper to Bullinger, March 27, 1550, in Robinson, ed., *Original Letters*, Vol. 1, p. 79.

31. "The Fifth Sermon Upon Jonas," in *Early Writings of John Hooper*, p. 534.

32. *Ibid.*, p. 535–537.

33. *Ibid.*, p. 535.

34. *A Declaration of the Ten Commandments, ibid.*, p. 347.

35. "The Third Sermon Upon Jonas," *ibid.*, p. 480.

36. Foxe, *Acts and Monuments*, Vol. 6, p. 114.

37. Peter Brooks, *Thomas Cranmer's Doctrine of the Eucharist* (London, 1965), p. 77, footnote 2.

38. This work is printed topically in Cranmer's *Writings Relative to Lord's Supper*, pp. 10–365.

39. *A Preface to the Reader, ibid.*, p. 6.

40. *Ibid.*, p. 4.

41. *Answer to Gardiner, ibid.*, p. 9.

42. *Explication and Assertion, ibid.*, p. 92.

43. *Ibid.*, pp. 334–335.

44. *Ibid.*, pp. 51, 202.

45. *Ibid.*, p. 340.

46. *Ibid.*, p. 51

47. This, of course, was the very thing Cranmer was *not* teaching in his version of the Catechism in the 1549 Communion Service.

48. *Explication and Assertion*, in *Writings Relative to Lord's Supper*, p. 55.

49. *Ibid.*, p. 90.

50. *Ibid.*, p. 62.

51. *Ibid.*, p. 63.

52. *Ibid.*, p. 325.

53. *Ibid.*, p. 70.

54. *Ibid.*, p. 79. This interpretation angered Cranmer. In the *Answer to Gardiner*, the Archbishop wrote: "The bread and wine be made unto us the body and blood of Christ (as it is in the book of common prayer,) but not by changing the substance of bread and wine into the substance of Christ's natural body and blood, but that in the godly using of them they be unto the receivers Christ's body and blood," *ibid.*, p. 79. The Standing Liturgical Commission of the Protestant Episcopal Church paradoxically argues more like Gardiner than like Cranmer on this point: "To be sure Cranmer in 1549 rendered 'fiat'

as 'may be' rather than 'may be made' which the Latin intended, but perhaps with no more consciousness of weakening the sense than the English Bible had of translating the Vulgate 'Fiat lux' of Gen. 1:3 as 'Let there be light,' " in *Prayer Book Studies IV*, p. 61.

55. *Explication and Assertion*, in *Writings Relative to Lord's Supper*, p. 83.

56. *Ibid.*, p. 340.

57. *Ibid.*, p. 229. For Gardiner's conviction that Christ alone is adored in true Christianity, see "Copy of the Letter of Stephen Gardiner sent to Master Ridley; containing Matter and Objection against a certain Sermon of the said Master Ridley, made at the Court," in *The Works of Nicholas Ridley*, Henry Christmas, ed. (Cambridge, Parker Society, 1848), pp. 495–504 (Appendix IV).

58. *Explication and Assertion*, in *Writings Relative to Lord's Supper*, p. 344.

59. *Ibid.*, p. 344.

60. *Ibid.*, p. 364.

61. *Ibid.*, p. 84.

62. We know of Cranmer's request from the words added to the title of the *Censura* by Conrad Hubert: ". . . *ad petitionem R. Archiepiscopi Centuariensis Thomae Cranmeri, conscripta*," in the title page of *Censura Martini Buceri super libro sacrorum seu ordinationis Ecclesiae atque ministerii ecclesiastici in regno Angliae*, in Martin Bucer, *Scripta Anglicana*, Conrad Hubert, ed. (Basle, 1577), p. 456.

63. *Ibid.*, pp. 456, 465.

64. *Ibid.*, p. 457.

65. *Ibid.*, p. 464.

66. *Ibid.*, p. 457.

67. *Ibid.*, p. 458.

68. Bucer to Hooper, [n.d.], *ibid.*, p. 708.

69. Peter Martyr to Henry Bullinger, Oxford, January 28, 1551, in Robinson, ed., *Original Letters*, Vol. 2, pp. 487–488.

70. John Burcher to Henry Bullinger, Strasbourg, December 28, 1550, *ibid.*, p. 675.

71. Bucer, *Censura*, in *Scripta Anglicana*, pp. 458–459.

72. *Ibid.*, p. 463.

73. *Ibid.*, p. 465.

74. *Ibid.*, p. 459.

75. *Ibid.*, p. 462.

76. *Ibid.*, p. 464.

77. *Ibid.*, p. 464.

78. *Ibid.*, p. 465.

79. *Ibid.*, p. 466.
80. *Ibid.*
81. *Ibid.*, p. 467.
82. See *supra*, p. 32.
83. *Censura,* in *Scripta Anglicana,* p. 468.
84. *Ibid.*, p. 473.
85. *Ibid.*
86. See *supra*, p. 34.
87. *Censura,* in *Scripta Anglicana,* p. 472.
88. *Ibid.*, p. 473.
89. Martin Bucer to Peter Martyr, Strasbourg, June 20, 1549, *ibid.*, p. 549.
90. Peter Martyr to Henry Bullinger, Oxford, June 1, 1550, in Robinson, ed., *Original Letters,* Vol. 2, p. 481.
91. Peter Martyr to Martin Bucer Concerning Their Review of the Book of Common Prayer, Lambeth, January 10, 1551, in Strype, *Memorials of Archbishop Cranmer,* Vol. 2, p. 662 (Appendix LXI).
92. *Ibid.*, pp. 661–662 (Appendix LXI).
93. *The Communion of the Sick,* in Ketley, ed., *The Two Liturgies of Edward VI,* p. 141.
94. Martyr to Bucer, in Strype, *Memorials of Cranmer,* Vol. 2, p. 662 (Appendix LXI).
95. *Ibid.*, Vol. 2, p. 662.
96. *Ibid.*, p. 663.
97. *Ibid.*
98. *Ibid.*

Chapter III. The Communion Services of 1552, 1559, and 1604

1. Blunt, *The Annotated Book of Common Prayer,* p. 84, footnote 1.
2. Quoted *ibid.*, page 20, footnote 4. For Cranmer's Ordinal, see Chapter I, *supra,* footnote on p. 44.
3. Thomas of Canterbury to Council, Lambeth, October 7, 1552, Blunt, *The Annotated Book of Common Prayer,* pp. 21–22.
4. *The Second Act of Uniformity,* quoted *ibid.*, p. 84, footnote 1.
5. Ketley, ed., *The Two Liturgies of Edward VI,* p. 193.
6. *Ibid.*, p. 195.
7. *Ibid.*, pp. 10–15.

8. *Ibid.*, pp. 187–192.

9. *Ibid.*, pp. 155–158; 197–199.

10. *Ibid.*, p. 197.

11. *Ibid.*, p. 198.

12. *Ibid.*, p. 199.

13. Thompson, ed., *Liturgies of the Western Church*, p. 245.

14. *Ibid.*, p. 269. All references to the Communion Service of 1552 are from Thompson ed., *Liturgies of the Western Church*, pp. 269–285. Reference to other Services in the Book of 1552 are from Ketley, ed., *The Two Liturgies of Edward VI* as indicated in a footnote.

15. See *supra*, pp. 25–26.

16. Ketley, ed., *The Two Liturgies of Edward VI*, p. 217.

17. *Ibid.*, p. 220.

18. Calvin and Luther had a similar rite in their Services. There is also considerable evidence that Reformers such as Pullain and Laski had the practice in their Services in England. See Brightman, *The English Rite*, Vol. 1, pp. clvi–clvii. However, since the thirteenth century in England the Decalogue was considered a necessary part of Christian instruction. The new rubric and rite may have come simply from this traditional English practice. See, for example, "The Injunctions given by Edmund Bonner, Bishop of London, to his Clergy," 1542, in Wilkins, ed., *Concilia Magnae Britanniae et Hiberniae*, Vol. 3, p. 865.

19. One noteworthy change occurred in the feasts for the Saints. That of Saint Mary Magdalene was dropped from the *Sanctorale*.

20. A rubric terminating the Service for The Churching of Women is consistent with this connection of Offering with support of the Minister. "The woman that cometh to give her thanks, must *offer* accustomed offerings: and if there be a Communion, it is convenient that she *receive* the holy communion." (Ketley, ed., *The Two Liturgies of Edward VI*, p. 322. Italics added.)

21. The great Evangelical Anglican Thomas Vogan stated: "our liturgy has no verbal oblation of the bread and wine; and, moreover, . . . our Church does not intend any such oblation; and if she had intended a virtual oblation, she would certainly not have omitted a verbal one," in *The True Doctrine of the Eucharist* (London, 1871), p. 496. Nor do Evangelicals of the Church of England today intend to allow a verbal oblation to the introduced into a revised Communion Service. See S. O. Buchanan, *The New Communion Service—Reasons for Dissent* (London, 1966), pp. 3–6. Buchanan is a member of the Evangelical Liturgical Committee of Latimer House, Oxford, and also a member of the Church of England Liturgical Commission. In his

published dissent, he objects strongly to the proposed addition of the words "we offer unto thee this bread and this cup." The views of such Evangelicals as those of Latimer House must be considered in any discussions or proposals for Eucharistic convergence between Anglicanism and the Church of Rome.

22. *The Two Books of Common Prayer Set Forth by Parliament in the Reign of King Edward VI,* E. Cardwell, ed. (Oxford, 1838), p. xxxii (Introduction by editor). See also Edward Lambe Parsons and Bayard Hale Jones, *The American Prayer Book: Its Origins and Principles* (New York, 1937), p. 187.

23. Parsons and Jones, *The American Prayer Book,* p. 190.

24. The rubrics for Communion of the Sick were also changed. This time there was no mention of reservation of the Sacrament. See Ketley, ed., *The Two Liturgies of Edward VI,* pp. 316–317.

25. See *supra,* pp. 50–51.

26. F. J. Smithen, *Continental Protestantism and the English Reformation* (London, 1927), p. 232.

27. John Utenhovius to Henry Bullinger, London, October 12, 1552, in Robinson, ed., *Original Letters,* Vol 2, pp. 591–592. In a footnote on page 591, Robinson remarks that Utenhovius probably erred in thinking that Knox was chaplain to the Duke of Northumberland.

28. This letter of September 27, 1552, was entitled "A letter to Grafton the printer to stay in any wise from uttering any of the books of the new Service, and if he have distributed any of them amongst his company, that then he give strait commandment to every of them not to put any of them abroad until certain faults therein be corrected," in Blunt, *The Annotated Book of Common Prayer,* p. 21.

29. Thomas of Canterbury to Council, Lambeth, October 7, 1552, in *ibid.*

30. *Ibid.*

31. *Ibid.,* p. 21.

32. *Ibid.,* p. 22.

33. James Parker, *An Introduction to the History of the Successive Revisions of the Book of Common Prayer* (Oxford, 1877), p. xxxvi.

34. Blunt, *The Annotated Book of Common Prayer,* p. 22.

35. Julius Terentianus to John ab Ulmis, Strasbourg, Nov. 20, 1553, in Robinson, ed., *Original Letters,* Vol. 1, p. 369.

36. Cecil McGarry, "The Catholic Character of Anglican Ecclesiology, 1945–1963" (unpublished S.T.D. dissertation, Pontifical Gregorian University, Rome, 1964), p. 33.

37. William Whittingham, *A Brief Discourse of the Troubles at Frankfort,* Edward Arber, ed. (London, 1908), pp. 26–93.

38. *Ibid.,* p. 37.

39. *Ibid.,* p. 38.

40. Knappen, *Tudor Puritanism,* pp. 133–144.

41. *Ibid.,* pp. 139, 143.

42. Christopher Goodman to Peter Martyr, Geneva, August 20, 1558, in Robinson, ed., *Original Letters,* Vol. 2, p. 769.

43. Knappen, *Tudor Puritanism,* p. 164.

44. Edwin Sandys to Henry Bullinger, Strasbourg, December 20, 1558, in *Zurich Letters Comprising the Correspondence of Several English Bishops and Others with Some of the Helvetian Reformers, During the Reign of Elizabeth,* Hastings Robinson, ed., trans., 2 Vols. (Cambridge, Parker Society, 1842–1845), Vol. 1, pp. 5–6.

45. Quoted in Dugmore, "The First Ten Years," in Archbishop of Canterbury, *et al., The English Prayer Book 1549–1662,* p. 29. Even if this were true, the Henrician party had "virtually disappeared" by 1558, and she would have received little support for a "Catholic without Rome" course, in T. M. Parker, "The Problem of Uniformity, 1559–1604," *ibid.,* pp. 41–42.

46. On Christmas day the Queen left her chapel during Mass because her chaplain insisted on elevating the host. She apparently failed to communicate three weeks later at her coronation; see Procter and Frere, *A New History,* pp. 96–97. The Sunday following the coronation she received "according to the Protestant rite, *sub utraque,* under both kinds," in Carl S. Meyer, *Elizabeth I And the Religious Settlement of 1559* (Saint Louis, 1960), p. 15.

47. Procter and Frere, *A New History,* p. 97.

48. John Knox to Queen Elizabeth, Edinburgh, July 20, 1559, in *John Knox's History of the Reformation in Scotland,* William Croft Dickinson, ed., 2 Vols. (London, 1949), Vol. 1, pp. 291–295.

49. John Calvin to William Cecil, Geneva, [n.d.], in Robinson, ed., *Zurich Letters,* Vol. 2, p. 34.

50. It is disputed whether this "Device" was merely a suggestion drawn up for discussion or a definite policy for revision that included the appointment of a committee to begin immediately. Henry Gee thinks it but a suggestion, in *The Elizabethan Prayer Book & Ornaments* (London, 1902), pp. 19–31.

51. *The Device for Alteration of Religion in the First Year of Queen Elizabeth, ibid.,* p. 197 (Appendix I).

52. Gee thinks Guest's letter should be dated 1552 (*ibid.,* pp. 32–50). Procter and Frere attribute it to the beginning of Elizabeth's reign

in *A New History,* pp. 98–99. Edward Cardwell agrees with the latter in *A History of Conferences, and Other Proceedings Connected with the Revision of the Book of Common Prayer, From the Year 1558 to the Year 1690* (Oxford, 1841), p. 21.

53. Guest to Sir William Cecyl, the queen's secretary, concerning the Service-book, newly prepared for the parliament to be confirmed; and certain ceremonies and usages of the church, *ibid.,* pp. 50–54.

54. *Ibid.,* p. 52.

55. *Ibid.*

56. *Ibid.,* p. 53.

57. *Ibid.,* p. 54.

58. Archbishop Parker and Others to Queen Elizabeth, [n.p.], 1559, in *Correspondence of Matthew Parker, Archbishop of Canterbury, Comprising Letters Written by and to Him, From A.D. 1535, to his Death, A.D. 1575,* John Bruce and Thomas Thomason Perowne, eds. (Cambridge, Parker Society, 1853), p. 94.

59. This is also the conclusion of G. J. Cuming in *The Durham Book, Being the First Draft of Revision of the B.C.P. in 1661* (London, 1961), p. xi (Introduction). A leading Evangelical scholar also concurs that Elizabeth would have preferred 1549, but due to Roman Catholic opposition, was forced to rely on Protestant support and accept 1552 with her three adjustments, in J. C. De Satge, "The Composition of the Articles," in J. C. De Satge, *et al., The Articles of the Church of England* (London, 1964), pp. 4–5.

60. Procter and Frere are of the opinion that the Pope was prepared early in the reign to recognize the 1559 Communion Service, in *A New History,* p. 111. This opinion most likely stems from a statement of Sir Edward Coke: "[the Pope] before the time of his excommunication against Queen *Elizabeth* denounced, sent his letter unto her Majesty, in which did allow the *Bible,* and Book of *Divine Service,* as it is now used among us, to be authentick, and not repugnant to truth. But that therein was contained enough necessary to salvation, though there was not in it so much as might conveniently be, and that he would also allow it unto us, without changing any part: so as her Majesty would acknowledge to receive it from the *Pope,* and by his allowance. . . . And this is the truth concerning Pope Pius Quartus as I have faith to God and men. I have oftentimes heared avowed by the late *Queen* her own words; and I have conferred with some *Lords* that were of greatest reckoning in the *State,* who had seen and read the Letter, which the Pope sent to that effect; as have been by me specified. And this upon my credit, as I am an honest man, is most true," in Blunt, *The Annotated Book of Common Prayer,* p. 24.

61. *AN ACT for the uniformity of COMMON PRAYER, and Service in the Church, and the administration of the Sacraments,* in *Liturgies and Occasional Forms of Prayer Set Forth in the Reign of Queen Eliizabeth,* William Keating Clay, ed. (Cambridge, Parker Society, 1847), pp. 27–28, 32.

62. *The Order for the Administration of the Lord's Supper or Holy Communion,* in Clay, ed., *Liturgical Services of Queen Elizabeth,* p. 195.

63. *The Order Where Morning and Evening Prayer shall be used and said, ibid.,* p. 53.

64. See, for example, John Knox, *A Godly Letter of Warning, or Admonition to the Faithful in London, Newcastle, and Berwick, 1554,* in *The Works of John Knox,* David Laing, ed., 6 Vols. (Edinburgh, 1846–1864), Vol. 3, p. 200.

65. James Pilkington and others to the Geneva congregation, Frankfort, January 3, 1559, in Whittingham, *Troubles at Frankfort,* p. 226. It should be noted that, despite the Acts of Supremacy and Uniformity, there was by no means uniformity of worship in England. The Romanist clergy still clandestinely said Mass from their worn missals; see J. R. H. Moorman, *A History of the Church in England* (New York, 1963), p. 216. Archbishop Grindal described the situation in London in 1565: "Some say the service and prayers in the chancel, others in the body of the church; some say the same in a seat made in the church, some in the pulpit with their faces to the people; some keep precisely to the order of the book, others intermeddle psalms in metre; some say in a surplice, others without a surplice: the Table standeth in the body of the church in some places, in others it standeth in the chancel; in some places the Table standeth altarwise, distant from the wall a yard, in some others in the middle of the chancel, north and south; in some places the Table is joined, in others it standeth upon trestles; in some places the Table hath a carpet, in others it hath not; administration of the Communion is done by some with surplice and cap, some with surplice alone, others with none; some with chalice, some with a communion cup, others with a common cup; some with unleavened bread, some with leavened; some receive kneeling, others standing, others sitting; some baptise in a font, others in a basin; some sign with the sign of the cross, others sign not; some with a square cap, some with a round cap, some with a button cap, some with a hat," quoted in Gee, *The Elizabethan Prayer Book,* pp. 164–165.

66. *A proclamation for the authorizing and uniformity of the Book of Common Prayer to be used throughout the realm,* Westmin-

ster, 1603, in Wilkins, ed., *Concilia magnae Britanniae et Hiberniae*, Vol. 4, pp. 377–378.

67. Thomas Fuller, *The Church History of Britain from the Birth of Jesus Christ, until the Year MDCXLVIII*, James Nichols, ed., 3 Vols. (London, 1868), Vol. 3, p. 189.

68. *A proclamation concerning such as seditiously seek reformation in church matters*, Wilton, 1603, in Wilkins, ed., *Concilia magnae Britanniae et Hiberniae*, Vol. 4, p. 371.

69. Quoted in Fuller, *History of Britain*, Vol. 3, pp. 193–194.

70. *The opinion of Matthew Hutton, Archbishop of York, touching certain matters, like to be brought in question before the King's most excellent Majesty, at the Conference at Court. Written October 9. 1mo Jacobi, to the Archbishop of Canterbury*, in Cardwell, *History of Conferences*, p. 160.

71. *The Works of That Learned and Judicious Divine, Mr. Richard Hooker: with an Account of his Life and Death by Isaac Walton*, John Keble, ed., 3 Vols. (Oxford, 1845), Vol. 2, p. 30. According to Horton Davies, for Hooker the Bible was the touchstone "in doctrine, but not in government or worship," in *The Worship of the English Puritans* (Westminster, 1948), p. 4.

72. Quoted in Cardwell, *History of Conferences*, pp. 134–135.

73. *The Humble Petition of the Ministers of the Church of England, Desiring Reformation of Certain Ceremonies and Abuses of the Church*, in Fuller, *History of Britain*, Vol. 3, pp. 215–217. References to this "Millenary Petition" will be taken from Fuller; but see also Cardwell, *History of Conferences*, pp. 130–133.

74. William Perkins, *The Workes of That Famous and Worthie Minister of Christ, M. W. Perkins*, 3 Vols. (London, 1616–1618), Vol. 1, p. 122.

75. All references to the Hampton Court Conference are taken from Fuller, *History of Britain*, Vol. 3, pp. 193–214. His account seems the most objective available. For Fuller as an historian, see Gee, *The Elizabethan Prayer Book*, p. 12. For other accounts of the conference see James Montague's in Cardwell, *History of Conferences*, pp. 138–141; see also Bishop Matthew's, *ibid.*, pp. 161–166; and William Barlow's, *ibid.*, pp. 167–212.

76. *Archiepiscopo Cantuariensi et aliis pro reformatione Libri Communis Precum*, in Cardwell, *History of Conferences*, p. 218.

77. *Ibid.*

78. *A proclamation for the authorizing and uniformity of the Book of Common Prayer to be used throughout the realm*, *ibid.*, pp. 226–227.

79. King James to some person unknown in Scotland; concerning the Conference at Hampton Court between him and the Puritans, [n.d., n.p.], *ibid.*, p. 161.

Chapter IV. The Communion Services of 1637 and 1662

1. William D. Maxwell, *A History of Worship in the Church of Scotland* (London, 1955), pp. 43–46.

2. For a description of the Five Articles, see Gordon Donaldson, *The Making of the Scottish Prayer Book of 1637* (Edinburgh, 1954), pp. 34–35.

3. *Ibid.*, pp. 39–40.

4. David Calderwood, *History of the Kirk*, Wodrow Society, ed., 8 Vols. (Edinburgh, 1842–49), Vol. 7, p. 569. This edition was edited by the Wodrow Society from the original manuscript of 1678.

5. H. R. Trevor-Roper, *Archbishop Laud 1573–1645* (London, 1963), p. 338.

6. For the history and a description of Cowper's Draft Liturgy, see Donaldson, *The Scottish Prayer Book*, pp. 35–39.

7. *The History of the Troubles and Tryal of the Most Reverend Father in God William Laud, Lord Arch-Bishop of Canterbury*, in *The Works of the Most Reverend Father in God, William Laud, D.D. Sometime Lord Archbishop of Canterbury*, William Scott and James Bliss, eds., Library of Anglo-Catholic Theology, 7 Vols. (Oxford, 1847–1860), Vol. 3, p. 427. Hereafter cited as *Works of William Laud*.

8. *Ibid.*

9. *Ibid.*

10. *Ibid.*, pp. 427–428.

11. *Ibid.*, p. 428.

12. *Ibid.*, p. 278.

13. Donaldson, *The Scottish Prayer Book*, p. 44.

14. *Ibid.* For a description of this copy, now called the "Haddington Book," see *ibid.*, pp. 84–86.

15. *Ibid.*, p. 47.

16. *History of the Troubles,* in *Works of William Laud*, Vol. 3, p. 337.

17. *Scottish Liturgies of James VI*, G. W. Sprott, ed. (Edinburgh, 1871), p. li (Introduction by editor).

18. Quoted *ibid.*, p. liii.

19. William of Canterbury to Dr. John Maxwell, [n.p.] in *Works of William Laud*, Vol. 6, p. 434.

20. *Ibid.*

21. *The Book of Common Prayer and Administration of the Sacraments and other parts of Divine Service for the use of the Church of Scotland, commonly known as Laud's Liturgy, 1637,* James Cooper, ed. (Edinburgh, 1904), pp. xviii–xix (Introduction by Editor).

22. William of Canterbury to James Wedderburn, Bishop of Dunblane, in *Works of William Laud,* Vol. 6, p. 456.

23. *Ibid.*

24. *Ibid.* For a description of this second annotated *Prayer Book,* see Donaldson, *The Scottish Prayer Book,* pp. 88–89.

25. Laud to Wedderburn, in *Works of William Laud,* Vol. 6, pp. 456–457.

26. Donaldson, *The Scottish Prayer Book,* p. 57. See also *A Proclamation for the authorising of the Book of Common Prayer to be used throughout the Realm of Scotland,* in *The Book of Common Prayer and Administration of the Sacraments and other parts of Divine Service for the use of the Church of Scotland,* p. 100; see *The Preface, ibid.,* pp. 101–102.

27. George B. Burnet, *The Holy Communion in the Reformed Church of Scotland, 1560–1960* (Edinburgh, 1960), p. 95.

28. *Ibid.,* p. 96.

29. *Ibid.,* pp. 96–97.

30. Laud confided to his diary: "No question, but there's a great concurrence between them and the Puritan party in England. A great aim there to destroy me in the King's opinion, &c.," in *The Diary of the Most Reverend Father in God William Laud, Archbishop of Canterbury,* in *Works of William Laud,* Vol. 3, p. 230.

31. Parsons and Jones, *The American Prayer Book,* p. 192.

32. *History of the Troubles,* in *Works of William Laud,* Vol. 3, p. 278.

33. *Ibid.,* p. 335.

34. *Ibid.,* p. 336.

35. *Ibid.,* p. 344.

36. *Ibid.,* p. 341.

37. *A Relation of the Conference between William Laud and Mr. Fisher the Jesuit, ibid.,* Vol. 2, pp. 339–341.

38. *Ibid.,* p. 341.

39. *History of the Troubles, ibid.,* Vol. 3, p. 358.

40. *Ibid.,* pp. 358–359.

41. *Ibid.,* p. 359.

42. *Controversarium de Eucharistia,* in *Ven. Cardinalis Roberti Bellarmini Politiani, S.J. Opera Omnia,* Justinus Fevre, ed., 12 Vols. (Paris, 1870–1874), Vol. 4, p. 423.

43. *The Reply to Mr. Harding's Answer,* in *The Works of John Jewel, Bishop of Salisbury,* John Ayre, ed., 4 Vols. (Cambridge, Parker Society, 1845–1850), Vol. 3, pp. 734–735.

44. *History of the Troubles,* in *Works of William Laud,* Vol. 3, p. 359.

45. *Conference with Fisher, ibid.,* Vol. 2, p. 307.

46. *Ibid.,* p. 306.

47. *Ibid.,* p. 364.

48. *Ibid.,* pp. 328–329.

49. *Ibid.,* p. 329.

50. *Ibid.,* pp. 320–321.

51. See *supra,* p. 61.

52. See *supra,* pp. 36–37.

53. *History of the Troubles,* in *Works of William Laud,* Vol. 3, p. 353.

54. *Ibid.,* pp. 353–354.

55. *Ibid.,* p. 354.

56. *Ibid.,* pp. 354–355.

57. *Ibid.,* p. 355.

58. *Ibid.*

59. *Ibid.*

60. *Ibid.,* pp. 355–356.

61. *Ibid.,* p. 357.

62. *Ibid.,* p. 347.

63. *Ibid.,* p. 348.

64. William of Canterbury to the Vice-Chancellor, Croydon, November 26, 1636, in *Works of William Laud,* Vol. 5, p. 156.

65. *Works of William Laud,* Vol. 3, pp. 356–357.

66. All references to this letter are taken from the letter of William of Canterbury to James Wedderburn, Bishop of Dunblane, in *Works of William Laud,* Vol. 6, pp. 455–459.

67. It is very significant that Wedderburn's sentences were the same as those used by Lancelot Andrewes in his *Preces Privatae.* Andrewes devised a Communion Service for use in his private chapel in which a clear distinction was made between offering of alms to the poor and offering of elements to God. He highlighted this distinction by having the congregation bring their "oblations" to the altar rails after the Creed while the new sentences were being read. Only after the Service, while the priest read the traditional Prayer Book sentences, did the people put alms in the poor box. See G. J. Cuming, "The Making of the Prayer Book of 1662," in *The English Prayer Book, 1549–1662,* pp. 84, 87.

68. Grisbrooke, *Anglican Liturgies,* pp. 4–5.

69. *The Order where and how Morning and Evening Prayer shall be said or sung,* in Donaldson, *The Scottish Prayer Book,* p. 128.

70. For concessions to Puritan sentiment see Donaldson, *The Scottish Prayer Book,* pp. 61–71; see also Grisbrooke, *Anglican Liturgies,* p. 5. For offensive features to Puritan sentiment see Davies, *Worship of English Puritans,* p. 131.

71. References to the English and Scottish Communion Services are taken from *The Order for the Administration of the Lord's Supper, or Holy Communion,* in Clay, ed., *Liturgical Services of Queen Elizabeth,* pp. 180–198, and *The Order of the Administration of the Lord's Supper, or Holy Communion,* in Donaldson, *The Scottish Prayer Book,* pp. 183–204.

72. The Scottish Bishops wished to reduce Saints' Days in 1637, but Charles increased the number of Saints' Feasts in the Kalendar. For a discussion of this see Donaldson, *The Scottish Prayer Book,* pp. 49, 74–75.

73. *An Ordinance of Parliament, for the taking away of the Book of Common Prayer, and for the establishing and putting in execution of the Directory for the Public Worship of God,* in Parker, *An Introduction,* p. lxvii.

74. *History of the Troubles,* in *Works of William Laud,* Vol. 3, pp. 241, 437.

75. For a description of the *Directory,* see Procter and Frere, *A New History,* pp. 158–162 (Additional Note).

76. Wilkins, ed., *Concilia magnae Britanniae et Hiberniae,* Vol. 4, p. 560.

77. Cardwell, *History of Conferences,* pp. 252–253.

78. *The King's Warrant for the Conference at the Savoy,* Westminster, March 25, 1661, *ibid.,* p. 300.

79. Procter and Frere, *A New History,* pp. 171–189. For practices the Puritans considered contrary to Scripture, see *ibid.,* p. 192, footnote 1.

80. Parker, *An Introduction,* p. cccc.

81. Charles R. To our Right Trusty and well beloved, the most reverend Father in God Acceptus Archbishop of York, Whitehall, November, 1661, *ibid.,* p. lxxxvi.

82. *Ibid.,* p. xci.

83. *An Act for the Uniformity of Publique Prayers and Administracion of Sacraments and other Rites and Ceremonies and for Establishing the Form of making ordaining and consecrating Bishops Priests and Deacons in the Church of England, ibid.,* pp. cccclxxxviii–cccclxxxix.

84. Brightman, *The English Rite,* Vol. 1, p. ccx.

85. Cuming, "Making of the Prayer Book of 1662," in Archbishop of Canterbury, *et al., The English Prayer Book 1549–1662*, p. 89.

86. *Ibid.*, p. 91. Cosin transcribed his own proposals and those of Bishop Matthew Wren in a folio Prayer Book known as the *Durham Book*. After Savoy his chaplain, William Sancroft, revised these changes in a more conservative direction. Finally, Sancroft transcribed them in a 1643 printing of the Prayer Book. This final version is known as the *Fair copy*. See also Cuming, *Durham Book*, pp. xxi–xxii (Introd.).

87. Parker, *An Introduction*, pp. lxxix–lxxx.

88. Cuming, "Making of the Prayer Book of 1662," in Archbishop of Canterbury, *et al., The English Prayer Book 1549–1662*, p. 94.

89. *Ibid.*, p. 99.

90. *Ibid.*, p. 99.

91. Brightman, *The English Rite*, Vol. 1, p. ccx.

92. Cuming, "Making of the Prayer Book of 1662," in Archbishop of Canterbury, *et al., The English Prayer Book 1549–1662*, p. 102.

93. *Ibid.*, p. 100.

94. *Notes and Collections in an Interleaved Book of Common Prayer, 1619*, in *The Works of the Right Reverend Father in God, John Cosin, Lord Bishop of Durham*, J. Sansom, ed., 5 Vols., Library of Anglo-Catholic Theology (Oxford, 1843–1851), Vol. 5, pp. 118–119.

95. *Ibid.*, p. 119. Cosin recommended placing the Prayer of Oblation immediately after the Consecration as more consonant "to the nature of this holy action," in *Particulars to be Considered, Explained, and Corrected in the Book of Common Prayer, ibid.*, p. 517 (Appendix I). He also urged a restoration of manual acts as "a needful circumstance belonging to this Sacrament." *Ibid.*, p. 516. He wanted "and Sacrifice" added to the Prayer of Consecration after "memory of that His precious death." *Ibid.*, p. 516. He also urged that the offerings or devotions of the people be brought to the priest and presented by him on the altar for such use as "be peculiarly named in the sentences then read by him." *Ibid.*, p. 514. Two things should be noted: first, all of these suggestions were intended to teach that the Communion was a Sacrifice; second, the Puritans too were in favor of manual acts, but for different doctrinal reasons.

96. *Notes and Collections in an Interleaved Book of Common Prayer, 1638*, in *ibid.*, p. 335.

97. *Ibid.*, p. 336.

98. *Ibid.*
99. *Ibid.*
100. *Ibid.*, p. 333.
101. *Ibid.*
102. A Sermon at the Consecration of Dr. Francis White, Bishop of Carlisle, *ibid.*, Vol. 1, p. 94.
103. *Notes and Collections, 1638, ibid.*, Vol. 5, p. 352.
104. *Notes and Collections, 1619, ibid.*, p. 119.
105. *Notes and Collections, 1638, ibid.*, p. 374.
106. *Ibid.*, p. 375.
107. *Notes and Collections, 1619, ibid.*, p. 104.
108. *Ibid.*, p. 124.
109. *Ibid.*, pp. 132–133.
110. *Ibid.*, p. 98.
111. *The History of Popish Transubstantiation to which is Premised and Opposed The Catholick Doctrin of the Holy Scripture, the ancient Fathers and the Reformed Churches, About the Sacred Elements and Presence of Christ in the Blessed Sacrament of the Eucharist, ibid.*, Vol. 4, p. 178.
112. *Transubstantiation*, in *ibid.*, p. 229.
113. *Ibid.*, pp. 168–169.
114. *Notes and Collections, 1619*, in *ibid.*, Vol. 5, p. 104.
115. *Ibid.*, pp. xviii–xix (Preface by editor). See also *Transubstantiation, ibid.*, Vol. 4, p. 174.
116. *Notes and Collections, 1638, ibid.*, Vol. 5, p. 356.
117. *Ibid.*, pp. 356–357.
118. *Particulars, ibid.*, p. 519. Whether or not this was Cosin's doctrine at the time of the 1661 Convocation is uncertain. The *Particulars* were probably written around 1640, and revised and used in 1661. If such is the case, Cosin's doctrine at time of revision was that the consecrated elements were still sacred after lawful use, and should be reverently consumed.
119. This may explain Cosin's difficulty with Presence after use, for Bucer denied perduring Presence and wished the elements returned to profane use.
120. *Notes and Collections, 1638, ibid.*, Vol. 5, p. 336.
121. *Transubstantiation, ibid.*, Vol. 4, p. 155.
122. *Ibid.*, p. 173.
123. *Ibid.*, pp. 173–174.
124. *Notes and Collections, 1638*, in *ibid.*, Vol. 5, pp. 345–346.
125. *Notes and Collections, 1619, ibid.*, pp. 108–109.
126. *Ibid.*, p. 121.

127. Sermon XII, *ibid.*, Vol. 1, p. 173.

128. *Notes and Collections, 1638, ibid.*, Vol. 5, p. 345.

129. *Transubstantiation, ibid.*, Vol. 4, p. 170.

130. *Ibid.*, pp. 156–157.

131. *Ibid.*, p. 174.

132. *Ibid.*, pp. 174–175.

133. *Ibid.*, p. 175.

134. *Ibid.*, p. 172.

135. Cuming, "Making of the Prayer Book of 1662," in Archbishop of Canterbury, *et al., The English Prayer Book 1549–1662*, p. 94. A monument to this power group still remains at the venerable University of Oxford, where the Sheldonian Theatre (named after the then Bishop of London) adjoins the Clarendon Building (named after the then Lord Chancellor).

136. *Ibid.*, p. 89.

137. *Ibid.*, p. 104.

138. Izaak Walton, *The Life of Dr. Robert Sanderson, Late Bishop of Lincoln*, in *The Lives of Dr. John Donne, Sir Henry Wotton, Mr. Richard Hooker, Mr. George Herbert, and Dr. Robert Sanderson: To Which are Added, The Autographs of Those Eminent Men, Now First Collected; An Index, and Illustrative Notes* (London, 1823), p. 425.

139. *The Preface*, in *The Book of Common Prayer, And Administration of the Sacraments, and other Rites and Ceremonies of the Church, according to the Use of The Church of England together with the Psalter or Psalms of David*, in *The Teacher's Prayer Book: being the Book of Common Prayer, with Introductions, Analyses, Notes, and a Commentary upon the Psalter*, Alfred Barry, ed. (London, 1813), pp. 7–8.

140. *Ibid.*

141. *Ibid.*, p. 8.

142. *Of the Liturgy*, in *The Works of Robert Sanderson, D.D. Sometime Bishop of Lincoln*, William Jacobson, ed., 6 Vols. (Oxford, 1854), Vol. 5, p. 39.

143. *Reasons of the Present Judgment of the University of Oxford Concerning the Solemn League and Covenant, the Negative Oath, the Ordinances Concerning Discipline and Worship, ibid.*, Vol. 4, p. 442.

144. *Of the Liturgy, ibid.*, Vol. 5, p. 39.

145. *Ibid.*

146. *Ibid.*, pp. 39–40.

147. *Ibid.*, p. 40.

148. In Bishop Sanderson and Bishop Wren, *Fragmentary Illustrations of the History of the Book of Common Prayer*, William Jacobson, ed. (London, 1874), pp. 22–29. All references to Sanderson's Office are from this edition.

149. Although Sanderson taught Real Presence in this prayer, he opposed Transubstantiation. *Ad Clerum*, in *Works of Robert Sanderson*, Vol. 2, p. 151; see also *A Discourse Concerning the Church, ibid.*, Vol. 5, p. 246.

150. There may have been another reason, in addition to the attempt to disguise the Service. Sanderson considered Purgatory and Invocation of Saints a Roman invention, in *Ad Clerum*, in *Works of Robert Sanderson*, Vol. 2, p. 151.

151. He considered the idea of a propitiatory Mass and private Masses the result of "a mass of human Traditions," *ibid.*

152. Brightman, *The English Rite*, Vol. 1, p. ccix.

153. Quoted in Sanderson and Wren, *Fragmentary Illustrations*, p. viii (Introduction by editor).

154. Cuming, "Making of the Prayer Book of 1662," in Archbishop of Canterbury, *et al., The English Prayer Book 1549–1662*, p. 90.

155. *Ibid.*, p. 100. In Cosin's absence, it seems that Wren introduced some changes into the *Durham Book* that displeased Cosin. *Ibid.*

156. *The most humble Answer of Matthew Wren, Bishop of Ely, to the Articles of Impeachment exhibited against him by the Honourable Commones House of Parliament for several Crimes and Misdeameanors*, in *Parentalia: or Memoirs of the Family of the Wrens; viz. of Mathew Bishop of Ely, Christopher Dean of Windsor, &c. But Chiefly of Sir Christopher Wren, Late Surveyor-General of the Royal Buildings, President of the Royal Society, &c &c.*, Stephen Wren, ed. (London, 1750), p. 74.

157. *Ibid.*, p. 75.

158. *Ibid.*

159. *Ibid.*, p. 77.

160. *Ibid.*, p. 78.

161. *Ibid.*, p. 92.

162. *Advising The   But Submitting All To The Judgment Of Our H. Mother, The Church of England*, in Sanderson and Wren, *Fragmentary Illustrations*, p. 55. The title of Wren's *Exceptions*, due to the poor condition of the first leaf of the manuscript, is only partially legible.

163. *Exceptions*, in *ibid.*, p. 74.

164. *Ibid.*, p. 76.

165. *Ibid.*, pp. 76–77.

166. *Ibid.*, p. 77.

167. *Ibid.*, p. 80.

168. *Ibid.*, p. 83.

169. *Ibid.*, p. 81.

170. *Ibid.*, p. 79.

171. *Ibid.*, pp. 82–83.

172. *Ibid.*, p. 81.

173. *Ibid.*, p. 84.

174. *Ibid.*, p. 77.

175. *Defence,* in Wren, ed., *Parentalia,* p. 81.

176. *Ibid.*, p. 82.

177. *Ibid.*, p. 103.

178. *Ibid.*, p. 104.

179. *Exceptions,* in Sanderson and Wren, *Fragmentary Illustrations,* p. 82.

180. *Ibid.*, p. 83.

181. *Ibid.*, p. 81

172. *Ibid.*, p. 81

183. A. Harold Wood, *Church Unity Without Uniformity* (London, 1963), p. 228.

184. Cuming, "Making of the Prayer Book of 1662," in Archbishop of Canterbury, *et al., The English Prayer Book 1549–1662,* pp. 104–105, 109–110.

185. All references to the 1662 Services are taken from Barry, ed., *The Teacher's Prayer Book.* The vestments rubric is taken from *The Order for Morning Prayer,* p. 37; *The Order of the Administration of the Lord's Supper or Holy Communion* is found in pp. 136–147. References to the 1559 Service are taken from *The Order for the Administration of the Lord's Supper or Holy Communion,* in Clay, ed., *Liturgical Services of Queen Elizabeth,* pp. 180–198.

186. Barry, ed., *Teacher's Prayer Book,* p. 140 (Commentary by Editor).

Chapter V. The Communion Services of 1718 and 1764

1. Roger Thomas, "Comprehension and Indulgence," in *From Uniformity to Unity,* Geoffrey F. Nuttall and Owen Chadwick, eds. (London, 1962), p. 242.

2. For a concise work on this subject, see J. W. C. Wand, *The High Church Schism* (London, 1951). See also John Dowden, *The*

Scottish Communion Office, 1764, With Introduction, History of the Office, Notes and Appendices, H. A. Wilson, ed. (Oxford, 1922), pp. 49–77.

3. Charles Booth was the last of what Neill calls a "shadow-episcopate" in *Anglicanism,* p. 175.

4. Thomas Brett, *A Collection of the Principal Liturgies Used by the Christian Church in the Celebration of the Holy Eucharist: Particularly the Ancient, viz. the Clementine, as it stands in the Book call'd The Apostolical Constitutions; the Liturgies of S. James, S. Mark, S. Chrysostom, S. Basil, &c. Translated into English by several Hands, With A Dissertation upon Them, Showing their Usefulness and Authority, and pointing out their several Corruptions and Interpolations* (London, 1720), pp. 358–362.

5. *Ibid.*

6. Henry Broxap, *The Later Nonjurors* (Cambridge, 1924), p. 47. See also J. H. Overton, *The Non-Jurors, Their Lives, Principles, and Writings* (London, 1902), pp. 290–308.

7. Quoted in Grisbrooke, *Anglican Liturgies,* p. 94.

8. The whole document is reproduced, *ibid.,* pp. 94–95.

9. *Ibid.,* p. 95.

10. *Ibid.,* pp. 297–316. Deacon's later rite deviated only in very minor points from the Service of 1718.

11. Dowden, *Scottish Prayer Book,* pp. 58–59.

12. Brett, *Dissertation,* pp. 261, 358; see also Thomas Brett, *Some Remarks on Dr. Waterland's Review of the Doctrine of the Eucharist, &c. With Regard to the Seeming Difference Between Him and Mr. Johnson's, Concerning the Sacrifice and Some Other Points. In Defence of Myself and Some Others Who Maintained Mr. Johnson's Opinion in our Late Answers to the Plain Account, &c.* (London, 1738), p. 1. See also Thomas Rattray, *The Ancient Liturgy of the Church of Jerusalem, Being the Liturgy of St. James, Freed from all Latter Additions and Interpolations of Whatever Kind, and so Restored to its Original Purity; by Comparing it with the Account Given of that Liturgy of St. Cyril in his Fifth Mystagogical Catechism, and with the Clementine Liturgy, &c. Containing in so many different Columns, I. The Liturgy of St. James as we have it at present, the Interpolations being only printed in a smaller character. II. The same Liturgy without these Interpolations, or the ancient Liturgy of the Church of Jerusalem. III. St. Cyril's Account of that Liturgy in his Vth Mystagogical Catechism. IV. The Clementine Liturgy. V. So much of the corresponding Parts of the Liturgies of St. Mark, St. Chrysostom and St. Basil as may serve for illustrating and confirming it. With an English Translation*

and Notes, as also an Appendix, containing some other Ancient Prayers, Of all which an Account is given in the Preface (London, 1744), p. xiii (Preface).

13. John Johnson, *The Unbloody Sacrifice and Altar, Unvail'd and Supported. Part the First. In which the Nature of the Eucharist is explain'd according to the Sentiments of the Christian Church in the first four Centuries, proving That the Eucharist is a proper Material Sacrifice, That it is both Eucharistic, and Propitiatory, That it is to be offer'd by proper Officers, That the Oblation is to be made on a proper Altar, That it is properly consum'd by Manducation, To which is Added, A Proof, That what our Saviour speaks concerning Eating his Flesh, and Drinking his Blood, in the VIth Chapter of St. John's Gospel, is principally meant of the Eucharist* (London, 1714), p. 297.

14. John Johnson, *The Unbloody Sacrifice and Altar, Unvail'd and Supported, Part the Second. Showing, The Agreement and Disagreement of the Eucharist with the Sacrifices of the Ancients, and the Excellency of the former. The great Moment of the Eucharist both as a Feast, and Sacrifice. The Necessity of frequent Communion. The Unity of the Eucharist. The Nature of Excommunication. And the Primitive Method of Preparation. With Devotions for the Altar* (London, 1718).

15. See, for example, *Answer to Gardiner*, in Cranmer, *Writings Relative to the Lord's Supper*, p. 85.

16. Johnson, *The Unbloody Sacrifice, II*, pp. 12–13.

17. Johnson, *The Unbloody Sacrifice, I*, pp. 71–72.

18. John Johnson, *The Primitive Communicant; in Three Discourses on the Sacrament of the Eucharist in which the Sacrifice of Christ and of the Church are fully explained* (Manchester, 1738), p. 51.

19. Johnson, *The Unbloody Sacrifice, II*, p. 60.

20. Johnson, *The Unbloody Sacrifice, I*, pp. 214–215.

21. John Johnson, *The Propitiatory Oblation in the Holy Eucharist Truly Stated, and Defended, from Scripture, Antiquity, and the Communion-Service of the Church of England* (London, 1710), p. 5.

22. *Ibid.*, p. 6.

23. Johnson, *The Unbloody Sacrifice, II*, pp. 150–151.

24. *Ibid.*, p. 60.

25. Johnson, *The Unbloody Sacrifice, I*, p. 146.

26. *Ibid.*, p. 208.

27. *Ibid.*, p. 231.

28. *Ibid.*, p. 208.

29. *Ibid.*, p. 232.

30. *Ibid.,* p. 215.
31. Johnson, *The Propitiatory Oblation,* p. 6.
32. Johnson, *The Unbloody Sacrifice, I,* p. 249.
33. *Ibid.,* p. 212.
34. *Ibid.*
35. Johnson, *The Propitiatory Oblation,* p. 28.
36. Johnson, *The Unbloody Sacrifice, I,* pp. 185–186.
37. *Ibid.,* p. 238.
38. *Ibid.,* p. 249.
39. Johnson, *The Unbloody Sacrifice, II,* pp. 175–181.
40. Alan Campbell Don, *The Scottish Book of Common Prayer 1929, Notes on its origin and growth, with illustrations from original documents* (London, 1949), p. 51.
41. Thomas Brett, *The Christian Altar and Sacrifice. A sermon, shewing that the Lord's Table is a proper altar, and the sacrament of the Eucharist a proper Sacrifice* (London, 1713), p. 10.
42. Thomas Brett, *A True Scripture Account of the Nature and Benefits of the Holy Eucharist &c.* (London, 1736), p. 77.
43. Brett, *Christian Altar,* p. 13.
44. *Ibid.,* pp. 2–3.
45. *Ibid.,* p. 13.
46. Thomas Brett, *The Divine Right of Episcopacy, and the Necessity of an Episcopal Commission for Preaching God's Word, and for the Valid Ministration of the Christian Sacraments, Proved from the Holy Scriptures, and the Doctrine and Practice of the Primitive Church, Together with an Impartial Account of the False Principles of Papists, Lutherans, and Calvinists, Concerning the Identity of Bishops and Presbyters, Also The Valid Succession of our English Bishops Vindicated, Against the Objections of Presbyterians and Romanists. And The Popish Fable of the Nags-Head Consecration of Archbishop Parker Fully Refuted* (London, 1718), p. 157.
47. *Ibid.,* p. 158.
48. Brett, *Christian Altar,* p. xiv (Introduction).
49. *Ibid.,* pp. 20–21.
50. *Ibid.,* p. 23.
51. Brett, *Dissertation,* p. 391.
52. *Ibid.,* p. 68.
53. *Ibid.,* p. 59.
54. *Ibid.,* pp. 380–382.
55. Brett, *Episcopacy,* pp. 195–196.
56. Brett, *Dissertation,* p. 391.
57. *Ibid.,* p. 169.

58. Thomas Brett, *A Discourse Concerning the Necessity of Discerning the Lord's Body in the Holy Communion, with a Preface, Giving an Account of the Erroneous Opinions of the Papists, Lutherans, and Calvinists, upon this Subject* (London, 1720), pp. xvii–xviii (Preface). See also Brett, *Remarks*, pp. 29–30.

59. Brett, *Christian Altar*, p. xiii (Introduction).

60. *Ibid.*, pp. xiv–xv.

61. *Dissertation*, p. 70.

62. *Ibid.*, p. 127.

63. *Ibid.*, p. 267.

64. *Ibid.*, p. 83.

65. *Ibid.*, p. 137.

66. Henry Broxap, *A Biography of Thomas Deacon, The Manchester Non-Juror* (Manchester, 1911), p. 43. Broxap was less inclined to attribute *exclusive* authorship to Deacon after further research in the Brett papers at the Bodleian Library, Oxford, England. See Grisbrooke, *Anglican Liturgies*, p. 95.

67. Broxap, *Thomas Deacon*, p. 47.

68. Thomas Deacon, *A Full, True, and Comprehensive View of Christianity: Containing a Short Historical Account of Religion from the Creation of the World to the Fourth Century after Our Lord Jesus Christ: As also the Complete Duty of A Christian in Relation to Faith, Practice, Worship, and Rituals, Set Forth Sincerely, Without Regard to any Modern Church, Sect, or Party, as it is Taught in the Holy Scriptures, was Delivered by the Apostles, and Received by the Universal Church of Christ During the Four First Centuries. The Whole Succinctly and Fully Laid Down in Two Catechisms, A Shorter and a Longer, Each Divided into Two Parts; Whereof the One Comprehends the Sacred History; the Other the Christian Doctrine. The Shorter Catechism Being Suited to the Meanest Capacity, and Calculated for the Use of Children; And the Longer for that of the More Knowing Christian. To which is Prefixed a Discourse upon the Design of these Catechisms, and upon the best Method of Instructing Youth in them* (London, 1747).

69. *Ibid.*, pp. 74–75.

70. *Longer Catechism*, in *ibid.*, p. 323.

71. *Ibid.*, p. 314.

72. *Ibid.*, p. 259.

73. *Ibid.*, p. 243.

74. *Ibid.*, p. 256.

75. *Ibid.*, p. 257.

76. *Ibid.*
77. *Ibid.*, p. 261.
78. *Ibid.*, p. 268.
79. *Ibid.*, pp. 275–276.
80. *Ibid.*, p. 279.
81. Quoted in Broxap, *Deacon*, p. 44.
82. Thomas Deacon, *Preface*, in *A Complete Collection of Devotions, both Public and Private; Taken from the Apostolical Constitutions, the Ancient Liturgies and the Common Prayer Book of the Church of England. In Two Parts. Part I. Comprehending the Public Offices of the Church. Humbly Offered to the Consideration of the Present Churches of Christendom, Greek, Roman, English, and all Others. Part II. Being a Primitive Method of Daily Private Prayers, Containing Devotions for the Morning and Evening, and for the Ancient Hours of Prayer, Nine, Twelve, and Three; Together with the Hymns, and Thanksgivings for the Lord's Day and Sabbath, and Prayers for Fasting Days; As Also, Devotions for the Altar, and Graces before and after Meal: All Taken from the Apostolical Constitutions and the Ancient Liturgies, with some Additions: And Recommended to the Practice of all Private Christians of Every Communion. To which is Added, An Appendix in Justification of this Undertaking, Consisting of Extracts and Observations, Taken from the Writings of very Eminent and Learned Divines of Different Communions. And to all is Subjoined, in a Supplement, An Essay to Procure Catholic Communion upon Catholic Principles* (London, 1734), p. 111.
83. Sermon, April 6, 1718, London, in Broxap, *Deacon*, pp. 30–31.
84. *Longer Catechism*, in Deacon, *Comprehensive View*, p. 297.
85. *Comprehensive View*, p. 69.
86. Dr. Deacon to Mr. Pierce, Manchester, May 4, 1750, in Broxap, *Deacon*, p. 139.
87. *Longer Catechism*, in Deacon, *Comprehensive View*, p. 281.
88. *Ibid.*, p. 307.
89. *Ibid.*, pp. 323–324.
90. All references to the 1718 Service are taken from Grisbrooke, *Anglican Liturgies*, pp. 275–296. All references to the 1549 Communion Service are from Thompson, ed., *Liturgies of the Western Church*, pp. 245–264; references to the 1637 Service are from Donaldson, *The Scottish Prayer Book*, pp. 183–204; references to the 1662 Service are from Barry, *The Teacher's Prayer Book*, pp. 136–147.
91. Brett, *Dissertation*, pp. 358–362.
92. Dowden, *Scottish Communion Office*, pp. 40–41. Dowden's

book is the standard and invaluable work for the history of the Scottish Communion Office. It should be read with caution, however, because Dowden wrote before the latest Scotch revision. Also, Dowden still labored under the false impression that few concessions were made to Puritan grievances in 1637, and that Maxwell and Wedderburn were the only Scottish prelates enthusiastic for the 1637 Communion Service.

93. *Ibid.* p. 40.

94. *Ibid.*, p. 71. For the complete title of Rattray's book see footnote 198, *supra*, p. 270.

95. Don, *The Scottish Book of Common Prayer*, p. 51.

96. Dowden, *Scottish Communion Office*, p. 233 (Appendix K).

97. *Journals of The Episcopal Visitations of the Right. Rev. Robert Forbes, M.A., of the Dioceses of Ross and Caithness, and of the Dioceses of Ross and Argyll, 1762 & 1770. With a History of the Episcopal Church in the Diocese of Ross, Chiefly During the 18th Century; and a Memoir of Bishop R. Forbes*, J. B. Craven, ed. (London, 1923), p. 16.

98. Quoted in Dowden, *Scottish Communion Office*, p. 78.

99. Don, *The Scottish Book of Common Prayer*, p. 51.

100. The notice is quoted in Dowden, *Scottish Communion Office*, p. 70.

101. *A Catechism Dealing Chiefly with the Holy Eucharist, Together with a Prayer at the Mixture of the Chalice*, John Dowden, ed. (Edinburgh, 1904). This book, indispensable for the doctrine of the 1764 and through 1764 the American Communion Service, is unavailable in this continent, but is available at the British Museum and the Edinburgh College Library.

102. *Ibid.*, p. 18, footnote 5.

103. *Ibid.*, p. 7.

104. *Ibid.*, pp. 7–8.

105. *Ibid.*, pp. 9–10.

106. *Ibid.*, p. 8.

107. *Ibid.*, pp. 8–9.

108. *Ibid.*, p. 10.

109. *Ibid.*, pp. 10–11.

110. *Ibid.*, p. 11.

111. *Ibid.*, pp. 11–12.

112. *A Prayer which may be used by the Priest when he is performing the Mixture, compos'd according to St. Cyprian's Explanation of this Usage*, in Forbes, *Catechism*, p. 22.

113. Dowden, *Scottish Communion Office*, pp. 118–121; all ref-

erences to the rest of the Service are also from Dowden's reprint of the Edinburgh edition of 1764, pp. 121–132.

Chapter VI. The American Service of 1789

1. Interestingly enough, the Anglicans of Australia still cling to the title "The Church of England in Australia."

2. William Wilson Manross, *A History of the American Episcopal Church* (New York, 1950), pp. 44–46.

3. Procter and Frere, *A New History,* pp. 234–235 (Additional Note 4).

4. William White, *Memoirs of the Protestant Episcopal Church in the United States of America From Its Organization Up to the Present Day* (New York, 1836), p. 23. When the English Bishops delayed, Seabury thought of approaching the Danes for the succession. But the young president of Magdalen College, Oxford, advised him to approach the Scottish Bishops. For this reason the presidents of Magdalen claim American Episcopalism was born within their walls. It is also of interest and significance that the same Dr. Routh, still living and still president of Magdalen in 1841, was the only Oxford president to support another young man in a quandary: John Henry Newman. See James Morris, *Oxford* (London, 1965), pp. 186–187, 184.

5. Quoted in Dowden, *Scottish Communion Office,* pp. 99–100. The original document is in the office of the Librarian at the General Theological Seminary in New York.

6. Standing Liturgical Commission, *Prayer Book Studies IV,* pp. 88–89.

7. Neill, *Anglicanism,* p. 283.

8. Dowden, *Scottish Communion Office,* p. 100.

9. For a collation of the Communion Service of Seabury and the Scottish Service, see Dowden, *Scottish Communion Office,* pp. 208–209 (Appendix F).

10. White, *Memoirs,* p. 30.

11. *Ibid.,* p. 154.

12. Standing Liturgical Commission, *Prayer Book Studies IV,* p. 87.

13. The testament of Seabury's consecration, signed by the three Bishops, is in the safe of the library at the General Theological Seminary in New York.

14. Raymond W. Albright, *A History of the Protestant Episcopal Church* (New York, 1964), p. 131.

15. J. W. C. Wand, *Anglicanism in History and Today* (London, 1963), p. 30.

16. Quoted in White, *Memoirs,* pp. 154–155. See also Dowden, *Scottish Communion Office,* p. 103.

17. Manross, *American Episcopal Church,* p. 199.

18. Samuel Seabury, *Address to the Ministers and Congregations of the Presbyterian and Independent Persuasions in the United States of America,* ([n.p.], 1790), p. 54.

19. Samuel Seabury, *Second Charge to the Clergy of his Dioceses Delivered at Derby in the State of Connecticut on the 22nd of September, 1786* (New Haven, [n.d.]), p. 12.

20. Samuel Seabury to William White, New London, June 29, 1789, in the Seabury papers, entitled *Papers, Books, and Printed Matter,* in St. Mark Library of the General Theological Seminary, New York. The Seabury papers are not yet completely indexed. There are two drawers of them in the office of the Librarian of the General Theological Seminary and others in a safe in the rare book room. These will hereafter be referred to as *Papers, Books, and Printed Matter.*

21. *Seabury's first Charge, to the Clergy of his Diocese,* in *The Address of the Episcopal Clergy of Connecticut to the Right Reverend Bishop Seabury with the Bishop's Answer, Seabury's First Charge, to the Clergy of his Diocese* (New Haven, [n.d.]), p. 14.

22. Seabury, *Second Charge to the Clergy,* pp. 17–18.

23. *Ibid.,* p. 18.

24. Samuel Seabury, *Of the Holy Eucharist,* in *Discourses on Several Subjects,* 2 Vols. (Hudson, 1815), Vol. 1, p. 147.

25. *Ibid.,* p. 148.

26. Samuel Seabury, *An Earnest Persuasive to Frequent Communion Addressed to those Professors of the Church of England in Connecticut, Who Neglect that Holy Ordinance* (New Haven, 1789), p. 19.

27. *Ibid.,* pp. 7–8.

28. *Ibid.,* p. 20.

29. See *infra,* p. 219.

30. Seabury, *Lectures Upon the Church Catechism,* p. 120, in *Papers, Books, and Printed Matter.*

31. *Ibid.,* pp. 120–121.

32. *Ibid.,* p. 121.

33. *Ibid.*

34. *Ibid.,* p. 123.

35. "On Frequent Communion," in Seabury, *Papers, Books, and Printed Matter.*

278 *The Anglican Eucharist in Ecumenical Perspective*

36. *Discourse Eight,* in Seabury, *Discourses,* Vol. 2, p. 107.
37. *Ibid.,* p. 119.
38. *Ibid.,* p. 129.
39. Samuel Seabury, *Discourse on II Tim. III. 16. Delivered in St. Paul's and St. George's Chapels in New York On Sunday the 11th of May, 1777* (New York, 1786), p. 8.
40. *Discourse VI,* in Seabury, *Discourses,* Vol. 1, pp. 148–149.
41. Seabury, *Second Charge to Clergy,* pp. 18–19.
42. *Discourse VI,* in Seabury, *Discourses,* Vol. 1, p. 149.
43. *Upon the Church Catechism,* p. 122, in Seabury, *Papers, Books, and Printed Matter.*
44. *Ibid.,* p. 123.
45. *Ibid.,* pp. 124–125.
46. Seabury, *Earnest Persuasive,* p. 15.
47. *Ibid.,* p. 8.
48. *Ibid.,* p. 9.
49. *Ibid.,* p. 21.
50. *Upon the Church Catechism,* p. 125, in Seabury, *Papers, Books, and Printed Matter.*
51. "On Frequent Communion," in Seabury, *Papers, Books, and Printed Matter.*
52. White, *Memoirs,* p. 27.
53. *Ibid.,* p. 28.
54. *Ibid.,* p. 141.
55. William White to Samuel Seabury, Philadelphia, August 16, 1789, in Seabury, *Papers, Books and Printed Matter.*
56. White, *Memoirs,* pp. 148–149.
57. *Ibid.,* p. 149.
58. *Ibid.,* p. 154.
59. To the Reverend the Clergy of the Protestant Episcopal Church in the States of Massachusetts and New Hampshire, Philadelphia, August 11, 1789, in the White papers, entitled *Letters, Sermons, Records,* in the General Theological Seminary, New York.
60. William White, *A Sermon on the Qualifications, the Authorities, and the Duties of the Gospel Ministry* (New York, 1804), p. 1.
61. William White, *An Address Delivered Before the Trustees, Faculty, and Students of the General Theological Seminary of the Protestant Episcopal Church in the United States, July 26, 1823* (New York, 1823), p. 10.
62. William White, *A Charge to the Clergy of the Protestant Episcopal Church in the Commonwealth of Pennsylvania* (Philadelphia, 1807), p. 10.

63. *Dissertation VIII,* in William White, *Lectures on the Catechism of the Protestant Episcopal Church* (Philadelphia, 1813), p. 398.

64. White, *Memoirs,* p. 154.

65. *Dissertation VIII,* in White, *Lectures,* p. 390.

66. *Ibid.,* p. 391.

67. *Commentaries Suited to Occasions of Ordination* (New York, 1833), p. 84.

68. *Ibid.,* p. 84.

69. *Letter I,* in William White, *A Voice From The Past. Two Letters of Bishop White to the Rev. John Hobart* (Philadelphia, 1789), p. 12.

70. *Commentaries,* p. 85.

71. *Letter I,* in White, *Voice From The Past,* p. 12.

72. *Commentaries,* p. 86.

73. *Letter I,* in White, *A Voice From The Past,* p. 12.

74. *Lecture V,* in White, *Lectures,* p. 127.

75. *Ibid.,* p. 130.

76. *Letter II,* in White, *A Voice From The Past,* p. 14.

77. *Ibid.*

78. *Ibid.,* p. 18.

79. *Ibid.,* pp. 18–19.

80. *Ibid.,* p. 18.

81. *Ibid.,* p. 19.

82. *Letter I,* in White, *A Voice From The Past,* p. 9.

83. *Lecture V,* in White, *Lectures,* p. 132.

84. *Letter II,* in White, *A Voice From The Past,* p. 21.

85. *Ibid.,* pp. 20–21.

86. *Dissertation VIII,* in White, *Lectures,* p. 396.

87. White, *Commentaries,* p. 201.

88. White, *An Address Delivered Before the Trustees, Faculty, and Students of the General Theological Seminary,* p. 11.

89. *Dissertation VIII,* in White, *Lectures,* p. 373.

90. White, *Commentaries,* p. 197.

91. *Ibid.,* pp. 197–198.

92. *Ibid.,* p. 198.

93. *Dissertation VIII,* in White, *Discourses,* p. 374.

94. White, *Commentaries,* p. 199.

95. *Ibid.*

96. *Lecture V,* in White, *Discourses,* p. 130.

97. To the Reverend the Clergy of the Protestant Episcopal Church in the States of Massachusetts and New Hampshire, in White, *Letters, Sermons, Records.*

98. White, *Memoirs*, pp. 154–155.

99. *Lecture V*, in White, *Discourses*, p. 128.

100. *Ibid.*

101. *Ibid.*, p. 131.

102. *Dissertation VIII*, in White, *Discourses*, pp. 384–385.

103. *Bishop White's Opinions on Certain Theological and Ecclesiastical Points, Being a Compilation from the Writings and in the Words of the Right Rev. Wm. White, D.D.,* "A Protestant Episcopalian," ed. (New York, 1846), pp. 95–96.

104. Horace Wemyss Smith, *Life and Correspondence of the Rev. William Smith, D.D.,* 2 Vols. (Philadelphia, 1880), Vol. 2, p. 118.

105. *Ibid.*, p. 275.

106. *Ibid.*, footnote, p. 289.

107. White, *Memoirs*, p. 154.

108. Procter and Frere, *A New History*, p. 245 (Additional Note 4).

109. *Sermon XVIII*, in *The Works of William Smith, D.D. Late Provost of The College And Academy of Philadelphia*, 2 Vols. (Philadelphia, 1803), Vol. 2, pp. 378, 379.

110. *Sermon XIII*, in *ibid.*, p. 249.

111. *Declaration of certain Fundamental Rights and Liberties of the Protestant Episcopal Church of Maryland, ibid.*, p. 519 (Appendix to *Sermon XXI*).

112. *Sermon XXII, ibid.*, p. 536.

113. William Smith, *Doctor Smith's Answer to Mr. Blatchford's Letter* (Newfield, 1798), p. 35.

114. William Smith, *An Address to the Members of the Protestant Church of Maryland, To Which Is Added A Sermon* (Baltimore, 1784), p. 27.

115. Smith, *Doctor Smith's Answer*, p. 35.

116. *Ibid.*, p. 31.

117. *Ibid.*, p. 35.

118. *Ibid.*, p. 33.

119. *Ibid.*, p. 30.

120. *Ibid.*, p. 34.

121. *Sermon V*, in William Smith, *Select Sermons of William Smith* (Philadelphia, [n.d.]), p. 75.

122. *Sermon VII, ibid.*, p. 94.

123. *Ibid.*, p. 97.

124. Smith, *Doctor Smith's Answer*, p. 38.

125. *Ibid.*, pp. 35–36.

126. *Sermon IX*, in Smith, *Works*, Vol. 1, pp. 143–144.

127. Smith, *Doctor Smith's Answer*, p. 38.

128. *Ibid.*

129. *Ibid.*, p. 34.

130. *Ibid.*, p. 32.

131. *Sermon VII*, in Smith, *Select Sermons*, p. 97.

132. Smith, *Doctor Smith's Answer*, p. 18.

133. *Sermon VII*, in Smith, *Select Sermons*, p. 101.

134. *Sermon XII*, in *ibid.*, p. 166.

135. All references to the 1789 Communion Service are taken from *The Order For The Administration of the Lord's Supper, or, Holy Communion,* in *The Book of Common Prayer, and Administration of The Sacraments, and Other Rites and Ceremonies of The Church, According to the Use of the Protestant Episcopal Church in the United States of America* (New York, 1835), pp. 138–149; all references to the 1662 Communion Service are from *The Order For The Administration of the Lord's Supper, or Holy Communion,* in Barry, ed., *The Teacher's Prayer Book,* pp. 136–147; all references to the 1764 Communion Service are from Dowden, *Scottish Communion Office,* pp. 118–132.

136. Standing Liturgical Commission, *Prayer Book Studies IV,* p. 90.

137. For the unfortunate misunderstandings over the curtailment of the Creeds in the "Proposed Book," see *ibid.*, pp. 88–89.

138. *Ibid.*, p. 92.

139. *Ibid.*, p. 87.

Conclusion

1. *Anglicanism, The Thought and Practice of the Church of England, Illustrated from the Religious Literature of the Seventeenth Century,* Paul Elmer More, and Frank Leslie Cross, eds. (London, 1962), p. 488.

2. Report of the fourth meeting of the Joint Commission on Anglican-Roman Catholic Relations in the United States of America, Milwaukee, Wisconsin, May 24–26, 1967; pub. in the *Journal of the General Convention, 1967* (Episcopal Church). See also *National Catholic Reporter,* III, 32, June 7, 1967, p. 1.

3. *The Reform of Liturgical Worship, Perspectives and Prospects* (New York, 1961), p. 104.

4. *Eucharistic Sacrifice,* pp. 267–268. See also Rudolf Schnackenburg, "The Dogmatic Evaluation of the New Testament," in *Dogmatic vs. Biblical Theology,* Herbert Vorgrimler, ed. (London, 1964), pp. 161–163.

5. Archbishops of Canterbury and York, *Answer of the Archbishops of England to the Apostolic Letter of Pope Leo XIII on English Ordinations* (London, 1954), p. 37.

6. "Anglicanism in the Seventeenth Century," in *Anglicanism,* p. xxxvii.

7. Walden Pell and P. M. Dawley, *The Religion of the Prayer Book* (New York, 1950), p. 132. See also Nelson R. Boss, *The Prayer Book Reason Why* (New York, 1963), p. 81.

8. *Prayer Book Interleaves* (New York, 1943), p. 157.

9. See note 2, above.

Bibliography

I. LITURGIES

Arnold, J. H., ed. *Anglican Liturgies,* Alcuin Club, Vol. 22. London, 1939.

Barry, Alfred. *The Teacher's Prayer Book: being the Book of Common Prayer, with Introductions, Analyses, Notes, and a Commentary upon the Psalter.* London, 1813.

Blunt, John Henry. *The Annotated Book of Common Prayer, Being an Historical, Ritual, and Theological Commentary on the Devotional System of the Church of England.* London, 1868.

The Book of Common Prayer, and Administration of the Sacraments and Other Rites and Ceremonies of the Church According to the Use of the Protestant Episcopal Church in the United States of America. New York, 1835.

The Book of Common Prayer and Administration of the Sacraments and Other Rites and Ceremonies of the Church According to the Use of the Protestant Episcopal Church in the United States. New York, 1945.

Brett, Thomas. *A Collection of the Principal Liturgies Used by the Christian Church in the Celebration of the Holy Eucharist: particularly the Ancient, viz. the Clementine, the Liturgies of S. James, S. Mark, S. Chrysostom, S. Basil, &c. Translated by several Hands. With a Dissertation upon them, shewing their Usefulness and Authority, and pointing out their several Corruptions and Interpolations.* London, 1720.

Cardwell, E., ed. *The Two Books of Common Prayer Set Forth by Parliament in the Reign of King Edward VI.* Oxford, 1838.

Clay, William Keating, ed. *Liturgies and Occasional Forms of Prayer Set Forth in the Reign of Queen Elizabeth.* Parker Society, Cambridge, 1848.

Collins, A. Jeffrey, ed. *Manuale ad Usum Percelebris Ecclesiae Sarisburiensis* Henry Bradshaw Society, Vol. 91. Chichester, 1958.

Cooper, James, ed. *The Book of Common Prayer and Administration of the Sacraments and other parts of Divine Service for the use of* the Church of Scotland, commonly known as Laud's Liturgy, 1637. Edinburgh, 1904.

Cuming, G. J., ed. *The Durham Book, Being the First Draft of Revision of the B.C.P. in 1661.* London, 1961.

Deacon, Thomas. *A Complete Collection of Devotions, both Public and Private; Taken from the Apostolical Constitutions, the Ancient Liturgies and the Common Prayer Book of the Church of England. In Two Parts. Part I. Comprehending the Public Offices of the Church. Humbly Offered to the Consideration of the Present Churches of Christendom, Greek, Roman, English, and all Others. Part II. Being a Primitive Method of Daily Private Prayers, Containing Devotions for the Morning and Evening, and for the Ancient Hours of Prayer, Nine, Twelve, and Three; Together with the Hymns, and Thanksgivings for the Lord's Day and Sabbath, and Prayers for Fasting Days; As Also, Devotions for the Altar, and Graces before and after Meal: All Taken, from the Apostolical Constitutions and the Ancient Liturgies, with some Additions; And Recommended to the Practice of all Private Christians of Every Communion. To which is Added, An Appendix in Justification of this Undertaking, Consisting of Extracts and Observations Taken from the Writings of very Eminent and Learned Divines of Different Communions. And to all is Subjoined, in a Supplement, An Essay to Procure Catholic Communion upon Catholic Principles.* London, 1734.

Dowden, John. *The Scottish Communion Office, 1764, With Introduction, History of the Office, Notes and Appendices,* H. A. Wilson, ed. Oxford, 1922.

Grisbrooke, W. Jardine. *Anglican Liturgies of the Seventeenth and Eighteenth Centuries,* Alcuin Club, Vol. 40. London, 1958.

Hall, Peter, ed. *Fragmenta Liturgica, Documents Illustrative of the Liturgy of the Church of England; Exhibiting the Several Emendations of it, and Substitutions for it, that Have Been Proposed from Time to Time, and Partially Adopted, Whether at Home or Abroad,* 7 Vols. Bath, 1848.

Ketley, Joseph, ed. *The Two Liturgies A.D. 1549 and A.D. 1552: with other Documents Set Forth by Authority in the Reign of King Edward VI.* Parker Society, Cambridge, 1844.

McGarvey, W., ed. *Liturgiae Americanae.* Philadelphia, 1895.

Rattray, Thomas. *The Ancient Liturgy of the Church of Jerusalem, Being the Liturgy of St. James, Freed from all Later Additions and Interpolations of Whatever Kind, and so Restored to its Original Purity; by Comparing it with the Account Given of that Liturgy by St. Cyril in his Fifth Mystagogical Catechism, and with the Clementine Liturgy, &c. With an English Translation and Notes, as also an Appendix, containing Some Other Ancient Prayers.* London, 1744.

Sprott, G. W., ed. *Scottish Liturgies of James VI.* Edinburgh, 1871.

Sprott, George Washington, and Leishmann, Thomas, eds. *The Book of Common Order of the Church of Scotland, Commonly Known as John Knox's Liturgy, and the Directory of Public Worship for the Public Worship of God Agreed Upon by the Assembly of Divines at Westminster, with Historical Introduction and Illustrative Notes.* Edinburgh, 1869.

Staley, Vernon, ed. *The Sarum Missal in English.* London, 1911.

Thompson, Bard., ed. *Liturgies of the Western Church.* Cleveland, 1962.

Wigan, Bruce, ed. *The Liturgy in English.* London, 1962.

Wilson, H. A., ed. *The Order of the Communion, 1548,* Henry Bradshaw Society, Vol. 34. London, 1908.

II. DOCUMENTS AND PRIMARY DOCTRINAL SOURCES

Archbishops of Canterbury and York. *Answer of the Archbishops of England to the Apostolic Letter of Pope Leo XIII on English Ordinations.* London, 1954.

Bellarmine, Robert. *Ven. Cardinalis Roberti Ballarmini Politiani, S.J., Opera Omnia,* Justinus Favre, ed., 12 Vols. Paris, 1870–1874.

Brett, Thomas. *A sermon of the Honour of Christian Priesthood, and the necessity of divine call to that office; with a preface to the Dissenters.* London, 1712.

————. *A Discourse concerning the Necessity of Discerning the Lord's Body in the Holy Communion, with a preface, Giving an account of the Erroneous Opinions of the Papists, Lutherans, and Calvinists, upon this Subject.* London, 1712.

————. *The Christian Altar and Sacrifices, A sermon shewing that the Lord's Table is a proper altar, and the sacrament of the Eucharist a proper Sacrifice.* London, 1713.

————. *The Divine Right of Episcopacy and the Necessity of an Episcopal Commission for Preaching God's Word, and for the Valid Ministration of the Christian Sacraments, Proved from the Holy Scriptures, and the Doctrine and Practice of the Primitive Church, Together with an Impartial Account of the False Principles of Papists, Lutherans, and Calvinists, Concerning the Identity of Bishops and Presbyters. Also the Valid Succession of our English Bishops Vindicated, Against the Objections of Presbyterians and*

Romanists. And the Popish Fable of the Nags-Head Consecration of Archbishop Parker Fully Refuted. London, 1718.

――――. *A True Scripture Account of the Nature and Benefits of the Holy Eucharist &c.,* London, 1736.

――――. *Some Remarks on Dr. Waterland's Review of the Doctrine of the Eucharist, &c. With Regard to the Seeming Difference Between Him and Mr. Johnson's, Concerning the Sacrifice and Some Other Points. In Defence of Myself and Some Others Who Maintained Mr. Johnson's Opinion in our Late Answers to the Plain Account, &c.* London, 1738.

――――. *A Supplement to the Remarks on the Reverend Dr. Waterland's Review of the doctrine of the Eucharist,* London, 1738.

Bucer, Martin. *Scripta Anglicana,* Conrad Hubert, ed. Basle, 1577.

――――. *Traduction française du Commentaire de Bucer sur l'Evangile selon Saint Matthieu,* Jacques Courvoisier, ed., and trans. Paris, 1933.

――――. *Résumé sommaire de la doctrine chrétienne,* François Wendel, ed., and trans. Paris, 1951.

――――. *Études sur la Correspondance,* J. V. Pollet, ed., and trans., 2 Vols. Paris, 1958–1963.

Cardwell, Edward, ed. *A History of Conferences, and Other Proceedings Connected with the Revision of the Book of Common Prayer; From the Year 1558 to the Year 1690.* Oxford, 1841.

Cosin, John. *The Works of the Right Reverend Father in God, John Cosin, Lord Bishop of Durham,* J. Sansom, ed., 5 Vols. Library of Anglo-Catholic Theology, Oxford, 1843–1851.

Cranmer, Thomas. *A Short Instruction into the Christian Religion, Being a Catechism Set Forth by Archbishop Cranmer in 1548. Together with the Same in Latin Translated from the German by Justus Jonas in 1539,* Edward Burton, ed. Oxford, 1829.

――――. *The Remains of Thomas Cranmer, D.D., Archbishop of Canterbury,* Henry Jenkins, ed. 4 Vols., Oxford, 1833.

――――. *Writings and Disputations of Thomas Cranmer Relative to the Sacrament of the Lord's Supper,* John Edmund Cox, ed. Parker Society, Cambridge, 1844.

――――. *Miscellaneous Writings and Letters of Thomas Cranmer, Archbishop of Canterbury, Martyr, 1556,* John Edmund Cox, ed. Parker Society, Cambridge, 1846.

――――. *Archbishop Cranmer on the True and Catholic Doctrine and Use of the Sacrament of the Lord's Supper,* Charles H. H. Wright, ed. London, 1907.

Deacon, Thomas, *The form of admitting a convert into the Communion of the Church.* London, 1746.

————. *A Full, True, and Comprehensive View of Christianity: Containing a Short Historical Account of Religion from the Creation of the World to the Fourth Century after Our Lord Jesus Christ: As also the Complete Duty of a Christian in Relation to Faith, Practice, Worship, and Rituals, Set Forth Sincerely, Without Regard to any Modern Church, Sect, or Party, as it is Taught in the Scriptures, was Delivered by the Apostles and Received by the Universal Church of Christ During the Four First Centuries. The Whole Succinctly and Fully Laid Down in Two Catechisms, A Shorter and a Longer, Each Divided into Two Parts; Whereof the One Comprehends the Sacred History; the other the Christian Doctrine. The Shorter Catechism Being Suited to the Meanest Capacity, and Calculated for the Use of Children; And the Longer for that of the More Knowing Christian. To which is Prefixed a Discourse upon the Design of these Catechisms, and upon the best Method of Instructing Youth in them*, London, 1747.

Edwall, P., Hayman, E., and Maxwell, W. D., eds. *Ways of Worship (Report of a Theological Commission of Faith and Order)*. London, 1951.

Forbes, Robert. *A Catechism dealing Chiefly with the Holy Eucharist, Together with a Prayer at the Mixture of the Chalice*, J. Dowden, ed. Edinburgh, 1904.

————. *Journals of the Episcopal Visitations of the Right Rev. Robert Forbes, M. A., of the Dioceses of Ross and Caithness, and of the Dioceses of Ross and Argyll, 1762 & 1770. With a History of the Episcopal Church in the Diocese of Ross, Chiefly During the 18th Century; and a Memoir of Bishop R. Forbes*, J. B. Craven, ed. London, 1923.

Hooker, Richard. *The Works of That Learned and Judicious Divine, Mr. Richard Hooker: With an Account of His Life and Death by Isaac Walton*, John Keble, ed., 3 Vols. Oxford, 1845.

Hooper, John. *Early Writings of John Hooper, D.D.*, Samuel Carr, ed. Parker Society, Cambridge, 1848.

————. *Later Writings of Bishop Hooper*, Charles Nevinson, ed. Parker Society, Cambridge, 1852.

Jewel, John. *The Works of John Jewel, Bishop of Salisbury*, John Ayre, ed., 4 Vols. Parker Society, Cambridge, 1845–1850.

Johnson, John. *The Propitiatory Oblation in the Holy Eucharist Truly Stated, and Defended, from Scripture, Antiquity, and the Communion-Service of the Church of England*. London, 1710.

————, *The Unbloody Sacrifice and Altar, Unvail'd and Supported. Part the First. In which the Nature of the Eucharist is explain'd according to the Sentiments of the Christian Church in the first* four Centuries, proving That the Eucharist is a proper Material Sacrifice, That it is both Eucharistic, and Propitiatory, That it is to be offer'd by proper Officers, That the Oblation is to be made on a proper Altar, That it is properly consum'd by Manducation, To which is Added, A Proof That what our Saviour speaks concerning Eating his Flesh, and Drinking his Blood, in the VIth Chapter of St. John's Gospel, is principally meant of the Eucharist. London, 1714.

————. The Unbloody Sacrifice and Altar, Unvail'd and Supported, Part the Second. Showing, The Agreement and Disagreement of the Eucharist with the Sacrifices of the Ancients, and the Excellency of the former. The great Moment of the Eucharist both as a Feast, and Sacrifice. The Necessity of frequent Communion. The Unity of the Eucharist. The Nature of Excommunication. And the Primitive Method of Preparation. With Devotions for the Altar. London, 1718.

————. The Primitive Communicant; in Three Discourses on the Sacrament of the Eucharist in which the Sacrifice of Christ and of the Church are fully explained. Manchester, 1738.

Kidd, B. J., ed. Documents Illustrative of the Continental Reformation. Oxford, 1911.

Knox, John. The Works of John Knox, David Laing, ed., 6 Vols. Edinburgh, 1846–1864.

————. John Knox's History of the Reformation in Scotland, William Croft Dickinson, ed., 2 Vols. London, 1949.

Laud, William. The Works of the Most Reverend Father in God, William Laud, W. Scott and J. Bliss, eds., 7 Vols., Library of Anglo-Catholic Theology. Oxford, 1847–1860.

Melanchthon, Philipp. Philippi Melanthonis Opera Quae Supersunt Omnia, Carolus Gottlieb Bretschneider, ed., Corpus Reformatorum, Vol. 5. Halis Saxonum, 1835.

More, Paul Elmer, and Cross, Frank Leslie, eds., Anglicanism, The Thought and Practice of the Church of England, Illustrated from the Religious Literature of the Seventeenth Century. London, 1962.

Parker, Matthew. Correspondence of Matthew Parker, Archbishop of Canterbury, Comprising Letters Written by and to Him, From A.D. 1535, to his Death, A.D. 1575, John Bruce and Thomas Thomason Perowne, eds. Parker Society, Cambridge, 1853.

Perkins, William. The Workes of that Famous and Worthie Minister of Christ, M. W. Perkins, 3 Vols. London, 1616–1618.

Pocock, N., ed. Troubles connected with the Prayer Book 1549, Documents now mostly for the first time printed from the originals in the Records Office, the Petyt Collection in the Library of the Inner

Temple, the Council Book, and the British Museum. Westminster, 1884.

Pusey, Edward B. *Eirenicon.* London, 1865.

Ridley, Nicholas. *The Works of Nicholas Ridley,* Henry Christmas, ed. Parker Society, Cambridge, 1848.

Robinson, Hastings, ed. and trans., *Zurich Letters, Comprising the Correspondence of Several English Bishops and Others with Some of the Helvetian Reformers, During the Reign of Elizabeth,* 2 Vols. Parker Society, Cambridge, 1842–1845.

————. *Original Letters Relative to the English Reformation, Written During the Reigns of King Henry VIII, King Edward VI, and Queen Mary: Chiefly from the Archives of Zurich,* 2 Vols. Parker Society, Cambridge, 1846–1847.

Sanderson, Robert. *The Works of Robert Sanderson, D.D., Sometime Bishop of Lincoln,* William Jacobson, ed., 6 Vols. Oxford, 1854.

Sanderson, Bishop and Wren, Bishop. *Fragmentary Illustrations of the History of the Book of Common Prayer,* William Jacobson, ed. London, 1874.

Seabury, Samuel. *The Address of the Episcopal Clergy of Connecticut to the Right Reverend Bishop Seabury With the Bishop's Answer, Seabury's First Charge, to the Clergy of his Diocese.* New Haven, [n.d.].

————. *Second Charge to the Clergy of His Diocese Delivered at Derby in the State of Connecticut on the 22nd of September, 1786.* New Haven, [n.d.].

————. *Discourse on II Tim. III. 16. Delivered in St. Paul's and St. George's Chapels in New York.* New York, 1786.

————. *An Earnest Persuasive to Frequent Communion Addressed to Those Professors of the Church of England in Connecticut, Who Neglect That Holy Ordinance,* New Haven, 1789.

————. *Address to the Ministers and Congregations of the Presbyterian and Independent Persuasions in the United States.* [n.p.], 1790.

————. *Discourses on Several Subjects,* 2 Vols. Hudson, 1815.

Smith, William. *Select Sermons of William Smith.* Philadelphia, [n.d.].

————. *An Address to the Members of the Protestant Episcopal Church of Maryland, To Which Is Added a Sermon.* Baltimore, 1784.

————. *Doctor Smith's Answer to Mr. Blatchford's Letter.* Newfield, 1798.

————. *The Works of William Smith, D.D., Late Provost of the College and Academy of Philadelphia,* 2 Vols. Philadelphia, 1803.

Strype, John. *Memorials of Thomas Cranmer,* 3 Vols. Oxford, 1847–1854.

Tomlinson, J. T. *The Great Parliamentary Debate in 1548 on the Lord's Supper.* London, [n.d.].

White, William. *A Sermon on the Qualifications, the Authorities, and the Duties of the Gospel Ministry.* New York, 1804.

——. *A Charge to the Clergy of the Protestant Episcopal Church in the Commonwealth of Pennsylvania.* Philadelphia, 1807.

——. *Lectures on the Catechism of the Protestant Episcopal Church.* Philadelphia, 1813.

——. *An Address Delivered Before the Trustees, Faculty, and Students of the General Theological Seminary of the Protestant Episcopal Church in the United States, July 26, 1823.* New York, 1823.

——. *Commentaries Suited to Occasions of Ordination.* New York, 1833.

——. *Memoirs of the Protestant Episcopal Church in the United States of America From Its Organization up to the Present Day.* New York, 1836.

——. *Bishop White's Opinions on Certain Theological and Ecclesiastical Points, Being a Compilation from the Writings and in the Words of the Right Rev. William White, D.D.,* "A Protestant Episcopalian," ed. New York, 1846.

——. *A Voice From the Past. Two Letters of Bishop White to the Rev. John Hobart.* Philadelphia, 1879.

Wilkins, David, ed. *Concilia Magnae Britanniae et Hiberniae Synodo Verolomiensi A.D. 446 Ad Londoniensem A.D. 1717. Accedunt constitutiones et alia ad historiam Ecclesiae Anglicanae spectantia,* 4 Vols. Bruxelles, 1964.

Wren, Stephen, ed. *Parentalia: or, Memoirs of the Family of the Wrens; viz. of Mathew Bishop of Ely, Christopher Dean of Windsor, &c. But Chiefly of Sir Christopher Wren, Late Surveyor-General of the Royal Buildings, President of the Royal Society, &c. &c.* London, 1750.

Zwingli, Huldreich, *Samtliche Werke,* Emil Egli, Georg Finsler, and Walter Kohler, eds., *Corpus Reformatorum,* 14 Bands. Leipzig, 1905–1935.

III. UNPUBLISHED PAPERS

Seabury, Samuel. A letter from Seabury to William White, New London, June 29, 1789, was used. His discourse on the Eucharist was used extensively. This discourse was found in a longhand collection of Lectures on the Catechism. An unpublished sermon on Frequent Communion was also helpful. Finally, a letter from

William White to Seabury, Philadelphia, August 16, 1789, was used. All these unpublished sources are in the Seabury papers in the St. Mark's Library of the General Theological Seminary, New York. As yet these papers are not completely indexed. Some are in two drawers in the Librarian's office; others are in a safe in the rare book room. An index card in the catalog simply lists the Seabury papers as *Papers, Books, and Printed Matter*.

White, William. A sermon was used, entitled To the Reverend the Clergy of the Protestant Episcopal Church, in the States of Massachusetts and New Hampshire, August 11, 1789. The sermon is in the White papers as St. Mark's Library of the General Theological Seminary, New York. The White papers are scanty and of little assistance for his Eucharistic doctrine. They are completely indexed and can be found among the papers of Protestant Episcopal Bishops. White's papers are entitled *Letters, Sermons, Records*.

IV. OTHER PUBLICATIONS

Albright, Raymond W. *A History of the Protestant Episcopal Church.* New York, 1964.

Allchin, A. M. "The Eucharistic Offering," *Studia Liturgica,* Vol. 1, No. 2, June, 1962, pp. 101–114.

Archbishop of Canterbury *et al. The English Prayer Book 1549–1662.* London, 1963.

Atwater, George Parkin. *The Episcopal Church.* New York, 1963.

Beckett, W. H. *The Reformation in England.* London, 1926.

Beckwith, R. T. *Priesthood and Sacraments, A Study in the Anglican-Methodist Report.* Plymouth, 1964.

Berton, Pierre. *The Comfortable Pew.* Winnipeg, 1965.

Bickersteth, Robert. *The Life of Archbishop Cranmer.* London, 1856.

Bosher, Robert S. *The Making of the Restoration Settlement: The Influence of the Laudians, 1649–1662.* New York, 1951.

Boss, Nelson R. *The Prayer Book Reason Why.* New York, 1963.

Brightman, F. E. *The English Rite,* 2 Vols. London, 1921.

Briloth, Yngve. *Eucharistic Faith and Practice, Evangelical and Catholic,* A. G. Hebert, trans. London, 1961.

Bromiley, G. W., *Thomas Cranmer Theologian.* London, 1956.

Brooks, Peter. *Thomas Cranmer's Doctrine of the Eucharist.* London, 1965.

————. "Cranmer Studies in the Wake of the Quatercentenary," *Historical Magazine of the Protestant Episcopal Church,* Vol. 31, No. 4, December, 1962, pp. 370–372.

Brown, P. Hume. *John Knox,* 2 Vols. London, 1895.

Brown, Raymond. *New Testament Essays.* London, 1965.

Broxap, Henry. *A Biography of Thomas Deacon, the Manchester Non-Juror.* Manchester, 1911.

————. *The Later Non-Jurors.* Cambridge, 1924.

Buchanan, C. O. *The New Communion Service—Reasons For Dissent.* London, 1966.

Burleigh, J. H. S., *A Church History of Scotland.* London, 1961.

Burnet, G., *The History of the Reformation of the Church of England,* N. Pocock, ed., 7 Vols. Oxford, 1865.

Burnet, George R. *The Holy Communion in the Reformed Church of Scotland, 1560–1960.* Edinburgh, 1960.

Calderwood, David. *History of the Kirk,* Wodrow Society, ed., 8 Vols. Edinburgh, 1842–1849.

Callahan, Daniel, Oberman, Heiko, and O'Hanlon, Daniel, eds. *Christianity Divided.* New York, 1961.

Calmeyn, J. *Origines de l'Anglicanisme.* Bruxelles, [n.d.].

Clark, Francis. *Anglican Orders and Defect of Intention.* London, 1956.

————. *Eucharistic Sacrifice and the Reformation.* Westminster, 1960.

————. *The Catholic Church and Anglican Orders.* London, 1962.

————. "Les ordinations anglicanes problème oecuménique," *Gregorianum,* Vol. 75, 1964, pp. 60–93.

Clarke, W. K. Lowther, and Harris, Charles, eds., *Liturgy and Worship: A Companion to the Prayer Books of the Anglican Communion.* London, 1959.

Constant, G., *The Reformation in England,* E. I. Watkin, trans., 2 Vols. London, 1942.

Couratin, A. H. "The Service of Holy Communion, 1552–1662," *The Church Quarterly Review,* 163 (1962), pp. 431–442; "The Holy Communion, 1549," *ibid.,* 164 (1963), pp. 148–159.

Courtuier, J. *The Book of Common Prayer and the Anglican Church.* London, 1930.

Davies, Horton. *The Worship of the English Puritans.* Westminster, 1948.

Delorme, J., *et al. The Eucharist in the New Testament, A Symposium,* E. M. Stewart, ed., and trans. London, 1964.

De Satge, J. C., *et al. The Articles of the Church of England.* London, 1964.

Dimock, N. *The History of the Book of Common Prayer.* London, 1910.

Dix, Gregory. *The Shape of the Liturgy.* Westminster, 1947.

————. "Dixit Cranmer et Non Timuit I," in *The Church Quarterly Review,* Vol. 145, No. 290, January-March, 1948, pp. 145–176.

————. *The Question of Anglican Orders, Letters to a Layman.* Westminster, 1956.

Dixon, R. W. *History of the Church of England, from the Abolition of the Roman Jurisdiction,* Henry Gee, ed., 6 Vols. Oxford, 1891–1902.

Don, Alan Campbell. *The Scottish Book of Common Prayer 1929, Notes on its origin and growth, with illustrations from original documents,* London, 1949.

Donaldson, Gordon, "The Relations between the English and Scottish Presbyterian Movements to 1604," (unpublished Ph.D. dissertation, Department of History, University of London), London, 1938.

————. *The Making of the Scottish Prayer Book of 1637.* Edinburgh, 1954.

Dowden, John. *The Workmanship of the Prayer Book,* 2nd ed. London, 1904.

————. *Further Studies in the Prayer Book.* London, 1908.

Dugmore, C. W. *Eucharistic Doctrine In England From Hooker to Waterland.* London, 1942.

————. *The Mass and the English Reformers.* London, 1958.

Eels, Hastings, "The Genesis of Martin Bucer's Doctrine of the Lord's Supper," *The Princeton Theological Review,* Vol. 24, January, 1926, pp. 225–251.

Foxe, John. *Acts and Monuments,* George Townsend, ed., 8 Vols. London, 1837–1841.

Frere, W. H., *The English Church in the Reigns of Elizabeth and James I, (1558–1625),* "A History of the English Church," Vol. 5, London, 1904.

Fuller, Thomas. *The Church History of Britain from the Birth of Jesus Christ until the Year MDCXLVIII,* James Nichols, ed., 3 Vols. London, 1868.

Garrett, Christian H. *The Marian Exiles.* Cambridge, 1938.

Gee, Henry. *The Elizabethan Prayer-Book and Ornaments.* London, 1902.

Gasquet, Aiden, and Bishop, Edmund. *Edward VI and the Book of Common Prayer.* London, 1928.

Goldie, F. *A Short History of the Episcopal Church in Scotland.* London, 1951.

Gorham, G. C. *Gleanings of a Few Scattered Ears during the Period of the Reformation in England.* London, 1857.

Grisbrooke, W. Jardine, "The 1662 Book of Common Prayer: its history and character," *Studia Liturgica,* Vol. 1, No. 3, September, 1962, pp. 146–166.

Hook, Norman. *The Eucharist in the New Testament.* London, 1964.

Hopf, Constantin. *Martin Bucer and the English Reformation.* Oxford, 1956.

Hughes, John Jay. "Ministerial Intention in the Administration of the Sacraments," *Clergy Review* No. 51, 1966, pp. 763–776; "Two English Cardinals on Anglican Orders," *Journal of Ecumenical Studies,* Winter, 1967, pp. 1–26; "The Papal Condemnation of Anglican Orders: 1896, *Ibid.,* Spring, 1967, pp. 235–267; and "Stewards of the Lord: A Reappraisal of Anglican Orders," Unpublished Doctoral Dissertation, Faculty of Theology of the University of Munster, 1967.

Hughes, Phillip. *The Reformation in England,* 3 Vols. London, 1952–1954.

Hurlbut, Stephen. *The Liturgy of the Church of Scotland Since the Reformtaion.* Charleston, 1950.

Hurley, Michael, ed. *Church and Eucharist.* Dublin, 1966.

Hutchinson, F. E. *Cranmer and the English Reformation.* New York, 1962.

Hutton, William Holden. *The English Church from the Accession of Charles to the Death of Anne (1625–1714),* "A History of the English Church," Vol. 6. London, 1913.

Innes, A. D. *Cranmer and the English Reformation.* New York, 1900.

Jeremias, Joachim. *The Eucharistic Words of Jesus.* Norman Perrin, trans., London, 1966.

Johnstone, Verney, and Evans, Ernest. *The Story of the Prayer Book.* London, 1949.

Kidd, B. J. *The Later Medieval Doctrine of the Eucharistic Sacrifice.* London, 1958.

Knappen, M. M. *Tudor Puritanism.* Chicago, 1963.

Ladd, William Palmer. *Prayer Book Interleaves.* New York, 1943.

Lahey, Raymond J. "The Historic Episcopate in the Context of the Contemporary Movement for Church Union with the Non-Episcopal Churches—1910–1963," (unpublished S.T.D. dissertation, Faculty of Theology, Saint Paul University). Ottawa, 1965.

Lamirande, Emilien. *What is the Communion of Saints?,* A. Manson, trans., "Faith and Fact Books," Vol. 26. London, 1963.

Lash, Nicholas, "The Place of the Priesthood," *New Blackfriars,* Vol. 47, No. 555, August, 1966, pp. 564–571.

Lautz, Boniface. "The Doctrine of the Communion of Saints in Anglican Theology 1833–1963," (unpublished S.T.D. dissertation, Faculty of Theology, University of Ottawa). Ottawa, 1964.

Leeming, Bernard. *The Vatican Council and Christian Unity, A Commentary on the Decree of Ecumenism of the Second Vatican Council, together with a translation of the text.* London, 1966.

Lorimer, Peter. *John Knox, and the Church of England.* London, 1875.

Manross, William Wilson. *A History of the American Episcopal Church.* New York, 1950.

Marshall, Romey P., and Taylor, Michael, J. *Liturgy and Christian Unity.* Englewood Cliffs, 1965.

Mascall, E. J. *Christ, the Christian, and the Church: a study in the Incarnation and its consequences.* London, 1946.

Mason, A. J. *Thomas Cranmer.* London, 1898.

Maxwell, William D. *A History of Worship in the Church of Scotland.* London, 1955.

———. *An Outline of Christian Worship.* London, 1961.

Maynard, Theodore. *The Life of Thomas Cranmer.* London, 1956.

McAdoo, H. R. *The Spirit of Anglicanism.* London, 1965.

McGarry, Cecil. "The Catholic Character of Anglican Ecclesiology, 1945–1963" (unpublished S.T.D. dissertation, Pontifical Gregorian University). Rome, 1964.

Messenger, Ernest C. *The Reformation, the Mass, and the Priesthood, A Documentary History with Special Reference to the Question of Anglican Orders,* 2 Vols. London, 1936–1937.

Meyer, Carl S. *Elizabeth I and the Religious Settlement of 1559.* St. Louis, 1960.

Michell, G. A. *Landmarks in Liturgy.* London, 1961.

Moorman, J. R. H. *A History of the Church in England.* London, 1963.

Morris, James. *Oxford.* London, 1965.

Muller, J. A. *Stephen Gardiner and the Tudor Reaction.* New York, 1926.

Neal, Daniel. *The History of the Puritans,* 3 Vols. London, 1937.

Nedoncelle, Maurice. *Trois aspects du problème Anglocatholique au XVIIe siècle.* Paris, 1951.

Neill, Stephen. *Anglicanism.* London, 1958.

Nuttall, Geoffrey F., and Chadwick, Owen, eds. *From Uniformity to Unity.* London, 1962.

O'Brien, John A., ed. *Steps to Christian Unity.* London, 1964.

Olmstead, Robert, "Anglican, Roman theologians see hope for intercommunion," *The National Catholic Reporter,* Vol. 2, No. 15, February 9, 1966, pp. 1, 10.

Overton, J. H. *The Non-Jurors, Their Lives, Principles, and Writings.* London, 1902.

Parker, James. *An Introduction to the History of the Successive Revisions of the Book of Common Prayer.* Oxford, 1877.

Parker, T. M. *The English Reformation to 1558.* London, 1950.

Parsons, Edward Lambe, and Jones, Bayard Hale. *The American Prayer Book: Its Origins and Principles.* New York, 1937.

Pell, Walden, and Dawley, Powel M. *The Religion of the Prayer Book.* New York, 1950.

Pollard, A. F. *Thomas Cranmer and the English Reformation.* London, 1904.

Powers, Joseph M., "Mysterium Fidei and the Theology of the Eucharist," *Worship,* Vol. 40, No. 1, January, 1966, pp. 17–35.

Powicke, Maurice. *The Reformation in England.* London, 1965.

Procter, Francis, and Frere, Walter. *A New History of the Book of Common Prayer: With a Rationale of Its Offices.* London, 1951.

Pullan, Leighton. *The History of the Book of Common Prayer.* London, 1901.

Rahner, Karl, *The Church and the Sacraments,* New York, 1964.

Rahner, Karl—Vorgrimler, Herbert, *Concise Theological Dictionary,* Cornelius Ernst, ed., Richard Strachan, trans., London, 1965.

Ratcliff, E. C. *Thomas Cranmer, 1489–1556, Three Commemorative Lectures Delivered in Lambeth Palace.* London, 1956.

———. "The English Usage of Eucharistic Consecration," *Theology,* 60 (1957), pp. 229–236, 273–280.

Richardson, C. C. *Zwingli and Cranmer on the Eucharist.* Evanston, 1949.

Ridley, Jasper, *Thomas Cranmer,* Oxford, 1963.

Romeu, Luis V., ed., *Ecumenical Experiences,* Rachel Attwater, trans., London, 1965.

Schillebeeckx, Edward, *Christ the Sacrament of the Encounter with God,* New York, 1963.

Shepherd, Massey H., Jr., *The Reform of Liturgical Worship, Perspectives and Prospects,* New York, 1961.

Smith, Horace Wemyss. *Life and Correspondence of the Rev. William Smith, D.D.,* 2 Vols. Philadelphia, 1880.

Smithen, F. J. *Continental Protestantism and the English Reformation.* London, 1927.

Smyth, C. H. *Cranmer and the Reformation under Edward VI.* Cambridge, 1928.

The Standing Liturgical Commission of the Protestant Episcopal Church in the United States of America, *Prayer Book Studies IV, The Eucharistic Liturgy.* New York, 1963.

Stanwood, Paul Grant, "John Cosin as Homilist 1595–1671/72,"

Anglican Theological Review, Vol. 47, No. 3, July, 1964, pp. 276–289.

Stone, Darwell, *A History of the Doctrine of the Eucharist*, 2 Vols., London, 1909.

Symonds, H. Edward, *The Council of Trent and Anglican Formularies*, London, 1933.

Tavard, George. *The Quest for Catholicity: A Study in Anglicanism*. London, 1963.

Taylor, Michael J., *The Protestant Liturgical Renewal*, Westminster, 1963.

Trevor-Roper, H. R. *Archbishop Laud 1573–1645*. London, 1963.

Van De Poll, G. J. *Martin Bucer's Liturgical Ideas*. Assen, 1944.

Van Hove, A., *Tractatus de sanctissima Eucharistia*, Mechlin, 1941.

Vogan, Thomas. *The True Doctrine of the Eucharist*. London, 1871.

Vorgrimler, Herbert, ed., *Dogmatic vs Biblical Theology*, London, 1964.

Walton, Izaak. *The Lives of Dr. John Donne, Sir Henry Wotton, Mr. Richard Hooker, Mr. George Herbert, and Dr. Robert Sanderson: To Which are Added, The Autographs of Those Eminent Men, Now First Collected; An Index, and Illustrative Notes*. London, 1823.

Wand, J. W. C. *The High Church Schism*. London, 1951.

——. *Anglicanism in History and Today*. London, 1963.

Wenger, A., "L'Eglise orthodoxe et les ordinations anglicanes," *Nouvelle Revue Théologique*, Vol. 76, No. 1, January, 1954, pp. 44–55.

Whittingham, William. *A Brief Discourse of the Troubles at Frankfort*, Edward Arber, ed. London, 1908.

Wood, A. Harold. *Church Unity Without Uniformity*. London, 1963.

Wordsworth, Christopher. *Notes on Medieval Services in England*. London, 1898.

Wordsworth, Christopher, and Littlehales, Henry. *Old Service Books of the English Church*, London, 1904.

Index